Praise for *Entitled*

"Kate Manne is the Simone de Beauvoir of the twenty-first century. In *Entitled*, she compellingly lays out the stubborn social assumptions behind our still-sexist cultural norms. Manne's writing is as breezy as it is sharp and unflinching, and will give any patriarchy-fighter the ammo she needs to keep fighting."

—AMANDA MARCOTTE, author of *Troll Nation*

"Manne's brilliant breakdown of male entitlement is essential to understanding the world we live in. Her thinking about this critical and complex topic is characteristically incisive, perceptive, and profound. Now, more than ever, *Entitled* is an absolute must-read!"

—SORAYA CHEMALY, author of *Rage Becomes Her*

"In *Entitled*, Manne gets right to the heart of gender, power, and inequality: what men presume they deserve, and what women learn we owe. The result is an unflinching indictment of male entitlement in nearly every aspect of modern life. *Entitled* is exactly what we need to understand our current moment—and to imagine something better."

—JILL FILIPOVIC, author of *The H-Spot*

"Manne tackles the kaleidoscopic manifestations of male entitlement with insights as invigorating as her subject matter is frustrating. Her thinking is so elegant and her theory of male entitlement as a symptom of a moral economy in which women are perpetually in men's debt is so groundbreaking that the book is sure to spark and inspire other feminist writers. *Entitled* is the work of a once-in-a-generation mind, and as always, Manne succeeds in leaving feminism richer and more robust than when she found it."

—MOIRA DONEGAN, columnist, *The Guardian*

"I wish this book didn't have to exist. I wish there was no need for a clear-eyed, razor-sharp deconstruction of male entitlement, and how that entitlement is killing us. But it is necessary, and Kate Manne is exactly the intellectual powerhouse I want to have written it."

—CARMEN MARIA MACHADO,
author of *Her Body and Other Parties*

"*Entitled* is a painful book that sets things right. Manne guides us through some of the most violent traumas our culture has to offer women, starting with #MeToo creeps and murderous incels and descending from there through just about every level of female Hell. Yet Manne's marvelous clarity and cool in the face of the unthinkable, her habit of crystallizing unspeakable problems into simple sentences that stay with you for years, makes her the most trustworthy possible guide through this house of horrors. One of the most essential voices of our times."

—SADY DOYLE, author of *Dead Blondes and Bad Mothers*

"Challenging, controversial, wide-ranging, and powerful, the eminent young philosopher Kate Manne brings to bear her well-known theory of patriarchy and misogyny on a range of contemporary issues, providing powerful evidence of its ubiquity and pervasiveness on everything from our ordinary interchanges with one another to our healthcare systems and elections."

—JASON STANLEY, author of *How Fascism Works*

"In lucid prose, Manne illustrates how male entitlement—to sex, power, and knowledge; to women's care, doctors' attention, and the benefit of the doubt—undergirds misogyny. Examining the special effects of misogynoir and transmisogyny alongside hostile behaviors that keep all women and non-binary people 'in their place,' Manne provides a thorough (if by no means exhaustive) look at the ways we prioritize cis men's needs and desires, to the detriment of half the population."

—KATE HARDING, author of *Asking for It*

"*Entitled* is a brilliant analysis of the systematic advantages and prerogatives awarded to men for nothing more than being men. Its deep engagement with real-world examples, eloquent prose, and compelling arguments provide a corrective lens through which to view the world without the blur and distortion that we don't even notice. This is the world we live in, and although the clarity can be painful, Manne also provides reason for hope."

—SALLY HASLANGER, professor of philosophy and women's and gender studies, Massachusetts Institute of Technology

"With eloquent prose and irrefutable evidence, Kate Manne gives voice to a twenty-first century rage. *Entitled* builds on Manne's earlier work on the forces of systemic patriarchy and the eternal frustration felt by generations of women forced year after year to fight for egalitarianism at the most fundamental levels. One of our most prophetic and gifted feminist voices today, Manne's work is as necessary as sunlight. Your anger may not be quelled by the final page, but at least you'll feel less alone."

—RACHEL LOUISE SNYDER, author of *No Visible Bruises*

ENTITLED

ENTITLED

HOW MALE PRIVILEGE
HURTS WOMEN

KATE MANNE

CROWN
NEW YORK

Published in the United States by Crown, an imprint of Random House, a division of Penguin Random House LLC, New York.

CROWN and the Crown colophon are registered trademarks of Penguin Random House LLC.

Hardback ISBN 978-1-9848-2655-8
Ebook ISBN 978-1-9848-2656-5

Printed in the United States of America on acid-free paper

randomhousebooks.com

1 2 3 4 5 6 7 8 9

First Edition

Book design by Susan Turner

To my daughter

CONTENTS

ONE Indelible—On the Entitlement of Privileged Men   3

TWO Involuntary—On the Entitlement to Admiration   14

THREE Unexceptional—On the Entitlement to Sex   33

FOUR Unwanted—On the Entitlement to Consent   56

FIVE Incompetent—On the Entitlement to Medical Care   75

SIX Unruly—On the Entitlement to Bodily Control   97

SEVEN Insupportable—On the Entitlement to Domestic Labor   120

EIGHT Unassuming—On the Entitlement to Knowledge   138

NINE Unelectable—On the Entitlement to Power   160

TEN Undespairing—On the Entitlement of Girls   184

ACKNOWLEDGMENTS   193

NOTES   195

INDEX   259

ENTITLED

Indelible—
On the Entitlement of Privileged Men

He was a picture of entitlement. Brett Kavanaugh, fifty-three, was red-faced, petulant, and shouted most of his answers. Clearly, he thought the proceedings were beneath him, a travesty. It was September 2018, and Kavanaugh was being questioned by the Senate Judiciary Committee regarding allegations that he had sexually assaulted Dr. Christine Blasey Ford, fifty-one, when they were both in high school. At stake was not only Kavanaugh's appointment to the U.S. Supreme Court; this was, more importantly, a tribunal on sexual assault, male privilege, and the workings of misogyny.

America did not pass the test. Despite highly credible evidence that Kavanaugh had indeed sexually assaulted a fifteen-year-old Ford some thirty-six years prior, Kavanaugh's nomination to the Supreme Court was confirmed by a slim majority.

Ford testified that she had been attacked by Kavanaugh, who, together with his friend Mark Judge, had "corralled" her into a bedroom at a party in Maryland. Ford alleged that Kavanaugh had pinned her to the bed, groped her, and ground his crotch against her. She said he tried to remove her clothes and covered her mouth to prevent her from screaming. Ford said she was afraid that Kavanaugh would accidentally smother and kill her. She said that she managed to escape when Judge jumped on the bed, knocking the two of them over.[1]

"Indelible in the hippocampus is the laughter," said Ford—a professor of psychology—in describing the incident and its traumatic aftermath. But even for many of those who professed to believe her, Ford's experience just did not matter enough to be worth depriving a man like Kavanaugh of his perceived due, given his background and reputation.[2] And, of course, there were also people who refused to believe her, saying she was either lying or mistaken.[3]

By the time the Kavanaugh hearings were front-page news, I had been thinking for quite some time about male privilege and the toll it takes on girls and women. The case seemed to encapsulate many of the social dynamics I'd been studying. It perfectly captured the concept of *entitlement:* the widespread perception that a privileged man is owed something even as exalted as a position on the U.S. Supreme Court.[4] This is a perception that Kavanaugh himself shared, judging by his aggrieved, belligerent, and, at times, borderline unhinged conduct during the hearings. In contrast with Dr. Ford's calm, tempered demeanor, and her poignant attempts to be "helpful" to the senators in responding to their queries, Kavanaugh was furious about being questioned. Especially, it might appear, when the questioner was a woman. Senator Amy Klobuchar asked him, in a now notorious exchange: "You're saying there's never been a case when you drank so much that you didn't remember what happened the night before, or part of what happened?" "You're asking about a blackout. I don't know, have *you*?" Kavanaugh replied, in a tone both contemptuous and whiney.[5]

The case also highlighted the phenomenon of *himpathy:* the way powerful and privileged boys and men who commit acts of sexual violence or engage in other misogynistic behavior often receive sympathy and concern over their female victims. Senator Lindsey Graham, fuming, epitomized such a himpathetic attitude:

GRAHAM: [*To Democrats*] What you want to do is destroy this guy's life, hold this seat open and hope you win in 2020. . . . [*To Kavanaugh*] You've got nothing to apologize for. When you see Sotomayor and Kagan, tell them that Lindsey said "hello," because I voted for them. [*To Democrats*] I would never do to them what you've done to this guy. . . . [*To Kavanaugh*] Are you a gang rapist?
KAVANAUGH: No.
GRAHAM: I cannot imagine what you and your family have gone through. [*To Democrats*] Boy, you all want power. God, I hope you never get it. I hope the American people can see through this sham. . . . You had no intention of protecting Dr. Ford—none. [*To Kavanaugh*] She's as much of a victim as you are. God, I hate to say it, because these have been my friends. But let me tell

you, when it comes to this, you're looking for a fair process? You came to the wrong town at the wrong time, my friend. Do you consider this a job interview?

KAVANAUGH: If the advice and consent role is like a job interview.

GRAHAM: Do you consider that you've been through a job interview?

KAVANAUGH: I've been through a process of advice and consent under the Constitution, which—

GRAHAM: Would you say you've been through hell?

KAVANAUGH: I—I've been through hell and then some.

GRAHAM: This is not a job interview.

KAVANAUGH: Yes.

GRAHAM: This is hell.

According to Graham, it was unconscionably hellish—and, beyond that, ridiculous—for a man in Kavanaugh's position to have to respond to serious, credible accusations of sexual assault, and undergo a truncated FBI investigation, in order to ascend to one of the highest positions of moral authority in America. And Kavanaugh clearly shared, and was further emboldened by, Graham's views here—not wasting the opportunity to indulge in self-pity. No comparable outpouring of feeling for Ford and her family was forthcoming from Graham, despite his giving lip service to the idea that she was "as much of a victim" as Kavanaugh in this process (referring to the supposed attempt on the part of Democrats to discredit Kavanaugh for political gain). "Miss Ford has got a problem, and destroying Judge Kavanaugh's life won't fix her problem," Graham fulminated on Fox News, later.[6]

Himpathy made Kavanaugh seem to Graham to be the *real*

victim in all of this. And not confirming a man like Kavanaugh to the Supreme Court became tantamount to ruining his life, not just withholding an opportunity.[7] It wasn't only men like Lindsey Graham spouting this kind of rhetoric and casting such aspersions on Christine Blasey Ford, either; many of the naysayers were women, and included other senators, journalists, and laypeople.[8]

Finally, the Kavanaugh case highlighted several aspects of misogyny's nature and function. In my previous book, *Down Girl,* I argued that misogyny should not be understood as a monolithic, deep-seated psychological hatred of girls and women. Instead, it's best conceptualized as the "law enforcement" branch of patriarchy—a system that functions to police and enforce gendered norms and expectations, and involves girls and women facing disproportionately or distinctively hostile treatment because of their gender, among other factors.[9] The sexual assault of Christine Blasey Ford (about which, for the record, I believe her) would certainly fit this description, since girls and women are significantly likelier to be subject to assaults of this kind than are their male counterparts.[10] In addition to this, misogyny is typically (though not invariably) a response to a woman's violations of gendered "law and order." The fact that Ford received abusive messages and death threats for speaking out about a powerful man's mistreatment of her exemplifies such punishment.[11]

In general, I think of misogyny as being a bit like the shock collar worn by a dog to keep them behind one of those invisible fences that proliferate in suburbia. Misogyny is capable of causing pain, to be sure, and it often does so. But even when it isn't actively hurting anyone, it tends to discourage girls and women from venturing out of bounds. If we stray, or err, we know what we are in for.[12] All the more reason, then, why Ford's testimony was so courageous.

In contrast to misogyny, I take sexism to be the theoretical and ideological branch of patriarchy: the beliefs, ideas, and assumptions that serve to rationalize and naturalize patriarchal norms and expectations—including a gendered division of labor, and men's dominance over women in areas of traditionally male power and authority. Though this book focuses more on misogyny than sexism, it's important to recognize that the two typically work in concert.

But we need to understand that someone can engage in misogynistic behavior without necessarily having sexist beliefs about women. Brett Kavanaugh's defense of himself against the allegations of sexual misconduct, on the grounds that he had employed an unusually large number of female clerks, is really no defense at all.[13] A man may believe that a woman is intellectually capable in law, business, or politics, say, and therefore be willing to have her serve as his subordinate in this domain, while still subjecting her or other women to misogynistic treatment—sexual assault, for example. More broadly, a man may be happy to extend a certain amount of power to a woman, as long as she does not threaten or challenge him. But if she does, he may engage in misogynistic behavior to put her in her place, and punish her for having ideas beyond her station. He would then be more of a misogynist than a sexist, on my analysis.

On the whole, though, my account of misogyny counsels us to focus less on the individual *perpetrators* of misogyny, and more on misogyny's *targets* and *victims*. This is helpful for at least two reasons. First, some instances of misogyny lack any individual perpetrators whatsoever; misogyny may be a purely structural phenomenon, perpetuated by social institutions, policies, and broader cultural mores.[14] Second, understanding misogyny as more about the hostility girls and women *face,* as opposed to the hostility men *feel* deep down in their hearts, helps us avoid a problem of psychological inscrutability. It's often difficult to know what someone's innermost states and ultimate motivations are, short of being their therapist (and even then, such knowledge may be elusive). But my account of misogyny doesn't require us to know what someone is feeling, deep inside, in order to say that they are perpetuating or enabling misogyny. What we need to know is something we are often in a much better position to establish: that a girl or woman is facing disproportionately or distinctively gendered hostile treatment because she is a *woman in a man's world*—that is, a woman in a historically patriarchal society (which includes, I believe, most if not all of them).[15] We don't need to show that she is subject to such treatment because she is a woman *in a man's mind*—which, in some instances, can't be the issue. After all, as I noted earlier, women as well as men can engage in misogynistic behavior—for example, by dismissing other women, or engaging in the kind of moralism that tends to let male counterparts off the hook, while harshly blaming women for that same behavior.

So I would argue that it is best to think of misogyny primarily as a property of the social environments girls and women navigate, wherein they are liable to be subject to hateful or hostile treatment because of their gender—together, in many cases, with their gendered "bad" behavior. Even so, I do not want to deny the reality of individual people who *do* deserve to be called misogynists. Admittedly, "misogynist" is a judgmental, pejorative term, and I don't think we should swing it about too freely, lest this important linguistic weapon lose its characteristic "punch" and power. So I propose defining a misogynist as someone who is an *overachiever* in perpetuating misogyny: practicing misogyny with particular frequency and consistency compared to others in that environment. This definition helps us acknowledge the important truth that we are *all* to a certain extent complicit in misogynistic social structures. But at the same time, for many people, especially those who are actively engaged in anti-misogynistic resistance efforts, it would be wrong to call us misogynists on the whole. That label should be reserved for the chief offenders. We will meet plenty of them in the ensuing pages.

When I wrote *Down Girl,* I focused on making an abstract argument that misogyny should be understood as the hostility girls and women face, which serves to police and enforce gendered norms and expectations. But this definition raised many of the questions I've been thinking about ever since: What *are* the gendered norms and expectations that misogyny polices and enforces, especially in my own milieu (the United States), with its reputation for being relatively egalitarian?[16] How might the resulting, sometimes subtle social dynamics constrain the possibilities for girls and women, together with non-binary people, in various spheres of life? And how do boys and men unfairly *benefit* from this system in its concrete daily operations? Throughout the process of thinking through these issues, I've become more and more cognizant of the way misogyny is inextricably bound up with the related social ills that an intersectional approach, as pioneered by Kimberlé W. Crenshaw, reminds us to attend to. These include racism (in particular, white supremacy), xenophobia, classism, homophobia, transphobia, and ableism, among other things.[17]

There is no universal experience of misogyny—not least because gendered norms and expectations always intersect with these other unjust systems to produce novel forms of oppression faced by different groups of girls and women. In what follows, I hope to shed some light (without claiming to be an authority) on the specific forms of misogyny faced by trans women and Black women in the United States—transmisogyny and misogynoir, respectively. Here, as a cisgender, heterosexual white woman myself, I have benefited immeasurably from the insights of Talia Mae Bettcher, Tressie McMillan Cottom, and Jazmine Joyner, among many other crucial voices on these topics.

Entitled tackles a wide range of ways in which misogyny, himpathy, and male entitlement work in tandem with other oppressive systems to produce unjust, perverse, and sometimes bizarre outcomes. Many of these stem from the fact that women are expected to *give* traditionally feminine goods (such as sex, care, nurturing, and reproductive labor) to designated, often more privileged men, and to refrain from taking traditionally masculine goods (such as power, authority, and claims to knowledge) away from them. These goods can in turn be understood as those to which privileged men are tacitly deemed *entitled,* and which these men will often garner himpathy for wrongfully taking from women—when it comes to sex, most obviously, though by no means exclusively.

All in all, this book shows that an illegitimate sense of male entitlement gives rise to a wide range of misogynistic behavior. When a woman fails to give a man what he's supposedly owed, she will often face punishment and reprisal—whether from him, his himpathetic supporters, or the misogynistic social structures in which she is embedded.

What's more, within this system, women are often unfairly deprived of their *genuine* entitlement to both feminine-coded and masculine-coded goods. This results in inequalities that range from a woman not receiving adequate care for her pain, to her not being able to take up traditionally male positions of power, to her not being granted her rightful authority to speak about subjects in which she is expert.

Some of the chapters that follow focus more on an illegitimate sense of male entitlement; others home in on the way girls and women, together with non-binary people, are deprived of goods to which they truly *are* entitled. These concerns are two sides of the same coin, in my book—though they will often require somewhat different analyses and solutions.

Exposing the underlying logic of these and other moral biases helps me address questions like the following: What do the anti-abortion and anti-trans movements have in common? Why are women still largely responsible for the "second shift" at home? Why do certain men so routinely get away with sexually assaulting girls and women, as well as other vulnerable people? And why is mansplaining still such a common occurrence?[18]

As I will show throughout this book, the forces that hold misogyny in place are powerful and prevalent. In part, women are punished and blamed—indeed, subject to misogyny—for daring to come forward and speak out about the reality of the problem. Many people feel that men are entitled not just to be deemed innocent until proven guilty, but to be deemed innocent, period, regardless of their misdeeds. Moreover, when misogyny makes its mark, the damage may be indelible. Dr.

Christine Blasey Ford was not only deeply traumatized by the original sexual assault, and quite possibly retraumatized by fulfilling what she felt was her civic duty to testify to its having happened; she was also subsequently driven out of her home, due to death threats against her and her family, following the hearings.[19] Brett Kavanaugh was not only appointed to the Supreme Court but may well soon play a role in lending crucial SCOTUS support to the anti-abortion movement in this country. At the time of writing, Donald Trump, credibly accused of sexually assaulting and harassing dozens of women, remains the nation's president.[20]

Still, progress fortunately does not rely—cannot, and has never relied—on universal agreement that what is patently unjust *is* unjust indeed. Instead, we can—and, I increasingly believe, must—take our cues from the daily acts of courage, creativity, and political resistance being undertaken, individually and collectively, in response to such injustices. I do not know, by any means, that this will be enough to bring about the right outcomes. But this I know: it is important and worthwhile to fight. And we can fight better when we are clear about what we are up against. It is with this conviction that I offer what's to follow.

TWO

Involuntary—
On the Entitlement to Admiration

On Friday, May 23, 2014, just after nine-thirty P.M., there was a loud knock on the door of the Alpha Phi sorority house at the University of California, Santa Barbara. At least forty female students would have been living there at the time. But it being Memorial Day weekend, relatively few of them were home to answer the door. And the knocking sounded unusually loud and aggressive, according to one of the women inside. They decided not to open up, even when the knocking continued for at least another full minute. In retrospect, it was wise, not to mention fortunate, that they made the decision they did. For the man who had come knocking, Elliot Rodger, twenty-two, had a loaded gun in his hand and was planning to annihilate all of them.[1]

"For the last eight years of my life, since I hit puberty, I've been forced to endure an existence of loneliness, rejection, and unfulfilled desires, all because girls have never been attracted to me. Girls gave their affection and sex and love to other men but never to me," Rodger explained in a YouTube video, which he uploaded immediately before driving to UCSB. "I'm twenty-two years old and still a virgin, never even kissed a girl. . . . It has been very torturous. College is the time when everyone experiences those things such as sex and fun and pleasure. In those years I've had to rot in loneliness; it's not fair," he complained. In a still more moralistic vein:

> You girls have never been attracted to me. I don't know why you girls aren't attracted to me, but I will punish you all for it. It's an injustice, a crime, because I don't know what you don't see in me. I'm the perfect guy and yet you throw yourselves at all these obnoxious men instead of me, the supreme gentleman.

Hence Rodger's plan, on his envisaged "Day of Retribution": "I am going to enter the hottest sorority house at UCSB and I will slaughter every single spoiled, stuck-up, blonde slut I see inside there."[2]

In the end, after being denied entry, he had to settle for shooting three other women (students from a nearby sorority house, Tri Delta) who were just then walking around the corner. He murdered two, and wounded one of them. He went on to murder one man and injure fourteen other people, in a subsequent drive-by shooting spree.[3]

• • •

When Kate Pierson heard three sharp bangs on the wall behind her, she thought the stereo in the hot yoga studio must have fallen from its shelf. But it was gunfire. A walk-in client, Scott Paul Beierle, forty, had driven more than two hundred miles to be there for the five-thirty P.M. class in Tallahassee, Florida. He paid his twelve dollars via credit card and asked how many people were expected. Disappointed that only eleven had pre-registered, he inquired about the studio's busiest times (Saturday mornings). Nevertheless, he stuck around as the women—and one man—trickled in for the class. The yoga teacher told him to stow his bag in the cubby outside the hot room. He told the teacher he had a question. Then he donned a set of hearing-protection earmuffs and pulled out a Glock. After pausing for a moment, gun in hand, he pointed it at the woman closest to him. He opened fire, seemingly indiscriminately: his objective being to kill women of the kind who had so enraged him since adolescence, when he had penned a revenge fantasy, "Rejected Youth." He ended up shooting six and murdering two of them.[4]

This was in November 2018. Prior to the shooting, Beierle had posted a video online, citing Elliot Rodger as inspiration. So did Chris Harper-Mercer, twenty-six, before he opened fire in a classroom at his Oregon community college—murdering eight students and an assistant professor, while injuring eight others. So did Alek Minassian, twenty-five, before driving a van into pedestrians in Toronto, killing ten people and wounding sixteen. "The Incel Rebellion has already begun! We will overthrow all the Chads and Staceys! All hail the Supreme Gentleman Elliot Rodger!" wrote Minassian beforehand, on Facebook.[5]

. . .

The term "incel" stands for "involuntary celibate." Ironically, the term was coined by a woman named Alana—a bisexual, progressive Canadian—who in the 1990s founded a website called Alana's Involuntary Celibacy Project.[6] It was intended to help others like her deal with their dating-related loneliness and sexual dissatisfaction.[7] But nowadays the term "incel" is used to self-identify almost exclusively by heterosexual men, most of them fairly young, who frequent anonymous or pseudonymous Internet forums devoted to incel ideology.[8] Incels believe they are entitled to, and have been deprived of, sex with "hot" young women, who are dubbed "Staceys." Sometimes incels also express an abstract longing for love, or for a girlfriend—or, more concretely, a woman to provide them with the attention and affection that Rodger lamented lacking. But an incel will typically want sex and love not only, and perhaps not even primarily, for their own sake. His rhetoric betrays a desire to have these goods for *instrumental* reasons: as currency to buy status in masculine hierarchies, relative to the "Chads." These are the supposed "alpha males," whose masculine prowess contrasts with the incel's (again, supposedly) lowly status. And an incel's plans for revenge may therefore target not just women but also the men they perceive as besting and thwarting them. Elliot Rodger said, in his aforementioned video:

> All those girls I've desired so much, they would have all rejected me and looked down upon me as an inferior man if I ever made a sexual advance towards them [*scoffs*] while they throw themselves at these obnoxious brutes. I'll take great pleasure in slaughtering all of you.
>
> You will finally see that I am in truth the superior

one. The true alpha male [*laughs*]. Yes. After I've annihilated every single girl in the sorority house, I will take to the streets of Isla Vista and slay every single person I see there. All those popular kids who live such lives of hedonistic pleasures while I've had to rot in loneliness for all these years. They've all looked down upon me every time I tried to go out and join them, they've all treated me like a mouse.

Well now I will be a god compared to you.

It might be tempting to dismiss this rant and its ilk as the ravings of lunatics. And that's not wrong, exactly: these cartoon villain rants *are* ludicrous, almost comical. But that is not sufficient reason to disregard them, unfortunately. For one thing, some of these men are obviously highly dangerous—all the more so because, often, by the time they lash out, they are despairing and at rock bottom. They feel they have nothing left to lose, and thus plan to take themselves out in a maximally violent (and hence, by their lights, glorious and gratifying) conflagration. Rodger, Beierle, and Harper-Mercer all ended their rampages by shooting themselves fatally; only Minassian, of the four, could be apprehended by law enforcement. And given the reality of copycat behavior, it is natural to be concerned that such violence may proliferate. So it's important to understand its nature and sources.

Moreover, and more subtly, incels are but a vivid symptom of a much broader and deeper cultural phenomenon. They crystallize some men's toxic sense of entitlement to have people look up to them steadfastly, with a loving gaze, admiringly—and to target and even destroy those who fail, or refuse, to do so. And, as will emerge here eventually, these men's sense of entitlement to such affection and admiration is a trait they often share with the far greater proportion of men who commit acts of domestic, dating, and intimate partner violence.

As I've already suggested, it's a mistake to think that incels are primarily motivated by sex. Not only are some incels also interested in love (or some outward simulacrum thereof), but their interest in having sex with "Staceys" is at least partly a means to an end—the end being to beat the "Chads" at their own game. Sex thus promises to soothe these men's inferiority complexes, at least as much as to satisfy their libidos.

It's also a mistake to accede too readily to an incel's self-reports about their lowly status in comparison with other men. With respect to male beauty standards, for example, a recent article on incels in *New York* magazine revealed photographs of perfectly ordinary-looking young men—some of them even handsome. They nonetheless hankered for different jaw lines, some going so far as to invest in exorbitantly expensive plastic surgeries, such as cheek implants and facial reshaping, to make them (in their own view) look more masculine.[9]

Yet another mistake is to think that sex would provide a solution to an incel's supposed problem. If an incel *does* start having sex, or gets into a relationship, who will he turn into? Contra several commentators, my guess is: not a nice guy.[10] A once-single incel may well become a female partner's tormentor. Anyone can feel lonely. But a wrongheaded sense of entitlement to a woman's sexual, material, reproductive, and emotional labor may result in incel tendencies prior to the relationship and intimate partner violence afterward, if he feels thwarted, resentful, or jealous. In other words, an incel is an abuser waiting to happen.

Incels differ in the degree to which they are proactive versus reactive. Elliot Rodger was largely the latter: he never made a serious effort to go on dates, by the lights of "My Twisted World," his so-called manifesto (really more of a memoir—and a lengthy one, at more than one hundred thousand words). He seems not to have actually approached the women of the Alpha Phi sorority house, simply assuming that they would reject him (which might, of course, have been an accurate prediction). Rather than try his hand, he preferred not to run the risk of failure, instead stalking them from a distance. Long before his final act of violence, he also engaged in numerous acts of petty vengeance against the happy-looking couples he saw out and about, who aroused his envy and outrage. He was particularly prone to throwing beverages in their faces—one time, hot coffee; another time, orange juice. This was about as close to physical contact with the "Staceys" as Rodger ever got, if his account is accurate.

Scott Beierle, in contrast, had a nasty habit of touching women without their consent. He was, in a word, handsy. At the time of the shooting, he had been fired from a temporary teaching job for touching a female student inappropriately (placing his hand on her stomach, just below her bra line, and asking her if she was ticklish). He had been discharged from the army for groping several women (an honorable discharge, notably). And he had been banned from the Florida State University campus in Tallahassee, where he had graduated with a master's degree in public administration and planning, after a series of incidents on campus. During one such, he had groped the buttocks of three young women in the dining hall—all of whom were wearing yoga pants.[11]

Beierle and Rodger were thus plausibly on different ends of a spectrum of entitled male behavior: from the domineering to the disappointed. While Beierle evinced his sense of entitlement to women's bodies by reaching out and subjecting them to unwanted touching, Rodger evinced his by harboring deep resentments to the women who did not reach out to *him* (metaphorically and literally). Rodger evidently expected a woman to turn up in his lap, or at least on his doorstep. And when one did not materialize, his sense of aggrieved entitlement led him to arrive on *her* doorstep with a plan for enacting vengeance.[12]

I do not want to suggest that either of these patterns of behavior is better than the other; it is a behavioral distinction that may not make for much of a moral difference. But it's important to be aware of both patterns, so that the superficial differences don't obscure the underlying similarities between the aggressive and the timid-seeming incel. The latter, in particular, is liable to be mistaken for a harmless "nice guy," even well after we have definitive evidence to the contrary.

Incels are often virulent racists. This is not to say that all incels are white; indeed, there are enough nonwhite incels to have given the racist terms "curry-cels" and "rice-cels" currency.[13] But incels who are not white typically *subscribe* to white supremacist ideology. Elliot Rodger, for example, was half Chinese and full of racist self-hatred, as his writings made apparent. He bemoaned his lack of whiteness, longing to be blond and Caucasian:

I was different because I am of mixed race. I am half White, half Asian, and this made me different from the normal fully-white kids that I was trying to fit in with.

I envied the cool kids, and I wanted to be one of them. I was a bit frustrated at my parents for not shaping me into one of these kids in the past. They never made an effort to dress me in stylish clothing or get me a good-looking haircut. I had to make every effort to rectify this. I had to adapt.

My first act was to ask my parents to allow me to bleach my hair blonde. I always envied and admired blonde-haired people, they always seemed so much more beautiful.[14]

Before driving to UCSB to attack the "hot, blonde sluts" whom he (falsely) perceived as having rejected him, Rodger fatally stabbed his two roommates and a guest of theirs. All three men were Asian—a factor that may well have played a role in this, his first three of six eventual murders.[15]

Rodger was also brimming with anti-Black bigotry. In "My Twisted World," he railed against interracial couples, especially those involving a Black man and a white woman. He described his first two housemates in Isla Vista (not his eventual murder victims) as "nice" but complained that

they kept inviting over this friend of theirs named Chance. He was [a] black boy who came over all the time, and I hated his cocksure attitude. Inevitably, a vile incident occurred between me and him. I was eating a meal in the kitchen when he came over and started bragging to my housemates about his success with girls. I couldn't stand it, so I proceeded to ask them all if they were virgins. They all looked at me weirdly and said that they had lost their virginity long ago. I felt so inferior, as it reminded me of how much I have missed out in life. And then this black boy named Chance said that he lost his virginity when he was only thirteen! In addition, he said that the girl he lost his virginity to was a blonde white girl! I was so enraged that I almost splashed him with my orange juice. . . .

How could an inferior, ugly black boy be able to get a white girl and not me? I am beautiful, and I am half white myself. I am descended from British aristocracy. *He* is descended from slaves. I deserve it more. I tried not to believe his foul words, but they were already said, and it was hard to erase from my mind. If this is actually true, if this ugly black filth was able to have sex with a blonde white girl at the age of thirteen while I've had to suffer virginity all my life, then this just proves how ridiculous the female gender is. They would give themselves to this filthy scum, but they reject *ME?* The injustice![16]

Scott Beierle expressed similarly noxious sentiments in a series of YouTube videos. For instance:

When I see an inter-racial couple I think one of two things . . . either the guy couldn't do any better, or the girl's a whore. . . . The army had plenty of this, I saw officers with Asian wives or black wives, and I thought,

This is what you're resigning yourself to: you couldn't do any better than this to provide you with companionship. I mean, even mail order . . . you can get a mail-order bride from Russia or the Ukraine. You don't have to resign yourself to some iguana, some lizard.[17]

Such vicious anti-miscegenation bigotry is obviously tightly connected with incels' fixation on masculine hierarchies—for example, the idea of a man lower down the racist social hierarchy gaining sexual and emotional access to a white woman is enraging to an incel.[18] His aggression toward both the man and the woman in this scenario may well be equal, and he may not be white himself. Even so, his hatred is clearly a product of white supremacist patriarchy and the sense of entitlement it can generate.

The notion of involuntariness in "involuntary celibate" is revealing—and jarring, upon reflection. Ordinarily, we use the modifier when the relevant term would otherwise incorrectly imply that the act was deliberately, intentionally, or freely undertaken. For example, the term "involuntary manslaughter" refers to a killing that was unintentional, albeit reckless. The term "involuntary servitude" similarly refers to work that is improperly coerced, not freely undertaken as the result of a negotiated contract.

The idea that a person's *celibacy* is involuntary—as opposed to merely a disappointing state of affairs—is therefore illuminating. It is distinct from, and much less innocent than, the idea of a person who is "single but looking" or "dateless and desperate." There is a strong implication that celibacy has somehow been *imposed* on the incel, even forced on him, against his will.

And when it comes to sex, that implication is deeply wrong-headed. Inasmuch as an incel regards himself as entitled to sex with women, and women as therefore obligated to have sex with him, he evinces an indifference to what would go against *her* will. For these reasons, it is clearly sexual *activity*, not celibacy, that should be thought of as voluntary or involuntary.

It might be tempting to conclude on this basis that incels are oblivious to the inner lives of women—that they regard women as mindless, thinglike, subhuman, or as nonhuman animals. And it's certainly possible to identify a basis for this temptation in some incels' rhetoric: witness Scott Beierle's slurring of the women above as iguanas or lizards.

I think we should resist this idea as too simple and too convenient. For one thing, an incel clearly *does* acknowledge the mental lives of women, inasmuch as he wants—indeed, demands—to be desired and admired by them. Rodger's writings are typical of the genre in this regard: he speculated bleakly, and at length, about why the women he wanted didn't seem attracted to him, and why they chose to "throw themselves" at the "obnoxious brutes" they preferred to him. "I don't know what you don't see in me," he complained. It seems clear that Rodger ascribed to these women agency, desires, and even an autonomous sexuality. Hence his outrage when they preferred other men to him, "the supreme gentleman."[19]

In other words, these women's freedom—their capacity to make choices for themselves—was not in doubt. But he resented that freedom when their choices did not favor him.

Recall too the title of Scott Beierle's novel, written during his adolescence: *Rejected Youth*. Although it was never released, *The Washington Post* described it as being a 70,000-word revenge fantasy of a middle school boy nursing hatred of the girls who had shunned and humiliated him. The protagonist, Scott Bradley, critiques their looks, ridicules their boyfriends and is enraged by their disdain. "The hot ones all detest me, and I haven't a clue why," he laments.

The boy murders them, brutally, one by one, even as he admires their bodies. In the final scene, he cuts the throat of the clique's ringleader before he throws himself off a roof with the cops closing in.[20]

Notwithstanding the parallels with Rodger's memoir and acts of violence, Beierle wrote this while he was in high school, in the late 1990s. Rodger was still in elementary school then—and, by his own account of things, enjoying a happy childhood.

So why do incels sometimes resort to such dehumanizing and objectifying language in speaking about women—for instance, by calling women "femoids" (or "foids," for short)?[21] As we have seen, it's not because they believe that women are literally nonhuman animals, mere sexual objects, robots, or similar. There is a simple alternative explanation: it is an expression of rage and the resulting desire to put women down. Incels are passionately invested in social hierarchies, including one that resembles the great chain of being, with god at the top, nonhuman animals at the bottom, and various ranks of human beings positioned in between them. So implying that a woman is something nonhuman may serve as the ultimate insult. But her supposed moral crime is a human, all too human, violation—the kind of act only human beings can commit—as is her proposed punishment. Nonhuman animals do not betray their owners, though they may disappoint them. And people typically don't take revenge on nonhuman animals either.[22] When they do, there is something conceptually awry, as opposed to simply ethically wrong, about the whole enterprise. That is the Cliffs Notes lesson of *Moby-Dick,* I take it.

There is also something far too convenient about the idea that incels don't see women as being fully human. It allows *other* men, who don't resort to calling women pigs or dogs, but who may still share aspects of an incel's entitled ideology, to defend themselves too easily. When accused of misogynistic behavior, men often respond by invoking their recognition of the humanity of their wives, sisters, mothers, or other female relatives. Far better that a man realize that no woman belongs to him—and that he is not entitled to have *any* woman's love, care, and admiration in an asymmetrical moral relationship. It is not hard, upon reflection, to recognize the obvious fact that a woman is fully human. The real challenge may be in recognizing that she is fully a human *being,* and not just a human *giver* of love, sex, and moral succor. She is allowed to be her own person, and to be with other people.

Incels are not amoral (though they are, of course, highly *immoral*); they are deep believers in a specific moral order. They feel not merely angry but aggrieved; they are not merely disappointed but resentful. They feel not merely let down but positively betrayed, by women in particular and by the world in general. They feel that the world owes them certain favors. And they often believe that they are vulnerable, victimized, and sensitive, even traumatized. Describing the first time he felt humiliated by a girl, when he was eleven, at summer camp, Rodger wrote:

> I was innocently playing with the friends I made, and they were tickling me, something people always did because I was very ticklish. I accidently bumped into a pretty girl the same age as me, and she got very angry. She cursed at me and pushed me, embarrassing me in front of my friends. I didn't know who this girl was. . . . But she was very pretty, and she was taller than me. I immediately froze up and went into a state of shock. One of my friends asked me if I was OK, and I didn't answer. I remained very quiet for the rest of the day.
>
> I couldn't believe what had happened. Cruel treatment from women is ten times worse than from men. It made me feel like an insignificant, unworthy little mouse.[23] I felt so small and vulnerable. I couldn't believe that this girl was so horrible to me, and I thought that it was because she viewed me as a loser. That was the first experience of female cruelty I endured, and it traumatized me to no end. It made me even more nervous around girls, and I would be extremely weary [sic] and cautious of them from that point on.

The words "trauma" and "traumatized" appear in Rodger's so-called manifesto on some ten other occasions, always in reference to himself. In this respect, he is far from an anomaly among his incel brethren. Such themes are ubiquitous in their writings. An anonymous user on incels.co wrote, "Our whole lives we've had to endure the pain of being so physically repulsive to females that they'd never even consider giving us a chance. We are actually so genetically inferior that they HATE us." He went on: "They need to suffer. Their hypocrisy is a crime [punishable by] torture for the rest of their slutty lives."

The sad truth is that, like many oppressors, incels perceive themselves as being the vulnerable ones. They feel like the true victims, even as they lash out violently against others. And they feel they are in the right, even as they commit the most deplorable acts of wrongdoing. All the more reason, then, that we should be skeptical about incels' self-reports about occupying a low rung, relative to other men, on an unjust hierarchy of attractiveness. More likely, they are *looking* for an unjust hierarchy to locate themselves on, thereby vindicating their preexisting feelings of inferiority and aggrieved resentment.[24] Often, we might suspect, there is little to these complaints: they are merely a post hoc rationalization for an extant, and unwarranted, sense of victimhood—of being oppressed or persecuted by people who aren't in reality wronging, thwarting, or even rejecting them. In particular, the women incels resent for these supposed sins are often just living their own lives and minding their own business.

These considerations also have implications for how we ought (and ought not) to deal with someone with an incel's entitled mind-set. A general ethical mandate says that when someone is in pain, we ought to try to soothe and assuage that pain if we can, all else being equal. Even if we aren't in a position to help, we should at least express our sympathies. And incels *are* clearly often in pain (though that pain may at times be overstated).[25] But when someone is in pain precisely because he has an overblown sense of entitlement to the soothing ministrations of others, which have not been forthcoming, stepping in to assuage his pain becomes an ethically fraught enterprise. Even expressing our sympathies runs the risk of feeding into his false, dangerous sense that other people—especially girls and women—exist to pander to the incel's needs and to gratify his ego.[26] So here, as elsewhere, we ought to resist the pressure to himpathize.

Incels have generated many headlines recently. It's easy to understand why, given the egregiously violent acts of misogyny some incels have committed. In truth though, such behavior is on a continuum with everyday occurrences that often slip under the radar, from domestic violence to rape to sexual predation and coercion. So strong is the continuity between the most extreme acts perpetrated by incels and the most extreme kinds of intimate partner violence that the two are sometimes mistaken for each other.

When Brandon Clark, twenty-one, killed Bianca Devins, seventeen, some early reports on Twitter described him as an incel. But, it seems, he wasn't; there's no evidence of his belonging to any such Internet community. True, the two had met on social media—on Instagram. However, they had dated for over two months in real life, in upstate New York, the victim's family clarified.[27] He had, in fact, become a trusted friend of the family during that time; therefore no one was concerned when the couple made plans to attend a concert together in New York City.[28]

It's not completely clear what happened that night, but some reports indicate that Bianca Devins flirted with or kissed another man at the concert, thereby enraging Brandon Clark. It *is* clear that they argued. He wound up slitting her throat so violently that some described it as a beheading. He then threatened to kill himself and wound up stabbing his own neck ineffectually, before the police arrested him and took him to the hospital. (He has since made a full recovery and been charged with second-degree murder.)[29] Before being apprehended, Clark posted pictures of his slain girlfriend, as well as selfies of his own wounds, on the chat app Discord—telling Bianca's followers, "You're gonna have to find somebody else to orbit." Seemingly, he begrudged her the attention she herself attracted, when she didn't give him quite enough of it.[30]

Of men like Clark, who post photographic evidence online of their crimes against women, law professor and privacy expert Lori Andrews commented, "They really expect viewers to empathize with them, to think they're entitled to teach her a lesson." Pamela Rutledge, director of the Media Psychology Research Center, noted that such behavior is a "misguided attempt to achieve social validation and feel special." "The drive for these sources of 'admiration' override any concerns of being caught," she added.[31]

As a result of Clark's grisly exercise in self-promotion, the story went viral. Even though he doesn't seem to have been involved in any incel-like forum, or even to have directly imbibed their ideology, Devins's murder was celebrated by incels on the Internet. "Her death pleases me," wrote one incels .co user. "Honestly, based on screenshots the THOT [that ho over there] was a horrible person anyway and reaped what she sowed," wrote another. "He orbits her for god knows how long, she belittles him makes him feel like human shit and treats him this way," offered yet another forum user, sporting an Elliot Rodger avatar.[32]

So many instances of domestic, dating, and intimate partner violence have much the same shape—the innocent-seeming beginnings, the indications of jealousy, and the brutal acts of retribution for some supposed act of betrayal—yet have little to no impact on our collective consciousness. Two to three women are murdered by their current or former intimate partner every day in the United States, on average.[33] And by far the most dangerous time for a woman with respect to intimate partner violence is when she either leaves, or threatens to leave, a relationship—thus provoking jealousy, rage, and feelings of abandonment in her male partner or ex-partner.[34] As the domestic violence expert Cindy Southworth put it, his subsequent crimes are "about dominating her world and wanting to be the only person who is important." So too, Southworth commented, when it comes to Bianca Devins:

> This is not an Instagram story. This is a story about dating violence and homicide, about power and control, about a man who felt entitled to take a girl's life and emboldened to post photos of it on a gaming platform.[35]

The story of Clark and Devins is not an incels story, either. The stories in this chapter are *all* stories, in the end, about the violence wrought by male entitlement.

THREE

Unexceptional—
On the Entitlement to Sex

Rae Florek, a Minnesota woman in her mid-fifties, had long been battling throat cancer. As of 2013, she had had some fifteen surgeries. She was often in pain. But that day, the pain was in her arm. "I had shoveled snow the day before and kind of thought, 'Wow, what did I just do?'" Her voice scratches.[1]

She had asked Randy Vanett, her on-again, off-again boyfriend, to bring her cigarettes and a six-pack of Twisted Tea (a mildly alcoholic beverage). He obliged, and laid down the receipt—seeming not to notice Rae's arm in a makeshift sling, fashioned from a dish towel. Rae paid him back immediately, then offered to make him lunch to thank him. But Randy didn't want lunch; he wanted sex. Rae demurred, saying: "I'm not feeling good, I just . . . no." Randy replied: "Well, that's okay, babe, because last time I was here I took you two more times after you crashed."

Rae needed a few moments to absorb what she was hearing. "You can't do that," she finally responded. "That's date rape."

Indeed, it's rape *simplicter*.[2] On the night Randy was referring to, Rae and Randy had consensual sex. Afterward, Rae took painkillers to soothe her sore throat and drank two Twisted Teas. She fell asleep and slept soundly. She slept through the two times Randy had sex with her—raped her—while she was unconscious.

Rae later reported that she felt "so betrayed . . . I had no say in it. I had no idea what he did to my unconscious body."[3]

After three weeks spent thinking over what to do, Rae contacted a friend whose husband was in law enforcement, who in turn called the sheriff. A deputy came to Rae's house, and Rae proposed secretly taping Randy confessing. The deputy said no, claiming—falsely—that this would be entrapment. Rae proceeded anyway, after buying a video camera at Walmart. She slit open the belly of a teddy bear and placed the camera inside it. She surreptitiously recorded two conversations in which Randy admitted to what he had done. In the first of these:

RAE: You knew I was out, passed out, because that's what you said that day in the kitchen. "Babe, that night after you passed out, I had you two more times."
RANDY: No, I didn't say "passed out."
RAE: What did you say? What did you say? I don't think you said "passed out." "Crashed."
RANDY: I have no idea. It wasn't "passed . . ." Yeah, well, we were sleeping.
RAE: "Crashed."

RANDY: Sleeping. When you were sleeping. I had you when you were sleeping.

RAE: "I had you when you were sleeping," that's right.

RANDY: Yeah.

RAE: Yeah.

RANDY: Yeah, and I did.

Rae wasn't sure the first recording had worked properly, so she invited Randy back over the next day. A snippet of their conversation over pizza:

RAE: Rand, I had to be gross when I'm crashed and you're fucking me, God.

RANDY: You're beautiful when you're crashed and I'm fucking you. Stop it. Stop bringing it up. You're beautiful.

Rae went to the police with the recordings. Her throat was bothering her particularly badly that day, so she spoke in a hoarse whisper and was at times barely audible. However, she was quite clear: Randy had had sex with her against her will, after she had taken her medication. ("Is that what you're reporting?" the detective, Dean Sherf, asked her. "Absolutely," Rae answered.) But Detective Sherf warned her repeatedly:

There's always two sides to every story, and nine times out of ten in cases like this, it's a he said–she said type deal, she said–he said, however you want to put it.

A week later, Sherf called Randy into the police station. Their conversation was cordial.

SHERF: Like I told you yesterday, I just want to talk to
you about what her report was and get your version of
how things played out. I'm not interested in locking
you up or anything. You . . . Whatever you tell me here
today, you're going to walk out of here, okay? You're
not charged with anything, you're not under arrest or
anything like that. It's just . . .

RANDY: Really is a sad deal.

SHERF: Well, I know. It's something no one wants to
deal with, but we gotta.

RANDY: I appreciate that.

SHERF: A report has been made, and in this case, it's . . .
She's alleging a fairly serious allegation, that there was
some sexual contact between you two when she was
under the influence of a prescription drug, is what she's
saying.

Randy told Sherf essentially the same story he'd told Rae:
he'd had sex with Rae while she was unconscious. "She didn't
say yes or no," he recalled. Randy denied that it was rape and
described what had happened as romantic. "This has and continues to be very painful to me," he added later, in an implicit
bid for himpathy.

Recall that himpathy, as I construe it, is the disproportionate
or inappropriate sympathy extended to a male perpetrator over
his similarly or less privileged female targets or victims, in cases
of sexual assault, harassment, and other misogynistic behavior.
Given that misogyny often involves punishing and blaming a

woman for her "bad" behavior—bad by the lights of patriarchal norms and expectations, that is—you can understand himpathy as the flip side of misogyny; its understudied mirror image; its natural (albeit highly unjust) complement. Misogyny takes down women, and himpathy protects the agents of that takedown operation, partly by painting them as "good guys."

Himpathy goes hand in hand with blaming or erasing the victims and targets of misogyny. When the sympathetic focus is on the perpetrator, she will often be subject to suspicion and aggression for drawing attention to his misdeeds.[4] Her testimony may hence fail to gain the proper uptake. Instead, those who are himpathetic find endless excuses for the perpetrator.

One striking case in point was that of Brock Turner, then nineteen, who sexually assaulted Chanel Miller, twenty-two, after a Stanford University fraternity party, while she was unconscious.[5] Despite the fact that Turner was caught in the act of violating Miller behind a dumpster (by two Swedish graduate students, who performed a citizen's arrest), many people expressed skepticism that Turner could possibly be a rapist.[6] One of his friends opined that Turner's crime was "completely different from a woman getting kidnapped and raped as she is walking to her car in a parking lot." "That is a rapist. I know for a fact that Brock is not one of these people," she wrote in a statement attesting to his good character. What had transpired was due to a "camp-like university environment" where "things get out of hand," she claimed. And she asked the judge not to base his sentencing on the testimony of "a girl who doesn't remember anything but the amount she drank." Many people *still* cite Miller's alcohol consumption as a decisive factor in this case. This, of course, is classic victim blaming.[7]

Instead of blaming the victim, others who expressed himpathy with Turner tried to erase Miller from the story—an act of "herasure," as I call it. Numerous news stories referred to Turner's swimming prowess and the loss of his bright future—never mentioning Miller's. Miller writes of Brock's many supporters:

> Even after the conviction, they believed he remained entitled to impunity. Their support was unwavering, they refused to call it assault, only called it *the horrible mess, this unfortunate situation*. And still they said, *Brock is not one to believe that he is above the law or has any special privilege. . . . As a woman, I have never felt intimidated by him whatsoever*. In his mother's three-and-a-half-page single-spaced statement, I was not mentioned once. Erasure is a form of oppression, the refusal to see.[8]

Meanwhile, Turner's father bemoaned the fact that his son could no longer enjoy a nice rib-eye steak fresh off the grill, having lost his appetite. The loss of Turner's "happy-go-lucky" and "easy-going" demeanor struck his father as being a travesty, rather than the appropriate outcome of his son's criminal wrongdoing. Yet more shockingly, the judge in this case, Aaron Persky, was prepared to take Turner's family and friends' word for it when it came to his being a "good guy." In response to Turner's aforementioned female friend, Persky said, "To me that just rings true. It sort of corroborates the evidence of his character up until the night of this incident, which has been positive." Similarly, Turner's father described his son's crimes as a mere "20 minutes of action out of his 20 plus years of life."

But, as we know, those who commit sexual assault are often repeat offenders—making these assumptions about Turner's otherwise good behavior likely too optimistic. After the trial it in fact emerged that Turner had leered at and made inappropriate comments to female members of the Stanford swimming team, for example.[9] Two young women had also reported Turner to the police for being "touchy" with them, and dancing with them in a "creepy" way, at another Stanford party at the same fraternity—just one week before he assaulted Miller (though the reports came six months after he committed his crimes against her). As Miller notes, these stories "were all absent from the image his loved ones and the media projected." *The Washington Post* had even called him "squeaky clean" and "baby-faced."[10]

Following these exercises in himpathy and herasure, Turner was sentenced to a mere six months in a county jail, of which he served just three (plus three years' probation). Persky worried that a lengthier sentence would have a "severe impact" on Turner's future.[11] What about the woman he had victimized, and those he might victimize going forward?

"Police: Maryland School Shooter Apparently Was Lovesick Teen," read the Associated Press headline. It was describing a seventeen-year-old boy, Austin Rollins, who had shot two of his classmates—including his ex-girlfriend, Jaelynn Willey. She was declared brain-dead and taken off life support one day later, thus making Rollins a murderer. Some people protested the sympathetic framing of the headline; but it proliferated, having been syndicated by many major news outlets, including ABC, MSN, and *Time* magazine.[12]

"Texas School Shooter Killed Girl Who Turned Down His Advances and Embarrassed Him in Class, Her Mother Says," read a headline in the *Los Angeles Times*.[13] A seventeen-year-old boy, Dimitrios Pagourtzis, subsequently confessed to opening fire and murdering ten people—including Shana Fisher, a girl who had rejected him. Shana "had four months of problems from this boy," according to her mother, Sadie Rodriguez. "He kept making advances on her and she repeatedly told him no."[14] Pagourtzis had reportedly increased the pressure until Shana stood up to him in class, embarrassing him in front of their classmates; he shot her a week later, along with seven others and two teachers.

Pagourtzis's family released a statement, saying they were "as shocked and confused as anyone else by these events that occurred." Moreover:

> We are gratified by the public comments made by other Santa Fe High School students that show Dimitri as we know him: a smart, quiet, sweet boy. What we have learned from media reports seems incompatible with the boy we love.[15]

These testaments to the shooter's "sweetness" may have been gratifying to his family. But they are grotesquely misleading and added deep moral insult to the victims' fatal injuries.

"Ex-NRL Player Rowan Baxter Dies Alongside His Three Kids, Estranged Wife in Brisbane Car Fire Tragedy," read one initial headline;[16] "Former NRL Star Rowan Baxter Appeared to Be a Fun-Loving Father Who Was Always Showering His Three Young Children with Love and Affection," read a caption to a photo accompanying another story about the incident.[17]

Baxter had killed his recently estranged wife, Hannah Clarke, and their three children—Aaliyah, Laianah, and Trey—by dousing their car with gasoline and setting fire to it. Baxter died shortly after the incident, due to self-inflicted stab wounds. Police detective Mark Thompson said he was keeping "an open mind" about these events in Queensland, Australia. Australian journalist Bettina Arndt commented on Twitter:

> Congratulations to the Queensland police for keeping an open mind and awaiting proper evidence, including the possibility that Rowan Baxter might have been "driven too far." But note the misplaced outrage. How dare police deviate from the feminist script of seeking excuses and explanations when women stab their partners to death, or drive their children into dams but immediately judging a man in these circumstances as simply representing the evil violence that is in all men.[18]

Arndt was honored earlier in 2020 by being appointed a member of the order of Australia (an honor similar to an OBE) "for significant service to the community as a social commentator, and to gender equity through advocacy for men."[19]

Himpathy often radically distorts the framing of men's violence against women, as well as children in some cases.[20] Himpathy imaginatively transforms presumptively brutal murders into understandable acts of passion or, alternatively, warranted desperation. And it imaginatively turns other crimes, such as rape, into mere misunderstandings and alcohol-fueled mishaps.

• • •

In the case of Rae Florek, Randy Vanett was never arrested, or charged, or prosecuted for the crimes to which he had admitted.[21] Dean Sherf, the detective who interviewed Rae and Randy, a sheriff's deputy in the county for almost three decades, has subsequently retired. Reporter Mark Greenblatt interviewed Sherf at his home about why this case never resulted in an arrest:

> GREENBLATT: Really, the substance of what the victim was alleging was that Randy had had sex with her while she was asleep or passed out.
>
> SHERF: Mm-hmm (affirmative).
>
> GREENBLATT: And that she didn't consent to that.
>
> SHERF: Right.
>
> GREENBLATT: Is that a crime?
>
> SHERF: It could be. Yeah, it is. I shouldn't say could be, it is, but are the rest of the elements there to convict him of that crime?
>
> GREENBLATT: What evidence would you need if the suspect acknowledges having sex with someone while they were asleep? Do you need more evidence than that?
>
> SHERF: Well, yeah. You have two people that the victim's saying one thing and the suspect's saying, "No, no, no, I didn't do that." That's what you have. There's nothing . . . There's no other physical evidence or any sort of a witness that you're going to prove that case. You had the interviews, you had no physical evidence, you had a he said–she said type deal, you had a recording.
>
> GREENBLATT: With respect, sir, what was he said–she said about it? He's acknowledging that he had sex with

someone that he thought was drunk and passed out. What's he said–she said about that?

It didn't matter in this case—nor does it matter in many cases like it—that it wasn't a he said–she said scenario in reality. What matters is the relevant clash of *interests,* even when there's no direct disagreement over the facts: no contradiction between what is asserted (by her) and what is denied (by him). In some cases, as in this one, he may just flat-out admit to his crime. But no action is taken against him; and to some, as we'll see, he may even be perceived as *her* victim. The interview went on:

GREENBLATT: In your mind, what does it take to convince you to make an arrest in a sexual assault case?
SHERF: A lot of things sometimes, and sometimes not . . . . It's a case-by-case deal.
GREENBLATT: When the suspect admits to it in front of you in a recorded interview, that's . . .
SHERF: I'm not going to argue the law with you. I decided not to arrest him. He didn't get charged. That's the way it is. I moved on to the next case. I don't know what else to tell you.

Earlier, the detective had commented on his rationale:

SHERF: Not to say that there wasn't proof beyond a reasonable doubt, but there just wasn't solid enough probable cause to make an arrest on that case. It was she said–he said, there was a time lapse from the time it was reported, they were in a consensual relationship. It wasn't an arrestable case.

The idea that there could be proof beyond a reasonable doubt but *not* probable cause is incoherent, it should be noted. The former standard of evidence for a crime is much higher than the latter.[22]

The interview concluded:

GREENBLATT: Is it not the case that a woman can be raped when she knows someone?

SHERF: Well, yeah. It can happen, but I would bet, if you went and gathered all of the cases of that sort that were investigated and compared it to how many people were even charged, it's going to be pretty minimal that were charged. It just don't happen for whatever reason. Again, that's up to the prosecutors and the courts and that's our fine system.[23]

The prosecutor, Todd Webb, said that one reason for their declining to prosecute Randy Vanett was that the victim in this case "cannot testify as to what happened because she has no personal knowledge of what happened." But that's hardly surprising, given that she was unconscious when she was assaulted. And the victims of a murder are in a considerably worse position to testify to the crime against them; but, somehow, prosecutors manage to press on in their absence.

Another prosecutor, Jim Alstead, said he thought that the teddy-cam recordings were unfair to Randy; he had been "set up." When asked why Rae would try to frame him—as opposed to having tried to pursue justice—Alstead replied, "Maybe she's on welfare." Or maybe she was lying about not being an illegal drug user, he then offered, without evidence.

When it comes to himpathy, herasure, and victim blaming, there's no shortage of possibilities. And so we see that rape involves so much more than individual bad apples. It involves bad actors who are enabled, protected, and even fostered by a himpathetic social system.

When it comes to the failings of this system, there's no shortage of possibilities, either. It's not just police officers declining to make arrests on an ad hoc basis and prosecutors declining to file charges. In many jurisdictions in the United States, rape cases are being routinely disposed of by what is known as "exceptional clearance." In 2018, *The Center for Investigative Reporting* journalists, in conjunction with reporters from ProPublica and Newsy, conducted a year-long investigation into this practice. They filed Freedom of Information Act requests to obtain data from 110 major cities and counties, although they succeeded in securing records for only about 60. They found that in almost half of these, police officers had used the designation of exceptional clearance to close the majority of rape cases.[24]

According to Lieutenant Tom McDevitt, commander of the sex crimes unit in Philadelphia, this classification applies, or is meant to apply, only to cases where "you know the crime, you're able to prove a crime occurred. You have a victim, you know where the person is and who they are. And either the prosecutor doesn't want to prosecute or the victim doesn't want to go forward with the case."[25] A Department of Justice official confirmed that exceptional clearances are supposed to be just that—exceptional—and to apply only when, despite sufficient evidence for an arrest, the arrest is unfeasible for some reason: for example, the suspect is already incarcerated or deceased, or the victim refuses to cooperate.[26] In cases of homicide, exceptional clearances tend to make up only around 10 percent of clearances; this means that around 90 percent of cleared cases are cleared by arrest (leaving, of course, a significant proportion of cases uncleared, "unsolved," or open).[27]

Yet when it comes to rape, many police departments appear to be flouting their own policies. In one of the cases the journalists followed from start to finish, a young woman had her rape case exceptionally cleared, despite her determination to move forward with it. A rape kit revealed that she had injuries and bruises consistent with the sexual assault she had reported. She cooperated fully with the police and said repeatedly she wanted justice. The police identified the man she had accused (who claimed that the alleged attack was consensual). Two years after going to the police, this woman received a letter out of the blue saying her case had been cleared two weeks earlier, exceptionally. There was nothing more she could do: case closed; it was over.[28]

Meanwhile, many cities and counties boast of high clearance rates, making no distinction between cases that actually resulted in an arrest and those cleared via exceptional means. Exceptional clearances thus threaten to skew public perception with regard to police efficacy.

While extremely high rates of exceptional clearances in rape cases may be news to many people, there is a growing awareness—

in liberal circles, at least—of the problem of untested rape kits. Recent testing of some 10,000 previously untested rape kits (discovered during a routine tour of a Detroit police storage warehouse) resulted in the identification of 817 serial rapists. According to Wayne County prosecutor Kym Worthy, there are an estimated 400,000 untested rape kits nationwide, and the existing evidence suggests that rapists commit between seven to eleven rapes, on average, before being apprehended. Worthy elaborated:

> We had many jurisdictions across the states . . . that have found these kits and are not doing anything. They're saying it didn't happen on our watch. . . . [But] I don't know how anybody can look at this problem square in the face and say that. No one would be saying this, and you wouldn't even have to ask that question, if we were talking about homicides . . . but because it's sexual assault, for whatever reason, it's very easy for some folks to sweep this under the rug.[29]

Another sobering reality: of the rape kits that had previously gone untested, some 86 percent of the victims were people of color—primarily girls and women. As Worthy puts it, "You're not going to find too many blond-haired, blue-eyed white women [with untested kits]. . . . Their kits are treated differently, their cases are solved. . . . Race is at the center of this in many ways as well, unfortunately; we know that across the criminal justice system."[30]

What explains this apathy, this hostile, pointed indifference?

Don't we regard rape as a heinous, monstrous crime? Yes, in the abstract. Very well then, but in practice, why do we refuse to hold certain perpetrators accountable vis-à-vis certain victims?

One explanation that has the virtue of not only parsimony but sheer coherence is that we regard certain men as *entitled* to take sex from certain women. A white man who is in a relationship with an equally or less privileged woman, or who was once in such a relationship, is often deemed sexually entitled to "have" her.[31] This is especially likely to be the case until she is otherwise spoken for—by another no less privileged man, not a woman or a man of color, at least typically. The most powerful of powerful men are deemed sexually entitled to "have" virtually anyone, with minimal repercussions. Consider Brett Kavanaugh; consider Donald Trump, who was credibly accused of sexual assault by multiple women prior to his election as president.[32] Consider too the now-notorious case of Jeffrey Epstein, a prominent investment banker and money manager, who was accused of sexual abuse by more than eighty girls, many of them underage. He allegedly groomed and molested these girls at his Palm Beach mansion, where he would ask them to give him a massage before touching them or masturbating, and sometimes sexually assaulting them. Yet until 2019, the consequences for him were minimal.[33]

For girls and women who are marginalized in multiple ways—in being Black, trans, or disabled, among other possibilities—the proportion of men who may rape them with impunity tends to be so large as to render their rape kit not worth testing. As such, the kit is liable to languish—and, with it, their basic entitlement to moral concern, to justice. "It was amazing to know I was going to get justice," said Tracy Rios, whose rape kit had gone untested for some fifteen years, after her rapist lured her into an empty apartment in Tempe, Arizona, in which he attacked her. "I lost faith in the system," she said. "I thought they didn't care."[34]

Rios's sexual assailant is now serving a seven-year sentence. But this is a rare outcome. If rape is theoretically punishable by, say, life in prison, what does it say about *your* value to society when your rapist walks free, despite damning evidence against him? What does that make you, other than a kind of cut-rate person?

This is not to say, of course, that rape *should* be punishable by life in prison. (Like many of my liberal ilk, I would strenuously deny this.)[35] The point here is simply to identify the negligence and double standards that plague certain victims with respect to certain perpetrators. Whatever we've identified justice as being (rightly or, most likely, wrongly), it's very clear that it's not being done in the vast majority of rape cases. Statistics from RAINN, the Rape, Abuse and Incest National Network, suggest that fewer than 0.6 percent of rapes will result in the rapist's incarceration.[36] This is a far lower rate than for comparable crime categories, including assault and battery, robbery, and so on.[37]

There is another aspect of rape culture that often goes under the radar: the sad, confronting reality of juvenile offenders. This problem, notably, defies both carceral solutions (whatever one's views about their viability in other cases) and ordinary notions of moral responsibility. The offenders are often far too young to blame, at least fully, for their wrongdoing.[38]

Roxane Gay wrote, in her devastating memoir *Hunger,* of the teenagers who brutally gang-raped her during her early adolescence. They were "boys who were not yet men but knew, already, how to do the damage of men." She did not speak of the rape, let alone write about it, for decades. Finally, in her book, she grappled with the memory:

> I remember their smells, the squareness of their faces, the weight of their bodies, the tangy smell of their sweat, the surprising strength in their limbs. I remember that they enjoyed themselves, and laughed a lot. I remember that they had nothing but disdain for me.[39]

And now, in the aftermath, as a woman of color, and a self-described fat woman, she has faced multiple forms of marginalization, myriad layers of hostile silence.

Recall from the introductory chapter that I take misogyny to be the hostility girls and women face, due to patriarchal forces, rather than the hostility men feel, deep down in their hearts. Given this, it seems clear that the sexual offenses perpetrated by (typically, adolescent) boys against girls count as misogyny. And this is so even if one holds that the perpetrators in such cases may *themselves* be in some sense the victims of misogyny and rape culture, which inflict moral damage partly via inculcating toxic behavior among those not yet old enough to know better—or even to know quite what they are doing, if they are very young.

This bears directly on the lessons to be learned from the Me Too movement, led by Tarana Burke for over a decade, and which celebrities like Alyssa Milano have helped to popularize since October 2017. As powerful man after powerful man has been exposed as a sexual wrongdoer, it's tempting to conclude that the ground has finally shifted. At last, we are taking their sexual misconduct seriously. Another possibility: something has changed about the perpetrators. The obvious factor is that they have gotten older, making it easier for people to cast them as "dirty old men"—albeit a more powerful variant of the ageist cultural trope, rather than a more pathetic figure. Notably, older men also tend to be less useful than young earners from the perspective of late-stage capitalism; their sell-by date is approaching. And so, in some such cases, they are more disposable than their younger counterparts.

But it is not as if sexual wrongdoers typically begin in their dotage, or even in middle age. The typical sexual assailant will commit his first offense during adolescence, according to self-report measures.[40] Moreover, even making the necessary exception for statutory offenses committed by younger persons (which make for cases that are rife with moral complexities), a significant proportion of sexual assault is committed by juvenile offenders—between a quarter and a third in the United States, according to recent estimates. These offenders are overwhelmingly male, just as with older perpetrators.[41]

The cases that generated the most headlines during the Me Too moment have to some extent borne this out. The allegations against Kevin Spacey and Harvey Weinstein currently date back to the early or mid-1980s (respectively). Spacey would have been around twenty-four; Weinstein, about thirty. We can readily envision each man as a sexual wrongdoer, looking back on it now; we read the older him back into the narrative, as recounted to us by his victims.

Yet when a woman came forward to testify that the English actor Ed Westwick, then age thirty, had raped her three years prior, a common attitude expressed on Twitter was: He's too young and hot to be a predator. Two more women have since testified against Westwick. The allegations still somehow failed to "ring true" to many people. The police dropped the charges, citing insufficient evidence. Plausibly, Westwick's youth and whiteness, among other forms of privilege, prevailed. He remains a golden boy. Therefore (or because?), he remains a moneymaker in Hollywood.

As we've seen, misogyny need not target girls and women universally; it often singles out those who are "bad" by the lights of patriarchal norms and expectations, and punishes them for their misdeeds, be these real or apparent. It's important not to misunderstand this point by overgeneralizing it, however. There is ample room in my framework to acknowledge the obvious fact that misogyny can target or victimize almost *any* girl or woman, regardless of her individual, gendered "good" behavior. This is partly because women are often treated as representative of a certain "type" of woman, and effectively blamed or punished for the misdeeds of the whole collective. It is also partly because misogynistic aggression can stem from myriad forms of dissatisfaction (resulting from men's being subject to capitalist exploitation, for example). And it may then involve displacement—colloquially, "punching down" behavior, directed at those who are vulnerable and available, who often happen to be women. If a woman faces this displaced aggression because she lives in a historically patriarchal world—in which men have long had, and continue to have, social permission to "act out"—she is still a victim of misogyny, according to my analysis. Finally, it bears mentioning that misogynistic social structures may have a reach that vastly exceeds their aim, and thus may punish a vast swath of women, beyond the intended or first-line targets.

All the same, it is important to recognize the ways in which women who directly flout patriarchal norms and expectations (as well as those who are merely perceived as doing so) may find themselves reliably subject to misogynistic reprisals. And the first rule of misogyny is that you do not complain about such mistreatment.

In the most egregious instances, women will effectively be punished for being, and claiming to be, the *victims* of misogyny. They will then be systematically disbelieved and maligned, notwithstanding strong evidence of the wrongdoing they have suffered.[42] In 2009, for example, a young woman in Washington State who told police she had been raped at knifepoint was fined $500 for supposedly filing a false report—a report that, it later turned out, had been accurate. This came to light in 2011 because the rapist, who had a distinctive egg-shaped birthmark on his calf, was subsequently accused of rape by another female victim in a nearby district.[43]

Between 2009 and 2014, more than one hundred women in the United Kingdom were prosecuted for making false rape allegations. One such was Layla Ibrahim, who was sentenced to three years in prison for perverting the course of justice. Her account of her sexual assault has never wavered, and both her mother and her lawyer have testified to the fact that she was regarded as a suspect almost from the outset.[44]

In late 2018, in Australia, a case involving actor Geoffrey Rush made headlines. Rush was publicly accused by his theater costar Eryn Jean Norvill of sexual harassment: putting his hand under her shirt and stroking her bare back, repeatedly making groping gestures, and sending her a text message containing a salivating (or, perhaps, panting) emoji—with the text "Thinking about you more than is socially appropriate." Norvill also alleged that Rush brushed her breast during their final scene in *King Lear*. Despite the concrete evidence of the harassment Norvill had provided, she was not believed.[45] And Rush was ultimately awarded nearly $2 million (or AUD$2.9 million) in damages for defamation.[46]

In 2006, seven queer women of color faced severe legal consequences for fighting back against sexual assault and harassment. Their assailant, a man named Dwayne Buckle, had become furious after his catcall was rebuffed. ("Mister, I'm gay!" said one of the women, trying to deter him.) He threatened to "rape them straight"; punches were thrown—there is dispute about who swung the first one. Buckle subsequently pulled hair from one of the women's heads and tried to strangle another. At some point, during the four-minute fight that ensued, Buckle was stabbed with a kitchen knife and had to be hospitalized. He described himself to *The New York Times* as "the victim of a hate crime against a straight man." Meanwhile, the women were depicted in the media as a "wolf pack" of "killer lesbians." In the end, each of the seven women was charged with felonies, including gang assault and attempted murder. Three of the seven wound up pleading guilty to assault charges, while the remaining four—who subsequently became known as "the New Jersey Four"—fought the charges and lost. They were sentenced to between three and a half and eleven years in prison.[47] Their supporters maintain that the women were guilty only of defending themselves.

And so we see that, for boys and men—especially those endowed with privilege—being held accountable for misogynistic behavior is often the exception, not the rule, even in rape cases. Meanwhile, for many girls and women, particularly those who are oppressed along other axes—race, class, sexuality, and disability, for starters—not only does their rapist or abuser often go unpunished; the women themselves may be punished for *protesting* this injustice.[48]

As for the story with which I began this chapter, it had a somewhat happier—if not exactly happy—ending. Rae Florek was eventually awarded $5,000 in emotional damages from Randy Vanett in a civil law suit. After hearing the decision about the settlement, Rae celebrated at a busy bar with her lawyer and some friends. Their conversation went as follows:

FRIEND: Cheers. What do you want to say?
RAE: Justice.
FRIEND: Victory. Yay.
RAE: Justice. I'm just reeling. I'm just reeling. I got more justice than I really ever expected.

She called it justice; he is contesting the verdict. Randy also posted pictures of Rae online, topless, in the aftermath of the court case. Such so-called revenge porn is punishable by jail time in Minnesota.[49] It remains to be seen whether or not he will be punished.

FOUR

Unwanted—
On the Entitlement to Consent

W hore." This—his—word is the last in the story, the story being "Cat Person," by Kristen Roupenian, which went viral late in 2017.[1] It paints a vivid portrait of a sexual encounter between a man and a woman: Robert, thirty-four, and Margot, twenty. Everything that happened between them that night was consensual, fairly clearly. But that's not to say it wasn't ethically problematic—not because of force or interpersonal coercion, but due to subtler factors.

Certainly, there are many criticisms one could make of Robert throughout the story. He is too old to be dating Margot, at least in my estimation. And he appears to engage in petty deception in order to attract her: ostensibly making up two cats to seem cuddlier by proxy. There is also his textbook misogynistic outburst after Margot breaks up with him. But the sex itself?

It is bad, awkward, unpleasant; it ought not to have happened. Yet it is difficult to fault Robert for not realizing something that Margot took great pains to conceal: after her initial enthusiasm wore off, she didn't want to be there. She went through with the sex only, or at least mainly, to avoid being rude to Robert.

As readers, we don't really know how Robert would have reacted if Margot had begged off politely (though we can easily guess, from his final word to her, what would have happened if she'd been candid or simply departed). Inasmuch as we suspect that he *would* have reacted badly, that counterfactual says something important about his character. But it does not tell us much about how to assess his actions. To channel *New York Times* columnist Bari Weiss's commentary on a different, albeit related case, some may hold that all Robert was guilty of was not being a mind reader.[2]

Weiss's not guilty verdict was rendered about a real-life case that unfolded a few weeks after "Cat Person" became an Internet phenomenon. A woman using the pseudonym "Grace," then twenty-two years old, testified to Babe reporter Katie Way that the actor-comedian Aziz Ansari, then thirty-four, had been responsible for a terrible night that had left her badly shaken.[3] One vital difference, however, between this and the fictional encounter in "Cat Person" was that Grace tried repeatedly to slow down and then stop what was happening: she was looking for an out, and Ansari was grossly insensitive to her wishes. There are various ways of envisaging what transpired between them—ranging from sexual assault via coercion to unethical but legal sex. But it seems clear, if we take Grace's word for it (as I, for one, am prepared to), that Ansari could, at a minimum, have done *much* more to glean that his date didn't want to have sex with him—if he didn't already realize this, at least tacitly, which he may well have.[4] This made Weiss's judgment inapt in Ansari's case, if not downright disingenuous, as well as cringeworthily himpathetic. One obvious ethical obligation when it comes to sexual activity is to actively try to glean whether or not your partner *wants,* deep down, to engage in it. If there is any real uncertainty, better to err on the side of caution, and cease and desist with alacrity.

All that, however, leaves open a possibility that may obtain in other cases: where the appearance of such unequivocal, enthusiastic consent (whatever exactly that amounts to) is merely a *performance.* And that is what "Cat Person" compels us to envisage. Margot is repulsed by Robert's body, his clumsy moves, his terrible kissing, and his sexual self-deceptions. (He declares himself "so hard," while being noticeably less than.) But she decides to go through with it anyway, and even manages to derive some sexual pleasure from the sense that Robert is taking great pleasure in *her* young, nubile body. To heighten the effect, she performs her role with ostensible enthusiasm, without feeling a shred of it.

None of this is politically or aesthetically comfortable; all of it is realistic. And it raises the specter of sex that is unwanted, and even coerced, but not *by* any particular person. Rather, the pressure derives from patriarchal social scripts and the prevalent sense of male sexual entitlement that would make it feel rude, even *wrong,* for Margot to walk out on Robert. We can imagine a variant of Robert who would have taken this exercise in sexual autonomy perfectly well, who would have handled the awkward aftermath with sensitivity and grace. Even so, we can still picture Margot—not knowing this, or not wanting to seem "spoiled and capricious" regardless—engaging in the same performance, out of deeply ingrained social programming.

The question thus becomes: Why, and how, do we regard many men's potentially hurt feelings as so important, so sacrosanct? And, relatedly, why do we regard women as so responsible for protecting and ministering to them?

"Cunt." This was a real-life case that began in much the same way "Cat Person" ended: a man sent this epithet as a one-word tweet to comedian Sarah Silverman—for no discernible reason, and with no further elaboration. Silverman responded that she had pored over this man's Twitter feed and knew that he was in pain: she saw him, she empathized, she believed in him, and so on. She forgave him and offered to pay for his rehab program for his addiction to prescription pain medication. This was generally presented as a heartwarming story—indeed, a "masterclass in compassion," according to one among many similar news headlines.[5]

Nobody in the media said the obvious, to the best of my knowledge: Silverman, though doubtless well-meaning and acting on prevalent (and, plausibly, gendered) social norms, nonetheless *indulged* this man's bad behavior. But not only was she not criticized for doing this; she was actively celebrated.

And so it goes: when women *do* minister to men's hurt feelings, they tend to be rewarded. And when they do not, they are liable to be punished.

"The Humiliation of Aziz Ansari," announced the headline by Caitlin Flanagan. Her piece in *The Atlantic* bemoaned the "temporary power" of "angry young women" like Grace—women who, the tagline announced, had suddenly become "very, very

dangerous."[6] The piece began with an expression of bafflement
about Grace's story. ("You understand the vocabulary and the
sentence structure, but all of the events take place in outer space.
You're just too old.") It then segued to a breathless recognition
of topicality. ("Like the recent *New Yorker* story 'Cat Person'—
about a soulless and disappointing hookup between two people
who mostly knew each other through texts—the account has
proved deeply resonant and meaningful to a great number of
young women.") Flanagan's own description of what happened
removed any doubt about where her sympathies ultimately lay:
squarely with Ansari, rather than with the victim of behavior
that was, by Flanagan's own admission, "not honorable."[7]

> Within minutes of returning [from dinner], [Grace]
> was sitting on the kitchen counter and [Ansari] was—
> apparently consensually—performing oral sex on her
> (here the older reader's eyes widen, because this was
> hardly the first move in the "one-night stands" of yes-
> teryear), but then went on, per her account, to pressure
> her for sex in a variety of ways that were not honorable.
> Eventually, overcome by her emotions at the way the
> night was going, she told him, "You guys are all the
> fucking same," and left crying. I thought it was the most
> significant line in the story: This has happened to her
> many times before. What led her to believe that this
> time would be different?

As well as engaging in garden-variety victim blaming, Flanagan takes liberties with Grace's words here. There is nothing
in her story that would suggest that this had happened to her

"many times before," as Flanagan surmises, rather than express-ing Grace's general disappointment with entitled male sexual behavior of myriad varieties.

Flanagan goes on to recommend that women do what women of a previous generation supposedly did in these situations: call her famous date "fresh," give him a slap, and thenceforth march out of there. But in a culture that no longer encourages the right thing for the wrong reasons—by giving a woman socially acceptable "outs" from uncomfortable sexual encounters, albeit in the name of preserving not her autonomy but her chastity—Grace prob-ably feared much the same thing the fictitious Margot did: being deemed rude, even a "bitch," by deflating a man's sexual ego. Flanagan is right that there's no real evidence that Grace was "fro-zen, terrified, stuck" (although it would certainly be understand-able if she *had* felt that way). But she lacked a socially graceful exit path. She must have known she was at risk of doing the very thing that Flanagan is so furious with her for eventually doing, albeit by another means: "humiliating" Ansari, causing him pain, and im-pugning his "good guy" self-image. She would have marched out of Ansari's apartment into a world in which women are regarded as feckless and irresponsible for drawing attention to a male date's genuinely feckless and irresponsible behavior. She will be the one who is blamed, while he is swiftly forgiven. Flanagan rails against Grace thus:

> What she and the writer who told her story created was 3,000 words of revenge porn. The clinical detail in which the story is told is intended not to validate her account as much as it is to hurt and humiliate Ansari. Together, the two women may have destroyed Ansari's career, which is

now the punishment for every kind of male sexual misconduct, from the grotesque to the disappointing.

"We certainly would be happy to make another season of *Master of None* with Aziz," said Netflix head of original content Cindy Holland about his TV series, a mere six months after Flanagan's dire speculations.[8] The streaming service also subsequently produced another of Ansari's stand-up comedy specials. Of course, one suspects that a white man may have enjoyed even more himpathetic rallying in his defense, and an even surer road to public redemption. Alternatively, as with the aforementioned rape allegations against Ed Westwick, the story may not even have made much of a dent—leaving his golden boy reputation largely untarnished.

Back to being rude, though: Why would a woman take such drastic actions—acting against her own will in such a fundamental way—simply to avoid this seemingly trifling social consequence? But we know from social and moral psychology that people often *do,* as a matter of fact, go to great lengths to avoid disrupting a social situation in which their behavior is culturally scripted—especially when it is prescribed or even suggested by some kind of authority figure.

This was revealed most dramatically in the famous Milgram experiments, conducted in the early 1960s, in which participants were directed by the experimenter to deliver an escalating series of electric shocks to a seemingly innocent man.[9] (In reality, he was a confederate of the experimenter, and a trained actor.) Naïve subjects met him and shook his hand; most reported finding him likable. They were also given a sample real electric shock of 45 volts so that they would have some sense of what he was in for if he gave incorrect answers to their prompts, in what was billed as a study of the effect of punishment on human memory. But despite participants' awareness of what they were putting the "learner" through, two-thirds of the subjects continued to follow the experimenter's instructions all the way, administering the entire series of shocks to their hapless seeming victim (who kept giving wrong answers). They went up to 450 volts, by pressing buttons with labels like "Caution: Severe Danger" and the ultimate, marked only "XXX." And they did so despite the man's audible moans, cries, agonized screams, his begging them to stop, pounding on the wall, and, eventually, eerie silence. To make matters even worse, he had complained of having a heart condition.

These results are now well known. What is less known, and bears careful reflection in this context, is that the vast majority of participants were visibly and viscerally *distressed* by their task. "They disagreed with what they were doing" even as they acted, according to Milgram.[10] Far from being indifferent to the pain they were inflicting, or operating with a "just following orders" mind-set pictured as rote and robotic, most people protested and tried to get out of the situation. In one recent analysis of audio footage for 117 subjects, 98 percent said things like "I don't want to" and "I can't" at some point in the proceedings.[11] But the majority were nevertheless prevailed upon to keep going by the experimenter's prompting. Those who completed their task did so while exhibiting stress in numerous ways: sweating, chain-smoking, crying, and, in one case, chanting.

The content of this man's chant was suggestive: "It's *got* to go on; it's *got* to go on."[12] This supports Milgram's point, which he argued for at length in his book *Obedience to Authority,* that participants labored under a false but strong sense of *moral obligation* to comply with the experimenter's orders.[13] It wasn't so much that people lost their moral conscience in the moment. It's that it was easy to instill a spurious but overriding, conflicting sense of duty to comply with an ad hoc authority figure in the form of the experimenter: in this case, a man in a lab coat, billed as a Yale scientist.[14] The participants had never met this man before, and he would play no foreseeable role in their lives going forward. They had been paid a mere four dollars (plus fifty cents for carfare) for their troubles. Yet most participants also saw compliance with his wishes as something to which he was *entitled.* When participants objected and tried to call a halt to the proceedings, the experimenter would issue one of the following prompts, in this order:

"Please continue" or "Please go on."

"The experiment requires that you continue."

"It is absolutely essential that you continue."

And, as a last resort:

"You have no other choice, you *must* go on."[15]

Interestingly, the last and most overtly coercive prompt also seems to have been the *least* effective. Each of the subjects who received it wound up making an exit.[16]

These experiments reveal the power of social scripts, especially when an authority figure is involved in them—someone whom one would have to resist, rudely, in order to break free of them.[17] Such situations can make perfectly ordinary people go so far as to torture an innocent victim, despite the strongest protestations of their conscience. The lesson of the Milgram experiments is not only what people are prepared to do to *others*, under such conditions. It is also about what they are prepared to do *despite themselves*, given such a setup.

"Please," said Harvey Weinstein, eleven times, to Ambra Gutierrez, a twenty-four-year-old model, over the course of two minutes. This was in secretly taped audio footage, published late in 2017, that helped occasion his downfall.[18] Weinstein, then sixty-five, had groped Gutierrez's breast the day before—hence her decision to go to the police and to consent to wear a wire during their next meeting. He was now determined to have her join him in his hotel room. He began in an explicitly coercive vein. (Weinstein: "I'm telling you right now, get in here." And shortly thereafter: "You must come here now." "No," Gutierrez responded, swiftly and decisively, albeit with audible difficulty.) Weinstein then shifted gears, abruptly and slyly, to something more like the first of Milgram's prompts. ("Please?" being his next utterance.) As he reiterated this "please" (as in, "please come here"), it became harder and harder—since less and less socially expected—for Gutierrez to keep demurring. Hence Weinstein's ostensibly light, but relentlessly applied, pressure. He was evidently not only indifferent to Gutierrez's mounting distress; he was *aiming* to cause it, to make her accede to him.

It's not that Gutierrez's no meant yes to Weinstein, exactly; it's that it meant *nothing*—it merely being his cue to keep asking, prompting, needling. He repeatedly reminded her of who he was ("I'm a famous guy"), as well as the script from which she was deviating ("Now you're embarrassing me"). She was refusing to take direction; she was being impossible to work with.

Weinstein's powerful persona—who he was in context, even independently of what he had it within his power to *do*—would surely have sufficed to make many of his targets vulnerable to his predation. Such a man is liable to create a spurious sense of obligation, in addition to (typically warranted) fear, in a female social subordinate who would otherwise resist his overtures. She may even be prevailed upon to be an active participant in his sexual hijacking of her person: she is just as averse to the sex as ever, but has been made *more* averse to continuing to say no to him. And so she may end up having sex she doesn't want for her own sake, nor for *its* own sake—not remotely. She does so in order to avoid the fallout women are socialized to circumvent.

Weinstein lured another of his targets, Emma de Caunes, to his hotel room and followed his modus operandi to the letter. When he emerged from the shower and asked her to lie down on the bed with him, she refused point-blank. He was startled. "We haven't done anything!" she remembers him exclaiming. He tried to convince her that the scenario was romantic. "It's like being in a Walt Disney movie!" he offered. (Another of his victims called his setup "a bad fairy tale.") De Caunes gathered her strength: "I looked at him and I said—it took all my courage, but I said, 'I've always hated Walt Disney movies.' And then I left. I slammed the door." Nevertheless, she was distraught, shaking, petrified.[19]

It's not just hyperprivileged men who can wield this kind of power, either. These things happen every day; they happen within marriages. In a recent Vox article, a woman wrote about what she described as "her deepest, darkest truth," which she had finally divulged in couples counseling: she had felt sexually violated by her husband all throughout their eight-year marriage.[20] "The unwanted sex at times made me sick," she related. "Once I had to run straight from bed to the bathroom, where I retched into the toilet." And yet, for the fifteen years following that counseling session, these awful realities were almost impossible for her to acknowledge. She was afraid to tell her husband that she didn't want to have sex with him; she was afraid to reject him; and she was even afraid to admit to herself what was happening. Instead, she writes, "I bargained my way out of sex as often as I could. I gloried in being sick enough to have the right to refuse," even though "I knew, intellectually, I was entitled to refuse sex" at any time. When she couldn't get out of it, she let her husband have sex with her, while she read a book to distract herself. She did say no to his kissing her. "That was the rule: You can fuck me, but you can't kiss me, and I don't have to pretend to like it. This satisfied him." She continues:

> Submitting to sex with a man who knew it was unwanted, who knew I felt deep pain at our lack of emotional connection, and who knew—who had been clearly told—that it felt like a violation, broke something in me. Knowing that he could still enjoy and feel emotionally fulfilled by that unwanted sex shattered my idea of our marriage. I felt like a sex doll. I felt unselfed.
>
> But I blamed myself.

The author began to reconsider this only during the Me Too movement, long after she'd left her husband. She writes:

> As I witness so much outrage on the behalf of women who have been shamed, coerced, and bullied into sex in so many other contexts . . . I wonder: How could my husband listen to me say what I said [about feeling sexually violated by him]—even once, even timidly—and sleep well that night, much less continue to insist on sleeping with me?

My answer, of course, is entitlement. But this story goes to show just how difficult it can be for a woman to resist a sense of male sexual entitlement that she has internalized, on his behalf. "How do you assert your agency when its price is the pain of others?" the author asks. At the time of writing, I have no real answer to this question.

The kicker? The author, who remained anonymous, is a humanities professor who regularly teaches feminist theory. But, she confesses, "all the feminist texts I had read could not drown out what I had absorbed from society and popular culture: that it was my duty to satisfy my husband, regardless of my own feelings."

In addition to being afraid of dire social consequences—from professional retribution to marital estrangement—a woman may experience intense guilt and shame for saying no to the men who feel entitled not just to sex but to her eager consent and participation.

Seen in this light, Caitlin Flanagan's concern about the humiliation of Aziz Ansari is curiously (if characteristically) lop-sided. A woman who thwarts a man's will on this score is often the one who feels shame and humiliation in the aftermath. And those painful emotions may then serve to secure her silence.[21]

This is essentially what the actor Salma Hayek wrote of Harvey Weinstein in a powerful *New York Times* piece, in which she broke her long-held silence about his abuse of her.[22] Weinstein made Hayek's creative dreams seem feasible; he gave her the sense that she might be somebody someday; and then, cruelly and vindictively, he lashed out at her when she failed to give him satisfaction. When she denied him sex, in particular, and said no to him in general, he treated her like a nobody. He belittled and threatened to kill her; his sexual coercion was just one move among many in his arsenal.[23]

When Hayek failed to play a sufficiently sexy Frida Kahlo for Weinstein, this enraged the famous producer, according to her narrative. Thus thwarted, he exploded: he isolated and humiliated her, before forcing her to perform a topless sex scene against which her very body protested. She writes of panicking, vomiting, and weeping at the thought of his eyes on her naked body—a visceral manifestation of the shame such men often weaponize against women.

But, again, it is not just powerful men like Weinstein who manage to do this (which is not to deny that the powerful do have extra leverage here). There are also those who are entitled but *aggrieved*, crestfallen, and disappointed, either by life in general or by women's reactions to them in particular. Kristen Roupenian's Robert is one such example, portrayed as a slightly crumpled, and easily wounded, person. Another is the character of Chuck Palmer, from HBO's *Girls*.[24] In the episode "American Bitch," which aired early in 2017, Hannah Horvath goes to the apartment of this acclaimed middle-aged writer. Palmer has been accused of exploiting his intellectual stardom to sleep with undergraduates while visiting college campuses around the country, giving lectures and master classes. It's not exactly clear whether the sex was consensual; and, indeed, that is part of the point. In a culture in which such men are deemed entitled to consent, the question of consent isn't all that needs to be asked, when it comes to what they may have to answer for, ethically speaking.[25] True, the consensual/nonconsensual distinction has come to mark the line between legal and criminal sex acts, by default if not by design. But there is more to ethical sex than merely not doing something criminal; the same goes for most areas of human life and moral conduct. For example, there is more to being honest than not committing fraud, burglary, or grand larceny.

In the show, Hannah (played by Lena Dunham, *Girls*' creator) is a writer herself—at twenty-seven, considerably younger than Palmer, and not yet famous. Hannah has written about Palmer's indiscretions—as he thinks of them—for an obscure feminist website. Despite his advantage in age and professional status, Palmer sees himself as Hannah's victim, and as being highly vulnerable to young women's power in general. They are now empowered to ruin his reputation by exposing his sexual exploits *as* exploitation. That is ostensibly why he has invited Hannah to his lavish, tasteful Manhattan home: to tell her his side of the story, as a pariah now racked with anxiety.

"Not rape, not quite that, but undesired nevertheless, undesired to the core"—this is how the character of David Lurie, a fifty-two-year-old professor, describes the sex he has with his twenty-year-old student Melanie in J. M. Coetzee's novel *Disgrace*. "As though she had decided to go slack, die within herself for the duration, like a rabbit when the jaws of the fox close on its neck."[26] Melanie moves of her own accord—even lifting her hips to help David undress her—but not quite of her own volition. When David knocked on her door that afternoon, surprising her in her slippers, she was cast into a cultural script in which such a man's sexual desire has outsize ethical importance.

Melanie would have to make her will hard and steely in order to resist David—soon to be disgraced and forced to resign from his university, due to his sexual misconduct and subsequent lack of remorse. Instead, Melanie goes limp. She is caught off guard; she freezes.

This makes the sex not quite rape. But what makes it morally gross, even to David himself—who slumps over his steering wheel, fighting dejection and shame after leaving Melanie's apartment—is that he is aware that it *might* have been rape had she been prepared for his onslaught. More precisely, if Melanie had had more in the way of agency and a sense of entitlement to deny him, she likely would have said no. And David, in knowing this, clearly took advantage (an old-fashioned expression, but a useful one here, for all that).

As it is, when he arrives, "nothing will stop him," and she does not even try. "All she does is avert herself—avert her lips, avert her eyes." She turns her back and removes herself—"So that everything done to her might be done, as it were, far away."[27] And so he has his way with her: his little death, his resurrection.

Later, Melanie arrives unannounced on David's doorstep and asks if she can stay with him. She plays her role in his life with some ostensible enthusiasm for a short while, as if to rewrite the ugliness and violence of that first time in her apartment. But "to the extent that they are together, if they are together, he is the one who leads, she the one who follows. Let him not forget that," he tells himself.[28] His words ring hollow.

This lack of desire at the core, this sexual Milgram experiment, this obedience to a culturally designated authority figure in the relevant domain—it goes beyond sex, too. Most obviously, it extends to other forms of manhandling that may or may not be sexual but are nonetheless proprietary and presumptuous. An eleven-year-old Hannah Horvath responded with a passivity similar to Melanie's when her English teacher, Mr. Lasky, was overly familiar with her, handsy (to invoke another old-fashioned, but again suggestive, turn of phrase). Hannah said she didn't mind, that she liked it, even: but for the wrong reasons, at the wrong time, in the wrong way, to invert Aristotle's famous formulation. She recalls to Chuck Palmer:

> He liked me, he was impressed with me. I did special creative writing: I wrote a little novel or whatever. Sometimes, when he was talking to the class he would stand behind me and he'd rub my neck. Sometimes he'd rub my head, rustle my hair. And I didn't mind. It made me feel special. It made me feel like someone saw me and they knew that I was going to grow up and be really, really particular. . . . Anyway, last year I'm at a warehouse party in Bushwick, and this guy comes up to me and he's like, "[Hannah] Horvath, we went

to middle school together, East Lansing!" And I'm like, "Oh my God, remember how crazy Mr. Lasky's class was? He was basically trying to molest me." You know what this kid said? He looks at me in the middle of this fucking party like he's a judge, and he goes, "That's a very serious accusation, Hannah." And he walked away.

Witness now David's similarly ponderous, judgmental reaction to Melanie's eventual accusations against him. He is not only defensive but deeply contemptuous, deeply patronizing:

> Abuse: he was waiting for the word. Spoken in a voice quivering with righteousness. What does she see, when she looks at him, that keeps her at such a pitch of anger? A shark among the helpless little fishies? Or does she have another vision: of a great thick-boned male bearing down on a girl-child, a huge hand stifling her cries? How absurd! Then he remembers: they were gathered here yesterday in this same room . . . [and] Melanie barely [came] to his shoulder. Unequal: how can he deny that?[29]

How indeed could David deny the power imbalance between them? But the basis on which he eventually affirms it—height—is maddeningly irrelevant. The relevant inequalities are a product of a patriarchal culture, and the subsequent threats and punishment leveled at girls and women who resist and challenge the will of male authority figures. Hence this particular form of internalized misogyny: the shame and guilt women often feel for not protecting a man who mistreats us. We do not want to hurt him or let him down; we want to be a good girl.

. . .

In the aforementioned episode of *Girls,* Chuck Palmer charms Hannah and wears down her defenses before too long. As they stand around swapping stories, she pulls a book down off his shelf: *When She Was Good,* by Philip Roth. Hannah says she loves the novel, loves Roth, regardless of his misogyny. The book had an alternate title: *American Bitch,* Hannah tells Palmer. He gives her his signed copy on the spot: a little reward for not being one.

In the next scene, Palmer lies down on his bed and asks Hannah to lie down next to him. He just wants to feel close to someone; he's not sleeping well; he's lonely. He lies with his back turned toward her; they are both fully clothed. Suddenly, uninvited, and without any warning, he turns around, jeans unzipped, and rubs his semierect penis against her thigh. He's expectant—and Hannah reaches down to jerk him off, instinctually. And then she jumps up, yelling, "I touched your dick!" repeatedly. She is utterly humiliated.

Chuck Palmer grins sardonically, even sadistically, as Hannah stands there yelling. He has won, and he knows it. She came to his apartment in order to confront him about his sexual predation. In showing her how it was done, and simultaneously undoing her, he has gotten what *he* wanted; she, meanwhile, is left undermined, sickened, flailing.

FIVE

Incompetent—
On the Entitlement to Medical Care

When the sociologist and writer Tressie McMillan Cottom was four months pregnant, she began to bleed. She was at work at the time, and after meeting her writing deadline, she called her husband to have him come pick her up. As she dryly remarks, "When you are a black woman, having a body is already complicated for workplace politics. Having a bleeding, distended body is especially egregious."[1]

McMillan Cottom went to her obstetrics office, which, she explains, she chose "based on the crude cultural geography of choosing a good school or which TJ Maxx to go to: if it is on the white, wealthy side of town, it must be good."[2] But it wasn't—at least not for her, as a Black woman.

Despite having called ahead to alert the staff to her condition, McMillan Cottom was left sitting for long enough that she began to bleed through the waiting room chair. When her husband asked if she could wait somewhere more private, the nurse "looked alarmed, about the chair." The doctor who eventually saw her "explained that [she] was probably just too fat and that spotting was normal."[3] He sent her home.

McMillan Cottom's pain began in earnest that night, "just behind the butt muscle and off to the side." After walking, stretching, and calling her mother, she finally called the nurse. The nurse dismissed the pain as constipation.[4]

For three days, McMillan Cottom's pain continued. She was unable to sleep for more than fifteen minutes at a time, over an almost seventy-hour period. When she went to the hospital, they admonished her for having probably eaten something "bad" for her, and they agreed to do an ultrasound only begrudgingly. What emerged was that McMillan Cottom had been experiencing labor pains all along—but they'd been discounted because the pain was in the "wrong" location. McMillan Cottom writes:

> The [ultrasound] image showed three babies, only I was pregnant with one. The other two were tumors, larger than the baby and definitely not something I had eaten. The doctor turned to me and said, "If you make it through the night without going into preterm labor, I'd be surprised." With that, he walked out and I was checked into the maternity ward. Eventually a night nurse mentioned that I had been in labor for three days. "You should have said something," she scolded me.[5]

McMillan Cottom's ordeal was still far from over: she was denied pain medication, since her pain wasn't deemed bad

enough for narcotics. As she was wheeled into a delivery operating room, she slipped in and out of consciousness. The pain
was in fact so bad that, at one point when she woke up, she
screamed, "motherfucker." The nurse on duty told her to watch
her language. When an anesthesiologist finally arrived to give
her the epidural she had requested, his reaction was not one of
compassion, or even professional coolness. Rather, McMillan
Cottom recounts: "he glared at me and said that if I wasn't quiet
he would leave and I would not get any pain relief." Then:

> Just as a contraction crested, the needle pierced my spine
> and I tried desperately to be still and quiet so he would
> not leave me there that way. Thirty seconds after the
> injection, I passed out before my head hit the pillow.[6]

McMillan Cottom gave birth to her daughter, barely breath-
ing, who she was told had come four days too early for the
hospital to attempt any medical interventions. The baby died
shortly afterward. McMillan Cottom held her daughter, and
consulted with the nurse about how to handle her remains. The
nurse then turned to her and said: "Just so you know, there was
nothing we could have done, because you did not tell us you
were in labor."[7]

According to recent estimates, Black women in the United
States are some three to four times more likely to die as the
result of pregnancy or childbirth than their white counterparts.[8]
These alarming rates of maternal mortality for Black women—
which cannot be explained by comparative poverty alone[9]—are

finally beginning to be discussed in white liberal circles, largely due to the intellectual labor of authors like McMillan Cottom and Linda Villarosa.[10] The harrowing experiences of tennis superstar Serena Williams—who nearly died after childbirth when her testimony about her history of blood clots was initially ignored or at least downplayed by medical staff—has also been a factor.[11] Such increased awareness is, of course, salutary and long overdue. But it also needs to be expanded beyond maternal healthcare. McMillan Cottom's essay "Dying to Be Competent," in which she narrates and analyzes the aforementioned experiences, sheds crucial light on just how wide and deep are the failures of healthcare for Black women, pregnant or no. As McMillan Cottom writes:

> Everything about the structure of trying to get medical care had filtered me through assumptions of my incompetence. . . . The healthcare machine could not imagine me as competent and so it neglected and ignored me until I was incompetent. Pain short-circuits rational thought. It can change all of your perceptions of reality. . . . When the medical profession systematically denies the existence of black women's pain, underdiagnoses our pain, refuses to alleviate or treat our pain, healthcare marks us as incompetent bureaucratic subjects.[12]

The converse holds as well, of course: if one is marked as incompetent, then one's pain is liable to be taken far less seriously. Women in general, and Black women in particular, routinely encounter medical professionals who regard them as hysterical, and subsequently treat their pain with skepticism.

In their groundbreaking and widely cited paper "The Girl Who Cried Pain," medical researchers Diane E. Hoffmann and Anita J. Tarzian canvassed the existing literature on gender differences in the experience and treatment of pain. For several painful procedures—including abdominal surgery, coronary artery bypass grafts, and appendectomies—they found that men received more pain medication than women (controlling for weight, when appropriate). For the last of these procedures, women were more likely to be given sedatives instead of pain medication. In one study, women at a pain clinic were prescribed "more minor tranquilizers, antidepressants, and non-opioid analgesics than men. Men received more opioids than did women."[13] These trends were not restricted to adult patients, either. For boys and girls who had undergone surgeries and subsequently complained of pain, boys were significantly more likely to be given codeine; girls, acetaminophen (the mild over-the-counter analgesic marketed in the United States as Tylenol).[14]

All of this is despite the fact that, as Hoffmann and Tarzian discuss in detail, there is some evidence that women may be prone to experiencing slightly *more* pain than men on the basis of the same noxious stimuli—submerging a person's hand in very cold water being a standard test for this—and would therefore presumably require more aggressive pain management. There are also numerous painful autoimmune and gynecological conditions for which girls and women constitute the majority or the vast majority of patients, respectively (along with, in the latter case, some trans and some non-binary patients). So, as Hoffmann and Tarzian write:

> Given that women experience pain more frequently, [and] are more sensitive to pain . . . it seems appropriate that they be treated at least as thoroughly as men and that their reports of pain be taken seriously. The data do not indicate that this is the case. Women who seek help are less likely than men to be taken seriously when they report pain and are less likely to have their pain adequately treated.[15]

Moreover, women tended to be portrayed as "hysterical and emotional" in the medical literature, resulting in more diagnoses of psychosomatic illnesses and perceptions of their emotional volatility, according to the researchers. Female chronic pain patients were hence likelier to receive a diagnosis of "histrionic disorder" (defined by "excessive" emotionality and attention-seeking behavior) than were their male counterparts.[16]

Hoffmann and Tarzian published their landmark article in 2001, and one might hope that the situation would have improved in the interim. This hope is rather dashed by a 2018 survey of more recent studies (published between 2001 and 2015), in which Anke Samulowitz and her coauthors found that

> women, compared to men, received less and less effective pain relief, less pain medication with opioids, and more antidepressants and got more mental health referrals. . . . A major finding is that women's pain in the reviewed studies was psychologized. . . . Women's pain

reports are taken less seriously, their pain is discounted as being psychic or nonexistent, and their medication is less adequate than treatment given to men.[17]

So, overall, the authors concluded: "the reviewed studies showed gender bias in the [medical] encounter, along with gender bias in prescribed medication. Differences in the treatment of men and women in these studies could not be explained by different medical needs."[18]

Samulowitz and her colleagues found a particular unwillingness on the part of medical professionals to believe women's pain reports for conditions without obvious physiological markers, such as fibromyalgia (which predominantly affects women).[19] Overall, when it came to such conditions, "women's narratives about their experiences with clinicians showed . . . how hard they have had to work to be taken seriously, believed, and understood in medical encounters."[20] And, in general, "women with pain can be perceived as hysterical, emotional, complaining, not wanting to get better, malingerers, and fabricating the pain, as if it is all in her head. Other studies showed that women with chronic pain . . . are assigned psychological [rather] than somatic causes for their pain." Meanwhile, "men were presented as being stoic, tolerating pain, [and] denying pain. . . . Further, men were described as being autonomous, in control, avoiding seeking health care, [and] not talking about pain."[21]

As we've seen, there is in fact some evidence that women may *experience* more painful sensations than men, on average, on the basis of the same noxious stimuli. But that doesn't speak to the question of whether men are more *stoical* than women—that is, whether they simply "soldier through" equivalent pain more readily. If there were good evidence for this proposition, then health-care providers might reasonably believe that if a man complains that he is in pain, he must *really* be in pain—or indeed in truly terrible pain, well beyond what his pain reports would indicate.

But despite its popularity, the notion that boys and men are comparatively stoical and inexpressive about their pain does not appear to have a robust empirical basis. True, some studies show that women consult with medical practitioners more frequently than do men, on average, particularly during their peak repro-ductive years. But, as this addendum suggests, women may also have more *reasons* to consult—for example, during pregnancy. So, as the researcher Kate Hunt and her colleagues note, this leaves open the question of whether women are more likely than men to seek consultations *for the very same painful conditions*. Their paper set out to answer this question, by comparing men's and women's consult rates for headaches and back pain. They found that the evidence that women consulted more than men for back pain was "weak and inconsistent." The evidence that women consulted more than men for headaches "was a little stronger . . . but by no means fully consistent."[22]

As Hunt and her coauthors acknowledge, several qualitative studies *do* show that men commonly vocalize their reluctance to seek help from medical practitioners. However, as the research-ers go on to point out, most of these studies are not compara-tive: they do not show that men are *more* reluctant than their female counterparts to seek help.[23] Notwithstanding this lack of data, "there is still a dangerous (often implicit) tendency to assume that, if men employ a public reluctance to seek help as one important way of demonstrating their masculinity, then this must necessarily suggest that women are *not* reluctant to seek help."[24] But women may indeed be reluctant to seek medical help, perhaps for different reasons (say, in anticipation of not being taken seriously, as opposed to being loath to admit weakness). So, as Hunt and her coauthors write, "The widespread assumption that men consult more readily than women needs to [be] empirically challenged and verified, refuted or refined" in order to ameliorate the risk of perpetuating injustice. They observe:

> As men's "under-usage" of the health care system is constructed as a social problem, there is a danger that a contrasting presumption that women "overuse" health care, consulting sooner and more often, sometimes for trivial symptoms which are self-limiting or amenable to self-management, is reinforced.[25]

Moreover:

> The often unchallenged but widespread assumption that women will consult more readily for *all* symptoms or conditions and that men will be more reluctant or will delay consulting may result in health care providers assuming that women have a lower level of symptom severity before deciding to consult.[26]

In other words, looked at from another angle, the perception of male stoicism may be the flip side of the perception that women are more likely to complain about comparatively little. In which case, this assumption would simply be another face of a prevalent gender bias.

This hypothesis is strengthened by evidence that people take male cries of pain more seriously than female ones long before socialization could possibly render boys hesitant to fully express their pain states. Two recent studies have shown that, when presented with footage of a crying infant (dressed in gender-neutral clothing), people tended to rate the infant as experiencing more pain when told the infant was a boy rather than a girl.[27] As the researchers note, the participants' implicit belief that "boys are more stoic" and "girls are more emotive" would neatly explain this finding.[28] But notice that, in this case, the belief itself is actually quite implausible, as this gender difference would have to be attributed to nature rather than nurture—not only that, but boys would have to be hardwired from *infancy* to express pain less intensely than girls do.[29] And even if this belief does turn out to be true, we do not yet have compelling evidence for its *being* true. This suggests that the documented tendency to perceive boys' pain cries as indicating greater pain is merely reflective of gender bias.

All in all, the evidence that boys and men are more stoical than girls and women seems significantly weaker than the corresponding assumption to that effect. And, in a way, this is not surprising. Such an unwarranted assumption serves a potent social function in a society in which men's experiences generally tend to be privileged over women's. In this case in particular, we should ask: Do we think men's pain should be taken more seriously because we tend to regard them as more stoical? Or do we regard them as more stoical because, at least in many settings, we tend to take their pain more seriously? The latter hypothesis is also bolstered by evidence that, when women are in pain, they are more likely than men to continue to perform household labor and family duties. Indeed, "an overload of responsibility for family, work, household, their pain, and their wellbeing seemed to be an obstacle for recovery for women with pain," researchers observed recently.[30]

None of this is to deny that there are extraordinarily stoical men. But there are extraordinarily stoical women too. Moreover, men may exhibit stoicism largely *in certain contexts*—for example, in front of other male peers or in certain hypermasculine, competitive settings. Around women and others who care for them, it may be a different story.

Whether or not it is true, the common presumption that boys and men are stoical means that their pain reports are generally taken seriously—*appropriately* seriously, in the vast majority of cases. When a privileged boy or man complains that he is in pain, there is a default tendency to believe that he really is in pain.[31] In virtue of this, he deserves sympathy and care, as well as medical attention and treatment, if required. This is all as it ought to be. But many people are not so fortunate. When girls and women complain of pain, they are liable to be dismissed, as the above research shows. The same plausibly holds for non-binary people, as well as many of the men who are *not* privileged, in terms of race, disability, sexuality, or class, among myriad other social factors. And, of course, for women who are subject to multiple, compounding forms of oppression on such bases, the situation is often far worse than for women who are privileged along these axes.

Pain thus turns out to be a powerful site of testimonial quieting, a concept developed by the philosopher Kristie Dotson, wherein "an audience fails to identify a speaker as a knower."[32] Because the audience doubts or impugns the speaker's competence, the speaker ends up effectively being silenced. She may complain of her pain, but her pain cries go unheeded. As Dotson shows, this kind of silencing is often enacted against Black women in America.

A similar kind of silencing occurs when someone's word is taken to be less credible than it ought to be, due to a prevalent prejudice against members of that social group. The philosopher Miranda Fricker calls this "testimonial injustice." To take one of her best-known examples, consider Marge Sherwood in the film *The Talented Mr. Ripley*. When Marge tries to air her warranted suspicions that her fiancé, Dickie Greenleaf, may have been harmed by his friend Tom Ripley, Marge is immediately dismissed by Dickie's father, Greenleaf Senior. "Marge, there's female intuition, and then there are facts," he tells her—relegating the basis of her utterance to the former, dismal category. Mr. Greenleaf treats Marge like the proverbial hysterical woman, whose word is not to be trusted. In other cases, women (as well as other minorities) may be dismissed not as hysterical or incompetent but as dissemblers or liars. Fricker argues that testimonial injustice has its roots in social stereotypes about either the competence or the truthfulness of a particular class of people.[33]

The above studies suggest that when women try to testify to their pain, they are routinely dismissed by the medical establishment on both of these bases—impugned as incompetent and hysterical, on the one hand, or as dishonest malingerers, on the other. And these injustices are often vastly worse—sometimes not merely in degree but in kind—for women who are multiply marginalized, because they are Black, queer, trans, and/or disabled. Tressie McMillan Cottom's essay "Dying to Be Competent" and her contrast between the experiences of white women and her own, as a Black woman, at her obstetrics office, draw vital attention to the compounding of injustice upon injustice here. This is misogynoir, to use a term coined by Black queer feminist Moya Bailey to capture the intersection of misogyny and anti-Black racism in America.[34]

Consider too in this connection the testimony of the Black disabled femme writer Jazmine Joyner. In seventh grade, Joyner began to experience sharp, throbbing pain in her lower left abdomen, during her track and field practices. "It felt like I was being burned and stabbed at the same time—it took the breath from my lungs," she recalls in a piece entitled "Nobody Believes That Black Women Are in Pain, and It's Killing Us."[35] "The pain would often show up as soon as I started running and I would fall to my knees on that dead grass, gasping for air and holding my side." Joyner's coach dismissed her pain as menstrual cramps, and Joyner tried to take her word for it, despite the pain's severity and constancy. When Joyner went to see her doctor and voiced her concern that the pain was relentless—not just there when she had her period—she was once again dismissed. She was told she was "overreacting and that it was normal" by the (female) doctor.

When Joyner's pain became more severe still—at least as bad, she later discovered, as the end stage of labor contractions—she hobbled to her mother's room in the middle of the night. Her mother (who had been a nurse for more than twenty years) took one look at her daughter and rushed her to the hospital. There, Joyner yet again encountered the insistence that she was just experiencing a bad period. It took her mom over an hour to persuade the staff to give her daughter an ultrasound. When they did—begrudgingly—they discovered a softball-sized cyst growing on her left ovary that had caused her fallopian tube to twist into a corkscrew shape. This agonizing cyst could have ruptured at any time, sending a blood clot to Joyner's heart, killing her. Fortunately, at this point, a lifesaving emergency surgery was performed. But Joyner lost her left ovary and fallopian tube—losses that were preventable, had her testimony been taken seriously to begin with.[36] Moreover, Joyner writes, this experience was merely a vivid preview of what was to come for her, as a Black, disabled woman, in the U.S. medical system:

> Over the years I have been diagnosed with several ailments and am both chronically ill and disabled. Each diagnosis took years to obtain. I have been gaslit by the medical community my entire life. My pain and knowledge of my body has been questioned at every turn by white doctors whose education has been historically steeped in anti-Blackness.

So, as helpful as Fricker's idea of testimonial injustice is for diagnosing part of the problem here, one may have doubts about whether it is equipped to do full justice to the relevant intersectional considerations. One cannot understand either McMillan Cottom's experiences or Joyner's as involving wholesale stereotypes about women; the testimonial injustice they faced was particular, and particularly egregious, due to their being positioned as Black women in a specific social context. As Joyner writes:

Yes, historically women have been dealt a shitty hand. . . .
Rather than being diagnosed with physical or mental
illnesses, including depression and anxiety, women were
routinely diagnosed with hysteria. . . . But to ignore the
specific misogynoir Black women and femmes experience within, and outside of the medical institutions of
the United States, is to erase the history of pain and
disrespect Black women's bodies experience every day.[37]

There is also a question about whether stereotypes, even
about specific *groups* of women, provide the best explanation of
the phenomenon of testimonial injustice (or, perhaps better, testimonial *injustices*). After all, for many women, their testimony is
considerably less likely to be dismissed in closely related medical
settings: when they are testifying as to the health of children in
their care, for example. Women are indeed often regarded as
supremely competent, trustworthy caregivers for their charges,
until proven otherwise (in which case the punishment for failures of "good womanhood" may be harsh, swift, and disproportionate).[38]

Why is the default to trust women in some contexts but not
others (as closely related as these may be)? A plausible explanation in this instance is that women are regarded as more than
entitled (indeed obligated) to *provide* care, but far less entitled to
ask for and receive it. Suppose she is positioned as the nurse or
the mother or the "mammy" (to invoke Patricia Hill Collins's
brilliant dissection of the "controlling image" of the "loving,
nurturing, and caring" Black woman who tends to "her White
children and 'family' better than her own").[39] Then, when it

comes to the well-being of the children who are her charges, she will often be regarded as at least as trustworthy as her male counterpart. But when she is the patient who is in pain—and asking for nurture, rather than giving it—she will tend to be regarded with much more suspicion and, sometimes, consternation. She will hence be in for dismissive, skeptical, and even contemptuous reactions.[40]

The problem then, at heart, may not be stereotypes about the trustworthiness of certain groups of women—for, as we've seen, these are deployed in an ad hoc manner to justify dismissing them in some, but only some, settings. The deeper problem here may be the sense that a woman is not entitled to ask for care for her own sake, or for its own sake—simply because she is in pain, and because that pain matters.

By the lights of this analysis, an exception will tend to arise when a woman clearly needs care for the sake of *others,* and for sanctioned instrumental reasons—for example, to help her be a better caregiver to those who are regarded as mattering more deeply. This helps explain some of the (superficially) bright and (truly) bleak spots when it comes to women's healthcare. For many white, privileged women, prenatal care in the United States is comparatively good—albeit geared toward the needs of the fetus, rather than that of the mother. When it comes to postnatal care, however, there is a marked and radical shortfall, as documented by Angela Garbes, author of *Like a Mother*—particularly for women of color. And for women of color, like Garbes, even prenatal care tends to be far from adequate. The same goes for many lesbian, queer, and non-binary people, who, as Garbes writes, "know that the 'normal' or 'average pregnant' person discussed in books does not refer to us."[41]

Seen through this lens, there is nothing accidental about such shortfalls in material care and moral concern for less privileged women. In a white supremacist milieu, a pregnant white woman, who is (presumptively and, in many cases, actually) carrying a white baby has the keys to the kingdom in her uterus.[42] Pregnant women of color, in contrast, may be perceived as dispensable, as disposable, or even as threats to white supremacy. Hence the resulting intolerable healthcare disparities described by McMillan Cottom and Villarosa—and their tragic outcomes, all too often.

There are still other structural sources of the aforementioned injustices. In her recent book *Invisible Women,* Caroline Criado Perez documents the tendency to regard men's bodies as the default—an instance of male-centeredness, or "andronormativity"—together with its pernicious effects on women's health and well-being. She writes:

> The evidence that women are being let down by the medical establishment is overwhelming. The bodies, symptoms and diseases that affect half the world's population are being dismissed, disbelieved and ignored.[43]

Criado Perez attributes these disparities in large part to "the still prevalent belief, in the face of all the evidence that we do have, that men are the default humans. They are not. They are, to state the obvious, just men."[44] Yet:

> Historically it's been assumed that there wasn't anything fundamentally different between male and female bod-

ies other than size and reproductive function, and so for years medical education has focused on a male "norm," with everything that falls outside that designated "atypical" or even "abnormal." References to the "typical 70kg man" abound, as if he covers both sexes (as one doctor pointed out to me, he doesn't even represent men very well). When women *are* mentioned, they are presented as if they are a variation on standard humanity. Students learn about physiology, and female physiology.[45]

It's important to add here that men and women differ not only from each other but also among themselves—sometimes in radical and fundamental ways. (Consider, for example, trans women, who would be particularly ill-served by this default conception of human embodiment.) All the more reason, then, to be concerned that a single "standard" (read: cisgender, white, nondisabled male) body is being treated as the paradigm.

In addition to this problem with medical training, many diseases are predominantly researched and understood with respect to such "standard" bodies.[46] This disparity is sometimes justified on the basis of people who menstruate being "difficult" research subjects, due to their characteristic monthly hormonal fluctuations. But, inasmuch as this isn't just an excuse for andronormativity, it is pretty cold comfort to the roughly half of the population whose bodies hence end up being underresearched. Either the fluctuations of the menstrual cycle make a difference when it comes to the safety and effectiveness of particular drugs, or they don't. If they do, then isn't it important that we know this? And if they don't, then, again, menstruating bodies should be included in these studies—as should the bodies of a diverse range of trans, non-binary, and intersex people, who are chronically excluded from medical research.

Such negligence can have disastrous results for diagnosis and treatment. Take the case of cardiac resynchronization therapy devices (CRT-D), a newer alternative to pacemakers that send electrical impulses to both lower chambers of the heart to help them beat together in synchronicity. As Criado Perez notes, women made up only around 20 percent of participants in trials for this device, according to a 2014 review of the FDA trial database. These numbers were so small that, until the results for men and women were combined and sex-disaggregated, no statistically significant difference between these different groups' needs was noticed—or used as a basis for different treatment. So the recommendation for men and women wound up being the same: they should have the device implanted only if their heart took 150 milliseconds or longer to complete a full electrical cycle. But when the more sophisticated data analysis *was* finally performed, it turned out that this recommendation was 20 milliseconds too long for women. Women with an electrical wave between 130–149 milliseconds enjoyed just over a 75 percent reduction in heart failure and death when they had a CRT-D implanted. Thus, as current guidelines stood, many women with heart trouble weren't getting the benefit of these devices.[47]

Failing women with respect to their hearts is hardly an anomaly, either. Cardiovascular disease has been the most common cause of death for women in the United States for the last three decades. And following a heart attack, women are more likely than men to die—partly due to the fact that women's symptoms (stomach pain, breathlessness, nausea, and fatigue) are often missed, since these signs are deemed to be "atypical," instead of typical for women. In Sweden, women suffering from heart attacks are given lower priority for ambulances and have to wait an average of twenty minutes longer at a hospital before receiving treatment.[48] In the United Kingdom, women are 50 percent more likely to be misdiagnosed following a heart attack. And young women who suffer from heart attacks are almost twice as likely to die in the hospital, compared with their male counterparts. Yet in the United Kingdom, research funding for coronary artery disease in men far exceeds that for women.[49]

This lack of research on non-male bodies has negative effects when it comes to more mundane medical matters too. Several common medications, including antidepressants and antihistamines, show menstrual-cycle effects, meaning they will affect a person who menstruates differently at different stages in their cycle. As a result of this, many of us may be taking the wrong dosage of the drugs we ingest on a daily basis.[50]

In view of such disparities, medical researchers have coined the term "Yentl syndrome" to capture the way women may have to present with typical male symptoms before receiving appropriate treatment. Even when it comes to disabilities and differences that should not be understood on a disease or illness model, but that may still require diagnosis, support, and management, girls and women are sometimes at a marked disadvantage. The received wisdom is that autism is some four times more common in boys than girls and that, when girls are affected, they are more profoundly affected (that is, more neuroatypical or divergent). Recent research, however, suggests that girls' socialization tends to mask signs of neuro-atypicality that ought to be recognized and appropriately accommodated.[51]

And when it comes to consumer safety, the tendency to treat privileged male bodies as the default may have far-reaching adverse outcomes. When women wearing seatbelts are involved in car crashes, they are 73 percent more likely than men to be killed or seriously injured. This appears to be due to the fact that, until very recently, all crash test dummies were modeled on cisgender men—ignoring potentially important differences between cis men and women in typical fat distribution, skeletal structure, and so on. When "female" crash test dummies *were* finally added, they were typically lighter and shorter than most actual women.[52]

Finally, medical problems that typically affect pregnant people are often chronically underresearched and underfunded. For example, more than eight hundred people around the world die every day from complications of pregnancy. Uterine failure, which results in weak contractions, accounts for around half of these deaths. Currently, there is only one available treatment for this condition: the hormone oxytocin, which typically works in only about half of these cases to allow the laboring person to give birth vaginally. Those for whom oxytocin doesn't work will require an emergency C-section. And there is currently no clinical test to tell whether or not a patient is likely to respond to oxytocin. Predictively speaking, it's a coin flip.

Imagine, then, the excitement of research that showed that patients with contractions too weak to allow them to give birth had more acid in their myometrial blood (located in the part of the uterus that initiates contractions). This was the finding of Susan Wray, a professor of cellular and molecular physiology and the director of the Centre for Better Births, in the United Kingdom. It had tremendous potential to improve outcomes—all the more so when Wray and her colleague Eva Wiberg-Itzel conducted a randomized control trial of a possible treatment for uterine failure consisting of a pantry staple: sodium bicarbonate, or baking soda. Those who did not receive this treatment were able to give birth vaginally in 67 percent of cases; for patients whose blood was made less acidic in this way, the number rose to 84 percent.[53] As the researchers noted, this treatment could potentially be made even more effective were it tailored to body weight and the amount of acid already in the patient's blood, and administered in repeat doses. So, as Criado Perez writes, the significance of this research can hardly be overstated: it could transform healthcare outcomes for the tens of thousands of pregnant people annually who undergo potentially avoidable major surgery. And it could be a lifesaver in contexts where C-sections are either unavailable or risky, such as in low-income countries. ("Not that you have to live in a low-income country for a C-section to be risky," as Criado Perez remarks. "You could just be a black woman living in the United States.")[54]

But if you're feeling optimistic, slow your roll. Wray's application for funding to continue her research in low- and middle-income countries was turned down. The research was "not a high enough priority," according to the British Medical Research Council.[55] The council members might as well have just come out and said it: the health of *women*—especially nonwhite and poor women—matters very little.

SIX

Unruly—
On the Entitlement to Bodily Control

On May 14, 2019, twenty-five white Republicans—all men—voted to pass the most restrictive abortion bill the United States had seen in decades, in the state of Alabama.[1] The bill was signed into law the following day by a white woman, Kay Ivey, Alabama's Republican governor. The law was ultimately blocked in federal court, but if it had gone into effect as planned that November, it would have criminalized abortions in the state—banning the procedure in almost every instance, including in cases of rape and incest.[2] The only exception would have been when carrying the fetus to term would jeopardize the physical or mental health of the person who would otherwise be forced to remain pregnant. Notably, the bill banned abortions at every developmental stage, thus violating the constitutionally protected right to obtain an abortion until the fetus reaches the point of viability (usually at around week twenty-four of pregnancy).[3]

Alabama's attempted abortion ban, extreme as it was, is only one of a litany of restrictive abortion laws recently passed in quick succession. Most of them have similarly received the bulk of their support from white Republican men, with conservative white women also playing an important role in crafting and promoting such legislation. So-called heartbeat bills, which seek to ban abortion after the point at which cardiac activity in the embryo can be detected, were engineered by one such conservative white woman, Janet Porter. Porter's chief contribution to the anti-abortion movement has been to further moralize abortion by depicting those who would choose to have one as cruel, callous, unfeeling. "To ignore that indicator, that heartbeat, is heartless," Porter declared, helping to shift the cutoff for abortion from around twenty-four weeks to just six or eight weeks (depending on the state in question).[4] At that stage in a pregnancy, many people do not know they are pregnant—and for those who do know, it was typically a planned outcome. So a heartbeat bill's ban on abortion would be close to total.[5]

The idea of a fetal heartbeat is clearly designed to tug on, well, the heartstrings. But calling it a heartbeat at six or eight weeks of someone's pregnancy (dating from the first day of their last menstrual period) is very much a misnomer. At this stage, there is no heartbeat—not least because there is no heart (nor a brain, nor a face).[6] There is no fetus, even: an embryo makes that transition at around week nine or ten. At six weeks of pregnancy, the embryo is approximately the size of a green pea.[7] On an ultrasound, a pulsing of cells that are specializing to become cardiac may or may not be detectable. In some pregnancies, such activity will not be detected until significantly later.

Meanwhile, when it comes to heartlessness, the shoe is on the other foot. The same day the Alabama law passed, news came to light that an eleven-year-old girl in Ohio had been abducted, raped multiple times, and was now pregnant.[8] A month earlier, Ohio had passed a heartbeat bill; it was slated to go into effect ninety days later, but it too was blocked by a federal court.[9] Under this law, the girl would have been forced to carry the pregnancy to term—thus compounding the trauma of one violation with what surely constitutes another. As the feminist writer Laurie Penny remarked about this case, "It's easy to see, by any sane moral measure, how a regime that forces a child to carry this pregnancy to full term and give birth is monstrous, heartless, and immoral."[10] Quite so; but, somehow, anti-abortion activists still purport to have the moral high ground.

It's one thing for someone who might get pregnant to oppose abortion on a personal level—to be disinclined to have one herself, or even to feel that it would be wrong for *anyone* in such a position to do so, on the basis of religious views she doesn't expect everyone to share, say. It's another thing entirely to think—especially as someone who cannot get pregnant, as a cisgender man—that anyone who becomes pregnant should be forced to bear the pregnancy to term, using the coercive power of the state, regardless of their age, beliefs, life circumstances, the traumatic manner of their becoming pregnant, or the devastating outcomes if they are not allowed to end it. The former is a reasonable manifestation of individual differences; the latter is a deeply draconian, deeply troubling attitude. Remember, the state doesn't regulate certain behaviors that most people think are immoral—lying to and cheating on one's partner, say—or behaviors that some people think are tantamount to murder—eating meat, for example. The social costs of coercion here seem to radically outweigh those of the possibility that some people will choose to do things that others believe they should not do, given the kinds of freedom to which they are entitled.

So, by all means, don't have an abortion, if you're personally opposed to them. But the state policing of pregnant bodies is a form of misogynistic social control, one whose effects will be most deeply felt by the most vulnerable girls and women. And this, in my book, is simply indefensible.

"The baby is born. The mother meets with the doctor. They take care of the baby. They wrap the baby beautifully, and then the doctor and the mother determine whether or not they will execute the baby." These words—outright lies—were uttered by President Donald Trump, during a rally in Wisconsin.[11] Many recent discussions of abortion have focused on early terminations, for understandable reasons, given the increasing impetus to ban them. But we should make sure that abortions that take place later aren't misrepresented either.

Of course, the heightened moral scrutiny of so-called late-term abortions belies the fact that only slightly more than 1 percent of abortions are performed after twenty weeks (about halfway through a typical pregnancy).[12] And these procedures are almost always undertaken due to severe fetal anomalies or serious health risks for the patient, should the pregnancy continue.

In one such case, Elizabeth (a pseudonym) was thrilled to be pregnant for a second time. (Her first pregnancy had ended at ten weeks, in a miscarriage.) At first, everything seemed to be going well. But at sixteen weeks, there were signs of serious trouble: the umbilical cord was positioned at the very edge of the placenta (instead of in the center), she was bleeding heavily, and her blood tests showed high levels of a protein that is meant to be mostly isolated in the fetus. A scan also showed that the fetus had club feet—not a big deal in itself, but potentially a sign of other developmental problems. This fear increased when doctors found that the fetus's fists were always closed during ultrasounds, which made them suspect muscular anomalies.

Despite these and other issues, and her mounting sense of trepidation, Elizabeth didn't seriously consider having an abortion at that stage. She and her husband wanted this baby badly; they nicknamed their son Spartacus, figuring that he should have a warrior name, given the odds he was up against. They were focused on seeing the pregnancy through various milestones—after week twenty-eight, their child would have a 75 percent chance of surviving, doctors told them. And he was still growing. At thirty weeks, they celebrated.

At thirty-one weeks, fetal growth had declined dramatically, from the thirty-seventh percentile right down to the eighth. And he wasn't swallowing. "This was the first time that we had been presented with this idea that there was something deeply wrong with the baby," Elizabeth told Jia Tolentino, in a moving interview.[13]

Elizabeth and her husband were finally confronted with the shocking news: her baby wouldn't be able to breathe, due to a muscular condition "incompatible with life," according to her doctors. If she carried the baby to term, Elizabeth would need a C-section, because a brain surgery she'd undergone two years earlier would make a vaginal delivery dangerous. Her doctors were afraid that if she pushed, she might suffer a fatal aneurysm. So at that point, they were considering putting her through major abdominal surgery for a baby that was never going to survive. There was also a significant risk that if she went into labor prematurely, she could suffer neurological complications—again, potentially fatal ones.

Under the circumstances, an abortion seemed to her the better option. Elizabeth had to fly to Colorado from her home state of New York (where the procedure would have been illegal) to have the procedure performed at thirty-two weeks, at a cost of $10,000. "To be clear," she said, "if the doctors thought there was any way he might make it, I would have taken that chance. I truly would have put myself through anything. What I came to accept was the fact that I would never get to be this little guy's mother—that if we came to term, he would likely live a very short time until he choked and died, if he even made it that far. This was a no-go for me. I couldn't put him through that suffering when we had the option to minimize his pain as much as possible."

In this case, and others like it, the choice to have a third-trimester abortion—by giving the fetus an injection that would stop his beating heart—was anything but heartless.[14] And yet, increasingly, those who are pregnant are not trusted to make such devastating decisions for themselves, in consultation with medical practitioners. Instead, they are maligned, policed, and even demonized.

• • •

As we've already begun to see, medical misinformation is a ubiquitous feature of anti-abortion activism. In 2012, Todd Akin, then a Republican representative from Missouri, opined that pregnancies resulting from rape were exceedingly rare—because "if it's a legitimate rape, the female body has ways to try to shut the whole thing down."[15] Akin thereby evinced magical thinking about the sorting power of the uterus, and mooted the category of "legitimate rape," which raises the question: Which rapes are *illegitimate*?

Such woeful ignorance of pregnant bodies has not deterred many of those who continue to try to regulate them. In February 2015, at a hearing to discuss a bill that would prohibit the prescription of abortifacients via telemedicine, a GOP lawmaker suggested to a doctor giving testimony that she and her colleagues might have patients swallow a camera to determine the state of their pregnancies—in a procedure similar to a colonoscopy. "Can this same procedure then be done in a pregnancy? Swallowing a camera and helping the doctor determine what the situation is?" No, she responded; the stomach does not provide a path to the uterus.[16]

Another GOP lawmaker suggested, in May 2019, that ectopic pregnancies should not be aborted: they should be reimplanted in the uterus from (in the vast majority of cases) the fallopian tubes.[17] This is manifestly not a thing. Ectopic pregnancies are generally agonizingly painful, almost never viable, and require urgent medical attention.[18] And, typically, the only feasible treatment is an abortion, which can be medical, using methotrexate to cause the cessation of the pregnancy and the reabsorption of fetal tissue, or, far more often, surgical. Without such treatment, the fallopian tube will rupture in 95 percent of cases; these potentially fatal medical emergencies cause a substantial percentage of pregnancy-related deaths.[19] And even if the patient does survive, they will often have trouble getting and staying pregnant in the future. So this stance makes little sense, even from the perspective of forced-birtherism.

Despite all of this, the conservative online magazine *The Federalist* recently published an article entitled "Is Abortion Really Necessary for Treating Ectopic Pregnancies?"[20] The piece, by pundit Georgi Boorman, advocated ending all legal abortion, including for ectopic pregnancies, despite the fact that this policy would cost lives. "Abortion is never the answer," she opined. Instead, she proposed leaving the affected fallopian tube to rupture, in the hopes that a small minority of embryos would somehow reimplant themselves "in a safer location." True, Boorman admitted, "knowing that a medical condition carries a very small chance of death is scary," but "is that very small chance enough to prompt you to suffer through purposely destroying your own child? Would you rather live with that on your conscience, knowing that in all likelihood it wasn't necessary?" In response to this combination of junk science (we know the chance of death is extremely high) and guilt-mongering, the world-renowned gynecologist Dr. Jen Gunter, author of *The Vagina Bible,* commented on Twitter: "STOP TRYING TO MAKE 'ECTOPIC PREGNANCIES ARE BABIES TOO' A THING. If you have never treated a woman with a belly full of blood from an ectopic you should shut the fuck up and sit down and learn before you get someone killed."[21] Exactly.[22]

There are evidently many men who feel entitled to regulate pregnant bodies without having the remotest idea about, or interest in learning, how they work. And there are evidently some women who are prepared to paint others as heartless for balking at these attempts to police and enforce their pregnancies.

The idea that extremely restrictive abortion laws are about protecting life is increasingly implausible. Many if not most of the Republicans who support these bans are also supporters of an administration that has overseen the tragic deaths of at least seven migrant children in detention during its tenure (while "losing" or, more accurately, stealing thousands of other children).[23] Many of the Republicans who support these bans also support the death penalty. A day after signing the most extreme anti-abortion legislation in the United States into law in Alabama, Kay Ivey declined to grant reprieve to a man sitting on death row; he was subsequently executed. Another man, who has a cognitive disability, awaits a similarly terrible death at the time of writing, due to be delivered via lethal injection.[24] Is life sacred or not? One wonders.

The vast majority of those who support such anti-abortion legislation have done nothing to address the shockingly high maternal mortality rates in the United States (particularly for Black, Native American, and Alaska Native women);[25] they show little to no interest in securing additional child support for children born into poverty; they appear unconcerned that poor-quality food and water (including, notoriously in Flint, Michigan) cause many Americans serious health problems; they actively work against the expansion of affordable healthcare; and they tend to be supremely indifferent to the police violence and state-sanctioned executions to which the Black Lives Matter movement has drawn urgent attention.[26]

Finally, anti-abortion activists are unmoved by the point that when abortion is made legal, the rates of abortion do not tend to go up. Rather, girls and women no longer need to seek out illegal abortions.[27] And illegal abortions have far worse health outcomes—sometimes harrowing ones, death included.

So the anti-abortion movement is not plausibly about life. It is not plausibly about religion, either—at least in the sense of owing directly to Christian religious doctrines now culturally associated with the movement. True, individual people may be sincere and truthful when they maintain that *their* anti-abortion stance is the result of their Christianity—understood as their participation in a local religious culture. But it's important to recognize that, in many cases, this local religious culture could easily have been otherwise. In particular, Evangelicals' attitudes toward abortion were deliberately manipulated in recent memory, for explicitly political purposes.

These purposes have drawn on anti-feminist sentiment from the outset. In an important series of papers, legal scholars Linda Greenhouse and Reva B. Siegel have shown that the contemporary anti-abortion movement in the United States had its roots in the "AAA strategy," spearheaded prior to the *Roe v. Wade* decision. The idea was to recruit Americans who had traditionally voted Democrat to the Republican Party by stressing the supposed moral threat of "acid" (LSD), amnesty (for so-called draft dodgers from the Vietnam War), and, finally, abortion—envisaged as a threat to the nuclear family. Greenhouse and Siegel write:

As [Nixon's] campaign progressed, Republican strate-
gists increasingly deployed abortion as a symbol of cultural trends of concern to social conservatives distressed
about loss of respect for tradition. In an August 1972
essay for *The New York Times* entitled "How Nixon Will
Win," realignment strategist Kevin Phillips boasted of
imminent Republican victory premised on the strategy
of courting Southerners who supported [George] Wallace in 1968. . . .

Phillips promised that a theme that the Republicans
would "attack aggressively is social morality," warning
that in the fall campaign Republicans would be "tag-
ging [Democratic frontrunner George] McGovern as
'the triple A candidate—Acid, Amnesty and Abortion,'"
and observing that "tactics like this will help link Mc-
Govern to a culture and morality that is anathema to
Middle America."[28]

Moreover, as the authors explain, "In this usage, attacks on
abortion were about more than abortion."[29] In a book published
the previous year, Greenhouse and Siegel had noted:

Triple-A attacks on McGovern condemned abortion
rights as part of a permissive youth culture that was cor-
rosive of traditional forms of authority. The objection
to abortion rights was not that abortion was murder,
but that abortion rights (like the demand for amnesty)
validated a breakdown of traditional roles that required
men to be prepared to kill and die in war and women

to save themselves for marriage and devote themselves to motherhood.[30]

The same was true of opposition to abortion in that era much more broadly. As Greenhouse and Siegel point out about the notorious anti-feminist Phyllis Schlafly: "[Her] attack on abortion never mentioned murder; she condemned abortion by associating it with the Equal Rights Amendment (ERA) and child care."[31]

All in all, then, anti-abortion activism has co-opted religion for the sake of supposed family values, rather than being driven by any grassroots religious movement. And these (again, supposed) family values aren't even about policing sex per se: witness the relative lack of interest in controlling *men's* sexual behavior or reproductive freedom. As Michelle Oberman and W. David Ball have recently pointed out, men have been almost entirely exempt from the wrath of anti-abortion activists, despite the fact that nine out of ten unwanted pregnancies happen within heterosexual relationships, and most patients who have abortions say that their partners agreed with their decision. Yet attempts to criminalize men's participation in such choices—still less their ill-considered ejaculations—are thin on the ground. As Oberman and Ball put it:

> The novelty of prosecuting men for abortion—despite the sound legal footing of such charges—tells us something important about the way we have, until now, framed the debate. Boys will be boys, but women who get pregnant have behaved irresponsibly. We are so comfortable with regulating women's sexual behavior, but

we're shocked by the idea of doing it to men. Though it might seem strange to talk about men and abortion, it's stranger not to, since women don't have unwanted pregnancies without them.[32]

It would be easy to continue detailing the hypocrisy of anti-abortion crusaders, while showing the thinness of such theoretical defenses as there may be. (Someone might argue, for example, that one can consistently support the death penalty while still opposing abortion vis-à-vis *innocent* life. Perhaps, in theory; but in practice, this defense falters, given the ubiquity of false convictions, particularly for Black Americans.) In many ways, though, there is no need: the words of anti-abortion activists increasingly betray them. "The egg in the lab doesn't apply. It's not in a woman. She's not pregnant," said Alabama state senator Clyde Chambliss, explaining why a bill claiming to protect fertilized eggs, embryos, and fetuses would not affect the legality of IVF procedures that involve selecting the strongest embryos for implantation and discarding the remainder.[33] This was a particularly brazen comment that made crystalline the true logic of anti-abortion activism: not preserving life, but controlling girls and women, and enforcing the prevalent expectation that women "give" designated men children.[34]

This is not to say that women are thereby perceived as subhuman creatures, nonhuman animals, or even mere vessels.[35] Indeed, a woman's humanity is conceptually crucial to the whole enterprise: what she is supposed to give to men, here as elsewhere, is a distinctively *human* service. She is not just supposed to *have* the child, in the style of *The Handmaid's Tale,* as an exercise in human breeding; she is meant to care for the child, afterward, in a self-effacing manner (and far in excess of the expectations placed on her male counterparts). But even if her humanity is not in doubt, it is perceived as owed to others. She is positioned not as a human *being* but, rather, as a human *giver*—of reproductive as well as emotional labor, material support, and sexual gratification, insofar as her male partner wants these. And he, correspondingly, is deemed entitled to take these goods from her, as a matter of his birthright. He is also deemed entitled to waive these goods. For many powerful Republican men, the most important exception to an abortion ban would be for a so-called mistress who got pregnant with a child who was, for him, unwanted.[36]

We can therefore conceptualize the anti-abortion movement as one of many misogynistic enforcement mechanisms designed to compel women's caregiving. A woman is not to opt out of the role of motherhood that the "AAA strategy" implicitly underlined. When she is pregnant, her habits of consumption will be subject to vigorous cultural policing—notwithstanding the evidence that the occasional alcoholic beverage, say, is unlikely to be harmful.[37] When she contemplates childbirth, so-called "natural" (that is, vaginal, unmedicated) birth will be lionized far in excess of the evidence of its benefits, either for her or for the infant.[38] And once she has an infant, she will be deemed obligated not only to care for her child with utter, selfless devotion but also to do so in a very specific manner. Consider the pressure to breastfeed, for example, which massively outstrips the evidence, or likely magnitude, of its benefits in contexts where clean water is available for formula as an alternative.[39] Heaven forbid that whatever putative benefits breastfeeding has for the infant should be soberly weighed against the pain, exhaustion, and lack of freedom it entails for many of those who try to do so.[40] (Of course, to make matters even more difficult, she is not to breastfeed in public, lest her unruly body result in squeamishness and shaming.)

Then, once a mother, she is always a mother—held disproportionately responsible for the emotional, material, and moral needs of those around her, in ways that extend well beyond being overtasked with the care of her own children. She is to be a mother to others too: a giver of succor and soothing, of nurture and love and attention. As we saw in the last chapter, she will be empowered to ask for such moral goods for her own sake comparatively seldom. And, as we'll see in the next, if she has children with a male partner, then he will be under comparatively little pressure to perform his fair share of their joint caregiving duties.

Given the perpetuity of maternal responsibilities, the urge to make women notional mothers at an earlier and earlier stage in their pregnancies is not difficult to explain. Nor is it hard to predict what will tend to happen if she attempts to resign from, or preempt her occupancy of, this role: she will be perceived as a *bad* woman. And she will be subject to misogyny, in the form of threats, punishment, and the impugning of her character. Designate her a mother as early as is imaginatively possible, by reenvisaging a tiny cluster of developing human cells as a fully fledged human being—indeed, a "natural person," to use an increasingly popular legal term of art. And once this notionally fully fledged human being is in the picture, terminating a pregnancy becomes a killing, becomes a murder—and the pregnant person, a murderer. For people who believe this, like Kevin Williamson, a correspondent for *National Review,* those who have abortions may even deserve the death penalty. As Williamson recently put it on a podcast:

> I would totally go with treating [abortion] like any other crime up to and including hanging—which kind of, as I said, I'm kind of squishy about capital punishment in general, but I've got a soft spot for hanging as a form of capital punishment. I tend to think that things like lethal injection are a little too antiseptic.

To which the blogger Charles Johnson aptly responded on Twitter: "You don't just want these women to die, you want them to suffer."[41]

That many women—especially white women—have internalized this moral code and would now consider *themselves* bad women for having an abortion is not difficult to explain, either. For those women who have much to gain by abiding by the norms of good womanhood, vis-à-vis the values of our white supremacist patriarchy, taking such a position is likely to be especially tempting. Witness the prominence of *privileged* white women, in particular—Kay Ivey, Janet Porter, Georgi Boorman, and Phyllis Schlafly—in this story already. Research shows that these women are not anomalous; in some states, white women are even likelier to oppose abortion than their white male counterparts.[42]

The predictability of their views does not, of course, absolve these women of moral culpability for their role in the anti-abortion movement. For when pregnancies are policed, it is predominantly poor and nonwhite women who are liable to pay for it—and not only with respect to access to abortion. One study on what has been dubbed "reproductive oppression," where pregnant people's physical liberty was restricted by means of law and public policy, canvassed more than four hundred such cases between 1973 and 2005. Under the auspices of the state, pregnant people have been arrested, incarcerated, and had time added to their sentences; they have been detained in hospitals, mental institutions, and treatment programs; and they have been subject to forced medical interventions, surgery included—such as a C-section even though they wanted to attempt a vaginal delivery.[43] The majority of these measures were responses to supposed threats that these pregnant individuals posed to their fetuses. And, as is the case with other forms of misogynistic social control, some women are believed to pose more of a threat than others. The researchers, Lynne M. Paltrow and Jeanne Flavin, found that:

> Overwhelmingly, and regardless of race, women in our study were economically disadvantaged, indicated by the fact that 71 percent qualified for indigent defense. Of the 368 women for whom information on race was available, 59 percent were women of color, including African Americans, Hispanic American/Latinas, Native Americans, and Asian/Pacific Islanders; 52 percent were African American. African American women in particular are overrepresented in our study, but this is especially true in the South. . . . Nearly three-fourths of cases brought against African Americans originated in the South, compared with only half of the cases involving white women.[44]

One such case was that of Regina McKnight, an African American woman from South Carolina. McKnight was twenty-one when she suffered an unexpected stillbirth—the result of an infection, as evidence would show later. But the state blamed McKnight's cocaine use. The jury took just fifteen minutes to deliberate, before pronouncing her guilty of homicide. McKnight was sentenced to twelve years in prison. Her conviction was eventually vacated, in 2008—but not before McKnight had spent some eight years incarcerated.[45]

Controlling pregnant bodies is only one of many ways in which the bodies of girls and women are regulated, policed, and, increasingly, (over)ruled. A particularly interesting—if often missed—parallel is with the anti-trans movement and its fixation on policing the bodies of *trans* girls and women, including by legal means. Take "bathroom bills," which propose to restrict access to multiuser restrooms, locker rooms, and other historically gender-segregated facilities, on the basis of the sex someone was assigned at birth. Bills of this nature have been considered in sixteen states in the United States at the time of writing, and in 2017, one was passed in North Carolina—though it was subsequently struck down in the federal courts.[46] Such legislation would force trans people to use a restroom that does not match their gender identity, subjecting them to potential social humiliation, increased risk of physical attacks, and the prospect of gender dysphoria. A recent survey of almost twenty-eight thousand transgender people showed that, unsurprisingly, even the routine extralegal policing of bathroom access has a significant negative impact: nearly 60 percent had avoided using a public restroom at least once during the previous year, due to a fear of being attacked or confronted.[47]

Like anti-abortion legislation, bathroom bills rely on the construction of an immoral—indeed, reprehensible—figure. In the case of abortion, it is a heartless cisgender woman, intent on killing her "unborn child"; in the case of bathroom bills, it is a predatory trans woman—or, alternatively, a cis man merely *pretending* to be a trans woman in order to gain restroom access. And like anti-abortion legislation, bathroom bills also rely on the construction of a notional victim. In the case of abortion, it is a heart-wrenchingly vulnerable fetus, who might also grow up to be the next Einstein; in the case of bathroom bills, it is a preyed-upon cis girl or woman. These notional victims then serve as a post hoc rationalization for the preexisting desire to police the supposed moral offenders.[48]

In reality, the number of trans women or cis men merely purporting to be trans women who have preyed on *any* restroom user is vanishingly small. Since 2004, such a crime has been reported roughly once per year in the United States, according to recent research. Meanwhile, cis men *not* bothering to pretend to be trans women attack women in restrooms with much greater regularity: the same team of researchers found that this had occurred more than 150 times during the same time frame.[49] So why do we hear so much from certain sources about the supposed threat of trans women (or, again, cis men purporting to be trans women), and so little about the very real threat that undisguised cis men pose to *all* women? The answer, surely, is transphobia—and, in particular, the transmisogyny that represents the dangerous, toxic intersection of misogyny and transphobia faced by trans girls and women.[50]

The fixation on the idea of predatory trans women, *or* predatory men pretending to be women, is not accidental. The disjunction conceals the fact that the two disjuncts—the two sides of the "or" statement—are often taken to be tantamount to the same thing by people steeped in transphobia. And when this is the case, violence against trans women is an all too likely and common outcome.

In an important series of articles, the philosopher Talia Mae Bettcher has shown that both the idea that gender presentation is code for *genital* presentation, and the insistence on an "alignment" of the two in the name of all that is natural and moral, lie deep in the heart of transphobic bigotry. She writes that, within a cis-sexist society,

> penises and vaginas [are] seen . . . as "legitimate possessions" to which males and females respectively have moral entitlements. In effect, the natural attitude about the metaphysics of sex is also a view about a moral order. This notion is useful in understanding a kind of transphobia thoroughly imbued with both moral and metaphysical considerations. It isn't uncommon for a trans person to be represented as "really a so and so, disguised as a such and such." A trans woman, for example, may be represented as engaging in a kind of "sexual deception."[51]

Specifically, a trans woman may be seen as either an "evil deceiver," pretending to be something she is not, or as a mere pretender, a faulty simulacrum of femininity.[52] For, as Bettcher writes, the trans woman's body is taken as intimately male. As such her vagina is seen as illegitimate, in part because it's not the completion of the moral structure of her body. In this case, the trans woman has not only "misrepresented" the structure of her body, she has "misrepresented" the genitalia to which she's entitled and which is the moral completion of that structure.[53]

An important corollary of the dynamic Bettcher identifies is the sense of entitlement, upon taking in someone whose gender presentation is that of a woman, to know her genital arrangements at a glance—even when she is fully clothed—without doubt or ambiguity. The entitlement to know a woman's *reproductive* capacities at a glance seems a plausible extension of this—which would imply her obligation not to *present* herself as a woman, if she is not capable of "giving" cisgender men heteronormatively sanctioned sex and biological children. Hopefully needless to say, this putative obligation is not a real one.[54]

As we've seen, the anti-abortion movement's supposed preoccupation with life belies the fact that it undermines the health and lives of cis girls and women, along with other people who may also become pregnant. Similarly, the anti-trans movement's supposed preoccupation with sexual safety belies the fact that it undermines the safety and lives of a particularly vulnerable class of people: namely, trans girls and women, who are disproportionately liable to be attacked, assaulted, and murdered, at rates that recently prompted the American Medical Association to declare this an epidemic.[55]

In one article, Bettcher considers the well-known case of Gwen Araujo, a seventeen-year-old trans girl from California who was viciously beaten and murdered in 2002.[56] Before her murder, Araujo had attended a party, where suspicions about her genitals had resulted in her being publicly and violently "outed," via forced genital exposure. As Bettcher notes, the subsequent declaration that "he is really a man" appears to have precipitated the vicious attack on Araujo by four young cis men—Jason Cazares, Michael Magidson, Jaron Nabors, and Jose Merel—who were eventually charged with her first-degree murder.[57] Notably, two of the men (Merel and Magidson) had had sexual contact with Araujo in the days prior to the party. Their subsequent violent rage was plausibly rooted in a sense of entitlement—to have Araujo's genitals and the sex she was assigned at birth match their expectations, given her gender presentation and their sexual desire for her.[58]

Rather than holding these young men responsible for Araujo's murder—after which they buried her battered body some 150 miles away, in the Sierra wilderness, before stopping at McDonald's—many people expressed empathy and support for them.[59] As Bettcher shows, they made excuses for the perpetrators, while embracing victim-blaming logic. "If you find out the beautiful woman you're with is really a man, it would make any man go crazy," said one of their mothers. "He was not honest with them and had he been, none of this would have happened," opined the student journalist Zach Calef—thereby misgendering Araujo, to add gross insult to moral injury. And despite the fact that these young men had *already* been speculating about Araujo's genitals several days prior to the killing, they were held to have acted "in the heat of passion," out of "extreme shock, amazement, and bewilderment," according to one of their attorneys. Indeed, they had experienced a provocation for the murder "so deep it's almost primal"—which sprang from Araujo's "sexual fraud, deception, betrayal." These claims reflect the idea that not only were these men entitled to read Araujo's genital status off her clothed appearance, they were entitled to "go crazy," even to slay her, when that sexual entitlement was challenged.

Dramatic as this example may be, there is a prevalent sense of entitlement on the part of privileged men to regulate, control, and rule over the bodies of girls and women—cisgender and trans alike. And as the direct result of this, those subject to such misogynistic policing are often impugned as moral monsters, even though *they're* the ones being made to suffer horribly.

SEVEN

Insupportable—
On the Entitlement to Domestic Labor

M en simply feel entitled to our labor," writes Darcy Lock-man, author of *All the Rage: Mothers, Fathers, and the Myth of Equal Partnership*. "The glow of this entitlement shines so bright."[1] It also casts a long shadow over many heterosexual households: mothers with male partners are doing far more than their fair share of the child-rearing and housework. And women's "second shift"—to use a term coined by sociologist Arlie Russell Hochschild in the late 1980s, to capture the extra month of "home" work that women perform annually—hasn't budged in decades.

This bleak picture of domestic inequality at home may be surprising. The image of the modern, involved father is prevalent in depictions of contemporary heterosexual couples—but it is, unfortunately, misleading. Although men's participation in child-rearing duties did increase in the United States from 1980 to 2000 (as women's labor force participation increased dramatically), there has been subsequent stagnation. In one representative study of the situation in the nation today, the sociologists Jill Yavorsky, Claire Kamp Dush, and Sarah Schoppe-Sullivan found that for male-female partners who both worked full-time (roughly forty-hour weeks), first-time parenthood increased a man's workload at home by about ten hours per week. Meanwhile, the increased workload for women was about twenty hours. So motherhood took double the toll as fatherhood, workwise. Moreover, much of the new work that fathers *did* take on in these situations was the comparatively "fun" work of engagement with their children—for example, playing with the baby. Fathers did this for four hours per week, on average, while dropping their number of hours of housework by five hours per week during the same time period. Mothers decreased their hours of housework by only one hour per week—while adding about twenty-one hours of child-rearing labor, including fifteen hours of physical child care—for instance, changing diapers and bathing the baby. And mothers *still* did more by way of infant engagement: about six hours per week, on average.[2]

A similar picture emerged via time-use diary statistics collected by Pew Research and the U.S. Bureau of Labor Statistics. In 2000, they found that working women took on around two-thirds of at-home child-care responsibilities, while their male partners did the remaining one-third. Again, women did double the work. And disturbingly, over the past two decades, these figures have held steady.[3]

A 2018 Oxfam report showed that women doing twice as much as men by way of unpaid care work and domestic labor is on the low end, globally speaking. Around the world, women average between two and ten times more of this work than their male counterparts. The global value of this work is estimated at $10 trillion annually.[4] Based on the current state of affairs, estimates of how long we have to go before reaching child-care parity between men and women range from seventy-five years (by the fatherhood campaign MenCare) to a still more dismal two hundred years (by the United Nations International Labour Organization).[5] Studies show there is but one circumstance in which men's and women's household work will tend to approach parity: when she works full-time and he is unemployed. And even then, the operative word is *approach*. She will still do a bit more. Equality is elusive, even in the supposedly egalitarian U.S. context.[6]

If anything, time-use studies may paint an overly rosy picture of male household participation. "I question what we know from time-use diaries," Kamp Dush told Lockman. "Our pattern of results, looking at couples on the same day, is different. It shows that men do even less."[7] Consistent with this is the fact that men appear to overestimate their contributions to shared household work. A recent *Economist* survey of parents in eight Western countries showed that while 46 percent of fathers reported being coequal parents, only 32 percent of mothers concurred with their assessment.[8] It is possible, of course, that women are *underreporting* their partner's contributions in time-use diaries, rather than men overreporting their own. But social scientists consider this unlikely. As sociologist Scott Coltrane put it:

> Because of the potential benefit of sharing family work,
> the rapid increase in women's labor force participation,

and increasing popular endorsement of equity ideals in marriage, many . . . predicted that the division of household labor would become more gender-neutral. Nevertheless, studies . . . seem to offer little support for this notion. This left researchers with a major unanswered question: "Why don't men do more?"[9]

One reason why men don't do more may well be obliviousness—a willful, and comparatively blissful, state of ignorance. As Kamp Dush writes, commenting on her own studies:

Interestingly, new fathers don't seem to realize that they aren't keeping up with their partners' growing workload. When we asked, both men and women perceived that they increased their total work by more than 30 hours a week each after they became parents. But our more accurate time diaries told a different story, one where parenthood added much more work for women than men.[10]

Another reason men don't do more is that, under such conditions, *asking* them to pull their weight is in itself a form of labor.

In the opening of *All the Rage,* Darcy Lockman recounts one of the incidents that led her to write her book. She had asked her husband, George, for a brief reprieve for Mother's Day: taking their two daughters to visit his mother, giving Lockman a rare opportunity to have some time for herself. Part of the tacit deal was that George would pack the children's suitcase, for the first time in the six and a half years since their eldest daughter's arrival. Lockman recalls her frustration at being asked if there was anything he might forget, and struggling to respond with equanimity. Shortly thereafter, the guilt kicked in. She writes:

> The devil on my shoulder—the one internalized over decades of white noise about women and their responsibilities and their relative place—eggs me on: You're not being fair to him. He's taking them away, after all. Just throw some stuff together. It's only a one-night trip. It'll take you thirty seconds. What's the goddamn big deal? I gather the iPad and some toys and put them in a bag, an offering to the devil, and to my husband, to whom I wish above all else to be fair.[11]

This inner dialogue captures the complex toll emotional labor often takes. Emotional labor encompasses, among other things, the *keeping track* and *anticipatory* work that so often falls to women: knowing what is where, who needs what, the grocery list, the family's budget, the family calendar, and so on—not to mention packing endless bags, from diaper bags to suitcases. (After Lockman declined to provide further assistance, her husband forgot their girls' pajamas; they ended up sleeping in their bathing suits.)

Including all of these forms of work under the heading of emotional labor is now fairly standard. In a recent guide to emotional labor pitched to a male audience, the concept received the following definition:

Free, invisible work women do to keep track of the little things in life that, taken together, amount to the big things in life: the glue that holds households, and by extension, proper society, together.[12]

Admittedly, such an expansion of the term has been resisted by its progenitor, Arlie Russell Hochschild, who originally used it to refer to *paid* work that requires maintaining a certain emotional affect—the cheery demeanor required of flight attendants, for example.[13] But this strikes me as an instance where the term has naturally evolved, in order to keep pace with the needs of language users. The idea of emotional labor is naturally construed as encompassing a multitude. As Gemma Hartley, author of *Fed Up: Emotional Labor, Women, and the Way Forward*, puts it:

> Housework isn't the only thing that becomes a drag. I am also the schedule keeper who makes appointments and knows what is on the calendar at all times. I am the person who has all the answers to where my husband left his keys, what time that wedding is, and what type of dress code is necessary, do we have any orange juice left, where is that green sweater, when is so-and-so's birthday, and what are we having for dinner? I carry in my mind exhaustive lists of all types, not because I want to, but because I know no one else will.[14]

Emotional labor also encompasses the work of managing the feelings *around* these kinds of tasks: not ruffling a male partner's feathers, for example, by pointing out that he has done something badly, and avoiding asking for too much of his "help" or "support" within a household. As a result, many women face a potent double bind: Don't ask, and you'll be saddled with far more than your fair share of material, domestic, and emotional labor. *Do* ask, and you'll be violating the implicit social code that tells women to keep the peace, nurture others, and not be too demanding. Hartley:

> Asking, and asking in the right way, is an additional layer of labor. Delegating, in many situations, requires repeating requests, which is often perceived as nagging. Sometimes it is simply not worth the effort of asking again and again, and continually asking in the right tone (and still risking being called a nag). So I do the task myself.[15]

Hartley's book begins with an incident strikingly similar to Lockman's opening anecdote: asking, for Mother's Day, for a housecleaning service for the bathrooms and floors of the apartment she shares with her husband and children. She explains:

> The gift, for me, was not so much the cleaning itself but the fact that for once I would not be in charge of the household office work. I would not have to make calls, get multiple quotes, research and vet each service, arrange payment, and schedule the appointment. The real gift I wanted was to be relieved of the emotional labor of a single task that had been nagging at the back of my mind. The clean house would simply be a bonus.[16]

But, alas, it was not to be. Hartley's husband elected to save the money and deep-clean the bathrooms himself. Meanwhile, she was tasked with caring for their children single-handedly, while the rest of the house fell into disarray around her. She described her subsequent anger at the "compilation of years and years of slowly taking on the role of the only person in our household who cared."[17]

It's easy to dismiss this as a first-world problem. It's also a red herring. The relevant comparison here is not between these women and their less privileged counterparts, who undoubtedly do face many distinctive problems—some of which we've already encountered, and of which more later. It's between women and their male counterparts who fail to take on an equitable proportion of the household caregiving burden. And there is no good reason for men's failures on this score: the all too convenient, sexist hypothesis that men and women "naturally" have different child-care proclivities or preferences has been debunked in part by studies showing that when men are the primary caregivers, their brains—being malleable—come to resemble those of women who are primary caregivers.[18] Men's failures in spite of this to participate properly in household and child-rearing labor appear to affect women in every demographic group.[19] This is not to say that rich and poor women are affected in exactly the same way, of course: when higher-income, predominantly white men fail to care, and their similarly wealthy (and, again, typically white) female partners become exhausted and desperate, they often end up "leaning down" and calling upon the labor of nonwhite and poorer women. So privileged white men's dereliction of their duties have deleterious effects not just on their wives, but also, by extension, on more vulnerable women, who may end up being exploited to do the work these comparatively privileged women should not have to cope with single-handedly.[20]

• • •

It's not just within the context of a household that men either fail or refuse to care. Even *paid* care work among men is strikingly unpopular. Economists have observed that men often prefer unemployment to taking on jobs in nursing (for example, as a nurse's assistant), elder care, or working as a home healthcare aide. Yet these are increasingly the jobs that are available and need doing, as traditionally male blue-collar work disappears from the U.S. economy. A *New York Times* article from June 2017 put the matter bluntly: "It seems like an easy fix. Traditionally male factory work is drying up. The fastest-growing jobs in the American economy are those that are often held by women. Why not get men to do them?"[21]

One barrier to male participation in paid care work is undoubtedly men's sense of entitlement to more traditionally masculine jobs: factory or bust, in other words, particularly for white men. But another barrier may be their female partners' preconceptions about the kind of work that befits a male partner's dignity. The sociologist Ofer Sharone found that even when a middle-aged professional man who had lost his job *was* willing to take lower-paying work in a traditionally feminine industry, his wife would often encourage him to keep looking.[22] Meanwhile, the percentage of men out of the labor force entirely (as opposed to being either employed, or unemployed but actively searching for work) has doubled—from just under 15 percent of men in 1950 to just over 30 percent of men in 2018.[23]

There has been much ink spilled about the crisis of modern American (predominantly white) masculinity. In many communities, especially rural ones, white men are increasingly not working. They are also at increasing risk for depression, drug dependency (especially on opiates), and even suicide. This can plausibly be read as, among other things, the result of a crisis in *meaning:* a lack of fulfilling roles that men have access to in these milieus. Yet care work not only needs doing; it is meaningful, not inherently exploitative, and has other advantages over many forms of traditionally masculine blue-collar labor, in generally tending to be less physically and environmentally damaging. In this case, men's sense of entitlement is not only hurting other vulnerable parties; it is hurting men *themselves,* and standing in the way of solutions to a gap between role supply and demand that desperately needs filling.

If men often feel entitled to certain kinds of paid work, they also feel entitled to far more by way of leisure, as compared with their female partners. As Darcy Lockman notes, multiple studies have found that "fathers who work long hours have wives who do more child care, while mothers who work long hours have husbands who sleep more and watch lots of television."[24]

Herein lies one of the answers to the question of how men are spending their time outside of paid work hours. But a chicken-egg question remains: Do men do so little because they engage in more leisure activities than their female partners? Or do they engage in more leisure activities in order to do so little?

When Gemma Hartley's husband, Rob, was laid off from work, they agreed that he would take over the morning routine, so that she could finish her book. She described one afternoon, about a month into this arrangement:

When I emerged from my home office, the two-year-old hadn't eaten lunch yet. I scrambled to make him ramen noodles and quickly put him down for a nap while Rob changed into his riding gear. . . . Abandoned coloring books, crayons, markers, printer paper . . . pencil shavings, and a library book I feared to look inside blanketed [the dining table]. There was kinetic sand in two colors, both of which were scattered in small lumps outside their designated trays and all over the floor. There were dishes from breakfast, half-eaten food taken off the plates, and milk hardening on the finished wood top of the table. . . . The house wasn't just a little messy. It was a disaster.[25]

While Hartley worked to resolve the chaos, her husband went mountain-biking. *Fed Up* makes it clear that this occurrence was far from unusual.

Jancee Dunn's husband, Tom, was also fond of bike riding; he got into the habit of going for long-distance rides when their daughter, Sylvie, was an infant. Dunn's book, somewhat ominously named *How Not to Hate Your Husband After Kids,* is a less scholarly work than either Lockman's or Hartley's. It is also addressed to a more particular audience: not to the men who might be behaving in loathsome, unfair ways, but to their female partners, who must find a way not to loathe them, somehow. This despite the fact that, in the case of Dunn and her husband—both freelance journalists with similar work schedules—he does just 10 percent of the housework. Dunn writes:

I wish his 10 percent effort was enough, but it isn't. I feel like he's a guest at the hotel I'm running. I'm constantly taking a silent feminist stand to see if he'll step up and lend a hand. The scorekeeping never ends. Adding to my resentment is that on weekends, Tom somehow manages to float around in a happy single-guy bubble. A typical Saturday for him starts with a game of soccer with his friends or a five-hour bike ride (he seemed to take up endurance sports right around the time our baby's umbilical cord was cut, like the sound of the snip was a starter's pistol to get the hell out of Dodge). This is followed by a leisurely twenty-minute shower, a late breakfast, a long nap, and then a meandering perusal through a variety of periodicals. Meanwhile, I am ferrying our daughter to birthday parties and playdates. On weekend evenings, Tom doesn't check with me before he meets friends for drinks; he just breezes out the door with the assumption that I'll handle bath time and bed.[26]

Dunn wonders whether her anger at the resulting situation is fair, given that she has "allowed this pattern to unfold." The answer, it seems to me, is yes, given that her husband is the one to have actually *committed* the bad behavior. A marriage counselor Dunn and her husband visited during this period—the well-known Boston-based therapist Terry Real, who charges $800 an hour for the benefit of his insights—is similarly unequivocal in his judgment about their situation. After Real asks them to walk him through a typical fight, Dunn explains that Tom had just returned from a bike trip through the Italian countryside for a magazine story he was writing. He was jet-lagged upon his return home, so he slept for two days, while Dunn continued to play single parent. When Tom finally woke up, Dunn was angry and yelled at him. "I got news for ya," Real says to Dunn: "I'm on your side."[27]

The therapist doesn't excuse some of Dunn's behavior in response to her husband's "selfishness and preciousness" (as Real calls it). Indeed, not mincing words, Real even labels Dunn verbally abusive (for regularly calling Tom an "asshole" and a "shitbag"). But Real is also clear in his assessment that, although Dunn's way of expressing her anger may be unacceptable, her anger itself is justified. "Volatile women generally don't feel heard," Real offers.[28]

Part of the reason why men get away with doing so little may be that, as recent research suggests, women in heterosexual couples are held to higher standards than their mates.[29] That is, women are more likely to be shamed and blamed for a messy home, eccentrically dressed children, or a lack of a perfect bento lunch box for Junior on every school day.[30] And another part of the reason may be that, even when men are doing woefully little, these are nevertheless the *good* guys, comparatively speaking. As Lockman writes:

> While father involvement in two-parent families has increased in recent decades, there are also fewer father-present families. Clearly, the men who stick around to love and shepherd their offspring are not only to be maligned.[31]

With the bar for men in general set so low, there is a temptation to compare a *present* male partner and father to his absent counterparts, and to find him morally admirable rather than wanting. Another invidious comparison turns on the fact that, currently, fathers do far more than *their* fathers usually did. The modern father *is* far more involved, on average, than his predecessor. But, again, it is vital to be clear about the most morally relevant comparison to make here: between male and female partners. And seen through this lens, women remain massively overburdened, while men often fail to do their fair share. This is particularly so because a man's female partner is nowadays much likelier to bring in a comparable amount of income, and to work comparable hours of paid labor.[32] So why should she do far more work than him at home, all else being equal? The answer, of course, is she shouldn't.

Despite this, women like Jancee Dunn struggle to recognize this. During their marathon five-hour therapy session, Real asks her and her husband why they don't split the domestic chores evenly, given their similar professional roles and commitments. Anything other than fifty-fifty would be unfair, he points out. Interestingly, that's when Dunn begins to make excuses for her husband. "But I think men have a problem with fifty-fifty," she ventures. "We're not talking about men, we're talking about Tom," Real replies. Then:

> [Real] asks Tom if he has a problem with splitting down the middle. "Well, entropy takes over sometimes, and I . . . ," Tom begins. "Look, I know what you're talking about," Real breaks in. "The inertia, the laziness. But it's also entitlement. And it's dumb."[33]

The exchange points to yet another reason why men often get away with this imbalance: many a woman unwittingly echoes and validates her male partner's illegitimate sense of entitlement to her labor, and to his leisure time. Despite her frustrations, she subsequently gives him mixed messages, and she is reluctant to insist on a more equitable arrangement. She exhibits himpathy—the disproportionate or inappropriate sympathy for a man who behaves in misogynistic or, I would now add, entitled ways, over his female victims—even though she herself is his victim in this scenario. During the beginning of their session, Dunn writes,

> To my profound discomfort, sudden tears are coursing down my cheeks. "I want to be kinder to Tom," I say, snuffling. "But I also want him to do more work around the house and not leave it all to me." I rub my eyes. "I wore mascara, how stupid was I?" Real pushes a box of tissues toward me.[34]

Similarly, Dunn recalls her emotional state during Real's dressing-down of her husband: she feels protective of him, even pities him, "jump[ing] in to add that with Sylvie, he is utterly unselfish, kind, and attentive." Such virtues are all to the good, of course; but the issue on the table, as Real points out, is how Tom treats *Dunn,* not how he treats their daughter. And, given the grim realities on this score, her pity is surely misplaced. But it is also understandable—and relatable. When a woman internalizes her putative obligations to care for others at the expense of herself, there is affective as well as behavioral fallout. She is likely to feel guilt and shame for holding a male partner accountable—

and, as Lockman points out, to feel an excessive sense of gratitude toward him, even for falling far short of fairness.[35]

Part of the problem here, then, may be *women's* sense of entitlement—or lack thereof. Some women may not feel entitled to equitable domestic arrangements and leisure time for themselves, on par with that of their husbands. Or they may feel entitled to this in theory but be unable to insist in reality, given the social forces around them that tell them *not* to insist and to "take one for the team" in perpetuity. Jancee Dunn even writes, in *How Not to Hate Your Husband After Kids,* of not feeling entitled to eat whole, undamaged crackers from the box. Instead, she eats the broken ones, saving the good ones for her husband and daughter. In the conclusion of her book, one of her take-home lessons reads as follows:

> **You don't always have to eat the broken crackers.**
> One of the most difficult things I had to do was develop a little entitlement of my own, and get fully behind the idea that I need help around the house, as well as rest and leisure time. It was tough to shake the attendant guilt, and the sense that somehow I should be able to handle everything. . . . [But] when I take time for myself, I come back and I'm more the mother I want to be. By taking care of myself, I become a better caretaker.[36]

Progress though this may be, there is something sad about the framing here. A woman is entitled to more than just "help" or "support" from a male partner. And she is entitled to as much rest and leisure time as he is for her own sake, not just for the sake of becoming a better caregiver.[37]

In Dunn's case, the involvement of her husband remained depressingly minimal by the end of the fourteen months during which she worked on both the book and her marriage. Her conclusion lists some good ideas for women in her situation, including getting couples counseling. ("Especially," writes Dunn, "if you can find a therapist who yells at your husband, 'Stop with your entitled attitude, get off your ass, and help her out!'"[38]) But it also canvasses some ideas that, throughout the book, seem to be addressing different, and much less pressing, problems than the sense of male entitlement that evidently dogs their marriage. The result is a Gretchen Rubin–style Happiness Project for partnership, rather than an egalitarian shake-up. Dunn and her husband engage in a variety of exercises— everything from a "sexperiment" (having sex ten days in a row, on the theory that the more you have, the more you want), to decluttering their apartment, to getting their daughter involved in chores. She even encourages Tom to employ official FBI strategies for "talking someone down," in an attempt to assuage her anger. Again, it seems to me that—whatever the acceptability of her means of expressing it—Dunn's anger was warranted. She recounts that, in the end, Tom has taken to making dinner one night a week; he occasionally takes his daughter to the park for forty-five minutes; and, for the first time ever, he attended a parent-teacher conference and took his daughter to the doctor. Dunn writes:

I don't care that it is not equal—I feel supported, and that perception is important. I am amazed (and sometimes a little dismayed) at how much mileage some of Tom's largely symbolic gestures have resonated with me. He doesn't need to toil with me side by side.[39]

Meanwhile, Dunn remains "the reluctant house manager, and likely always will be. I still must continually insist, quietly but firmly, that Tom do his share around the house."[40] By her reports, he still doesn't. Despite this, Dunn's book concludes with an expression of profound gratitude toward him: "And, most importantly, I am forever grateful to my husband, Tom. I can't think about what you mean to me without reaching for a box of tissues."[41]

EIGHT

Unassuming—
On the Entitlement to Knowledge

On February 9, 2019, *The Guardian* tweeted out an article called "Me and My Vulva: 100 Women Reveal All."[1] The article featured an intimate photo series by Laura Dodsworth that was intended to destigmatize and educate people about the vulvas of women (both cis and trans), as well as of gender-nonconforming people with the relevant body part. Shortly thereafter, a man saw fit to weigh in on the article's title. "The correct word is vagina," opined one "Doktor Paul Bullen" on Twitter. The corrections came swiftly and in no short supply: "vulva" is, of course, the correct terminology for the external anatomy pictured; the vagina is an internal organ leading to the uterus, comparatively difficult to photograph. The corrections also came from authoritative sources—gynecologists, for example.[2] Even Dictionary.com got involved—with a tweet that read, "Well. Actually" and a link to the word "vulva"'s online definition.[3]

Paul Bullen was not deterred, however. In a truly remarkable feat of doubling down, he maintained that his usage was, in fact, the correct one. He wrote (in a since-deleted tweet): "I consider the recent attempt to replace vagina with vulva as an affectation."[4] In response to the inevitable and apt point that this was an especially egregious case of mansplaining, Bullen was similarly recalcitrant. "That's an incorrect use of the word mansplaining," he chimed in. "Not that I want to legitimize the term, but by its own definition it requires more than just having a man who is explaining something. Even if some in the audience are women."

Bullen was actually right about "mansplaining" meaning more than just a man explaining something. But his tweet *did* meet the further relevant conditions. A paradigmatic act of mansplaining consists of a man presuming to "explain" something incorrect(ly) to a more expert female speaker or set of speakers—and in an overly confident, arrogant, or overbearing manner, which often results in his not backing down or admitting to his mistake after it has been authoritatively pointed out to him. So, when it came to mansplaining, Paul Bullen's tweet was a perfect exemplar. (Indeed, his after-the-fact quibbling only cemented its status.)

One can argue about whether an action that deviates somewhat from this paradigm still counts as mansplaining; as with the concepts expressed by most terms in natural language, its extension can be fuzzy and shift over time. (In which case, I'd be tempted to understand the key questions as being: How ought we to understand the term? How would it most productively be defined and understood?)[5] But for the purposes of this discussion, I'm more interested in the kind of attitude that underlies and perpetuates mansplaining.[6] And my answer, in short, is *entitlement:* entitlement of the epistemic variety, which relates to knowledge, beliefs, and the possession of information.

In particular, I believe that mansplaining typically stems from an unwarranted sense of entitlement on the part of the mansplainer to occupy the conversational position of the *knower* by default: to be the one who dispenses information, offers corrections, and authoritatively issues explanations. This is objectionable when and partly because he is *not* so entitled: when others, namely women, happen to know more than he does—and he ought to anticipate this possibility, rather than assuming his own epistemic superiority from the get-go. Dr. Paul Bullen ought to have anticipated, for example, that the woman who produced the photo series and was subsequently interviewed for an article entitled "Me and My Vulva," Laura Dodsworth, would know the correct terminology with which to refer to her own subject matter—not to mention, her own anatomy.[7]

Earlier in this book, I introduced Miranda Fricker's concept of epistemic injustice—specifically, testimonial injustice, where a speaker's word is taken to be less credible than it should be, due to prejudices against members of her social group (for example, as a Black woman) in the relevant domain of knowledge (such as her bodily experiences, pain, illness, and so on). Her status as a knower vis-à-vis that subject matter is thereby unfairly denied or disregarded. The concept of epistemic entitlement, which I'm introducing here, is obviously closely related to the idea of testimonial injustice. But they are distinct and complementary. Whereas testimonial injustice involves unfairly dismissing a less privileged speaker—typically, after she has attempted to make a contribution—epistemic entitlement involves peremptorily assuming greater authority to speak, on the part of a more privileged speaker.[8] Understood in this way, we can see that epistemic entitlement is a common precursor to, and cause of, testimonial injustice.[9]

On other occasions, manifestations of epistemic entitlement may result in a less privileged speaker deciding not to make her intended or fitting contribution to the conversation. This will then often constitute what the philosopher Kristie Dotson calls "testimonial smothering," where a speaker *self*-silences, due to her anticipating that her word will not receive the proper uptake, and may instead place her in an "unsafe or risky" situation.[10] This may happen because there is something about the specific *content* of her testimony that makes it unsafe or risky for a speaker like her to utter. Or she may self-silence because it is unsafe or risky for a speaker like her to venture to say anything at all, or to interrupt the relentless flow of a man's pontificating. A mansplainer may be nigh on uninterruptable.

This point is epitomized by an incident recounted by Rebecca Solnit, in her classic and galvanizing essay "Men Explain Things to Me." (Solnit did not herself coin the term "mansplaining," and she reports a degree of ambivalence about it; but her essay nevertheless inspired the coinage and much of the subsequent discourse.) Solnit had attended a dinner party with a female friend, where she'd been prevailed upon by the older, "distinguished" male host to linger after dinner to talk about her writing. "I hear you've written a couple of books," he offered genially. "Several, actually," she ventured. "And what are they about?" he inquired, in a patronizing tone—much "the way you encourage your friend's seven-year-old to describe flute practice," as Solnit puts it. She nevertheless obliged and began to describe her most recent book at the time, which was about Eadweard Muybridge, an English American photographer and pioneer of motion pictures. She didn't get far, however. Solnit recalls:

> He cut me off soon after I mentioned Muybridge. "And have you heard about the very important Muybridge book that came out this year?" So caught up was I in my assigned role as ingénue that I was perfectly willing to entertain the possibility that another book on the same subject had come out simultaneously and I'd somehow missed it. He was already telling me about the very important book—with that smug look I know so well in a man holding forth, eyes fixed on the fuzzy far horizon of his own authority.[11]

The very important book, Solnit's female friend soon realized, was Solnit's. The friend tried to interject this point three or four times. But the mansplainer failed, somehow, to hear her. When he finally registered this news, his face fell; he turned "ashen." Solnit writes:

> That I was indeed the author of the very important book it turned out he hadn't read, just read about in the *The New York Times Book Review* a few months earlier, so confused the neat categories into which his world

was sorted that he was stunned speechless—for a moment, before he began holding forth again.

Of the many insights Solnit offers us here into the nature of mansplaining, one of the most striking is the way *both* speakers in this exchange are assigned roles, which are then difficult to break from. Solnit's host was the authority, of course; and she was cast as the naïve one—"an empty vessel to be filled with [his] wisdom and knowledge," she writes, "in some sort of obscene impregnation metaphor." Because of the social dynamics in play here, it then became very difficult to change the course of the conversation. Even Solnit's female friend's powers of intervention were strictly limited. And without such an active bystander, one wonders whether the correction would have been issued whatsoever. In part, it would depend on whether Solnit had the confidence to insist that the book was indeed her own—which, as she points out, as a distinguished and prolific author (not to mention a white woman), she was in a comparatively good position to muster. It still wouldn't have been easy for many of us, me included. And, at least as importantly, it would also have depended on whether Solnit was willing to do something socially jarring, liable to be perceived as rude, in asserting herself in this manner. Of course, she would have been completely within her rights—entirely entitled—to do so. But the skewed sense of epistemic entitlement that structured the exchange left her host's face "ashen" when he finally registered his error. She was in danger of humiliating him. Still, he was only momentarily deterred: he proceeded to explain *other* things when unceremoniously deprived of that fledgling site of epistemic domination.

Such incidents serve as a powerful reminder to women "that the truth is not [our] property, now or ever." They keep us in our place. Sure, women can be arrogant, and "explain" things to more expert parties incorrectly on occasion, as Solnit freely acknowledges. But the point here is that mansplaining is systemic; it is part of a (much) broader system. Solnit aptly describes this system as a male "archipelago of arrogance"—and, I would add, entitlement.

If the truth is not our property, then neither is authority. Listening to women becomes superfluous, except for instrumental reasons—a mere performance, intended to mollify or, perhaps, to virtue-signal. Of course, this problem is far worse, and sometimes in sui generis ways, for women who are subject to multiple compounding forms of oppression. In her brilliant essay "Girl 6," Tressie McMillan Cottom writes of calculating the number of Black women whom David Brooks and Jonathan Chait each followed on Twitter at the time. The number was 6 apiece. Just 6, out of 322 and 370, respectively. McMillan Cottom:

> A Professional Smart Person can be so without ever reading a black woman, ever interviewing a black woman, ever following a black woman, or ever thinking about a black woman's existence.[12]

Black women are not just dismissed, then; they are not heeded in the first place by many of those overly endowed with epistemic privilege.

.   .   .

As we've seen, a sense of epistemic entitlement can be maintained blithely, with utmost (unearned) confidence. It can also be jealously guarded and defended—sometimes to the point of engaging in creepy, controlling, and even abusive behavior. One of the darkest manifestations of epistemic entitlement in this vein is gaslighting.

"Gaslighting" takes its name from the 1938 Patrick Hamilton play *Angel Street,* which was performed onstage as *Gas Light.*[13] The play was heavily adapted into two different movies by the latter name—a British and an American version—both of which have become better known than the original. But the play is to my mind richer than either film, and so forms the basis of the discussion here.

In *Gas Light* (as I'll refer to it), Jack Manningham appears to be intent on driving his wife, Bella, insane. His original motives for doing so become apparent only during the play's second act, but—importantly—his behavior is intelligible right from the beginning, lending the play its claustrophobic, indeed suffocating, atmosphere. Act One is a vivid depiction of domestic terror. Mr. Manningham wrong-foots and undermines his wife at every turn—humiliating her in front of their servants, correcting her constantly, and even impugning the anxiety he is thereby instilling in her as irrational and baseless. (Mr. Manningham: "Why are you so apprehensive, Bella? I was not about to reproach you." Mrs. Manningham: [*Nervously . . .*] "No, dear. I know you weren't."[14] He goes on to reproach, indeed berate, her shortly thereafter.)

In a particularly cruel, long-running series of manipulations, Mr. Manningham leads his wife to believe that she is going out of her mind, and losing possession of her rational

faculties, by regularly hiding their belongings and then holding her responsible for their disappearance. And he holds her
responsible not merely causally, but *morally:* depicting her as
mischievous and wicked, as well as confused and delusional.
(He also accuses her—most painfully of all—of deliberately
hurting their pet dog, thus painting *her* as the cruel and abusive
one.) This combination of accusations is of course incoherent, as Bella Manningham tries repeatedly to point out to her
husband. If she really *is* confused and delusional, and cannot
help her behavior, then surely he ought to treat her kindly and
try to help her, rather than getting angry.[15] But Mr. Manningham ignores this, as he does all of his wife's attempts to prevail
upon his goodwill. She is truly powerless, utterly subject to her
husband's control, within their household. And she is nobody
outside of it, since her husband has deliberately isolated her
from all of her friends and relatives.[16] She hence has no choice
but to defer to him—and, even then, it does little to appease
his seething temper.

The effect of Mr. Manningham's behavior—a devastating
portrait of a recognizable pattern of abuse that subsequently
became known as gaslighting, for reasons that will emerge
shortly—is to deprive Bella of her *own* sense of entitlement to
state even the most basic realities. Toward the end of Act One,
in an arguably disappointing deus ex machina, a detective comes
to visit her and ultimately tells her the terrible, albeit liberating
truth: her husband is the diabolical Sydney Power, who murdered the former owner of their house, Alice Barlow, in order to
steal her rubies. He slit Alice's throat to silence her, some fifteen
years prior, before prevailing on Bella to use her inheritance
to buy the residence. But he may never have managed to *locate*

the rubies, Detective Rough suspects, as he confides to Bella. Might Power still be looking for the jewels on the top floor of their home—which is shut up, off-limits to her and even to the servants? He might indeed, Bella realizes:

> MRS. MANNINGHAM: It all sounds so incredible [but] when I'm alone at night I get the idea that—somebody's walking about up there—[*Looking up.*] Up there—At night, when my husband's out— I hear noises, from my bedroom, but I'm too afraid to go up—
> ROUGH: Have you told your husband about this?
> MRS. MANNINGHAM: No. I'm afraid to. He gets angry. He says I imagine things which don't exist—
> ROUGH: It never struck you, did it, that it might be your own husband walking about up there?
> MRS. MANNINGHAM: Yes—that *is* what I thought—but I thought I must be mad. Tell me how you know.
> ROUGH: Why not tell me first how *you* knew, Mrs. Manningham.
> MRS. MANNINGHAM: It's true, then! It's true. I knew it. I knew it![17]

Bella Manningham did indeed know, deep down, that her husband was creeping about upstairs. For, as she goes on to explain, ten minutes after he ostensibly left the house every evening (before, in fact, sneaking straight back into their attic via a skylight), the gas light would ebb. Then, ten minutes before he came through the front door again, it would return to its former full flame. That meant another light must have been turned on, then off again, somewhere in the house—since the glow of each light would diminish as another lamp siphoned gas pressure away from it. But Bella Manningham was forced to deny—and could barely admit to herself—what she knew. Her husband's epistemic domination over her was so total that she didn't dare question his movements, let alone his motives. And his sense of epistemic entitlement—to maintain that kind of domination, to dictate the terms of her reality—was so great that *she* was the one who felt guilty for entertaining even the slightest doubts about her scurrilous, lying husband. From the very beginning of the play, exchanges like the following show how little latitude she has to question either the rightness of his beliefs or the benevolence of his actions. In Act One, she ventures hopefully:

> Mrs. Manningham: Oh, Jack dear. You have been so much kinder lately. Is it possible you're beginning to see my point of view?
> Mr. Manningham: I don't know that I ever differed from it, did I, Bella?
> Mrs. Manningham: Oh, Jack dear. It's true. It's true.[18]

In the context of the play as a whole, it is clear that she is not allowed to question his kindness: a particular cruelty.

Gaslighting can thus have a distinctively moral dimension, as well as an epistemic one: via a variety of techniques, the victim may effectively be prohibited from disputing the gaslighter's version of events, his narrative, or his side of the story.[19] She would be committing a grievous sin within the context of the relationship by questioning his authority, challenging his claims to knowledge, or even disagreeing with him regarding certain matters.[20] As the philosopher Kate Abramson argues in her groundbreaking work on gaslighting, "What makes the difference between the fellow who ignores or dismisses evidence . . . and the one who gaslights is the inability to tolerate even the possibility of challenge."[21]

Real-life cases of gaslighting scarcely less extreme than the foregoing fictional one are not hard to come by. And they highlight the fact that gaslighting is a common occurrence within families, as well as in intimate relationships. Take Kyle Stephens, one of the many girls the Michigan State University gymnastics team doctor Larry Nassar victimized. She was forced to apologize to *him* for impugning his good name by reporting his abuses to her parents. Who forced her to apologize? Her parents. Her *parents.* It's not just that they didn't believe her (which would be bad enough, in this context). They also punished her for coming forward, and regarded her as having wronged the good doctor—whose narrative about what transpired became effectively unimpeachable. And, like many victims of such gaslighting, Stephens subsequently came to doubt her own memory. "I began to feel brainwashed," she testified in court, during Larry Nassar's trial in January 2018. "It was as if I had never accused him. I felt I was losing my grip on reality. I started to question whether the abuse ever happened." She would replay the traumatizing incidents again and again in her mind, in an effort to retain her hold on the truth—and so she wouldn't forget that *she* wasn't the liar.[22]

Another real-life case of gaslighting was explored at length in the recent hit podcast *Dirty John.* The eponymous John's victim, Debra Newell, a divorcée in her late fifties, had entered the dating scene after a previous relationship had ended. Initially, John Meehan—who she met online—swept her off her feet. He was romantic, attentive, and, she believed, gainfully employed as an anesthesiologist. After the pair moved in together, and had gotten married, Debra discovered that her new husband's back-story was almost entirely fabricated (as her children had long suspected).[23] He was not, as he claimed, an anesthesiologist or, indeed, any kind of doctor but, rather, had trained as a nurse anesthetist. And he was no longer that either, his license hav-ing been suspended after he'd stolen drugs intended for patients (some of whom were on the operating table at the time, and thus would have been left in agony). When Debra and John first met, he had just gotten out of prison for felony drug theft—unbeknownst to her, until much later. He had a long-standing addiction to prescription pain medication. And he had a long history of broken relationships with women—including a pre-vious marriage—that had ended in their taking out a restrain-ing order against him. He was a con artist, but more than that; many people who met him reported finding his presence deeply unsettling, with a threat of violence lurking just beneath the surface. Here, in part, is how he earned his moniker:

> John would pick up women on dating websites; often he used match.com or Plenty of Fish. On dates, he would wear medical scrubs and pretend to be a doctor. He would induce women to send him intimate photos of themselves, which he then used to blackmail them. He sent them to their families. He sent them to their kids' school. An Irvine woman told me that he cut and pasted her photo for match.com and sent flyers to our neigh-

bors, calling her a slut and a home wrecker. A judge gave her a 5-year restraining order and he retaliated by asking for a restraining order on her. A Porter Ranch woman told police he wrote her an anonymous letter insinuating that he had raped her while she was unconscious and had taken photos of it. "You are my project for years to come," he wrote, "this I promise. Do you think I joke? Every breath I take will be to ruin your surgically implanted life. Thanks for the pictures."[24]

"Just the most devious person I've ever met . . . the most devious, dangerous, deceptive person" was how one career cop described John Meehan.

After discovering documents in his possession revealing much of his past (police reports, restraining orders, and jail and prison records), Debra moved out of their luxury home in Newport Beach, California. She hid out in hotels—changing locations every few days, to avoid being tracked down by him, on the recommendation of a detective whose help she had solicited. In the meantime, John went into the hospital for back surgery and was laid up with a bowel obstruction. *Los Angeles Times* journalist and *Dirty John* host Christopher Goffard recounts:

[John] began texting [Debra] accusations that she could not make sense of. That she had hit him, that she'd stolen $10,000 from his wallet. He threatened to call the police on her. He had become unrecognizable. . . . He had seduced her with lavish, unending compliments about her beauty. Now he denigrated her looks, mocked her age, ridiculed her attempts to stay attractive at 59. "Five marriages and a family that hates you. You want to see how this plays out? I sure do. You want to see how bad this turns out? You hit me. You threatened me." She replied, "Enough. You're evil."

Notwithstanding Debra's initial assertiveness, and the fact that there was absolutely no truth to these accusations, John continued to paint himself as her victim. And somehow, eventually, despite everything, she forgave him. Here's Debra's account of how this happened:

DEBRA: So twenty-three days go by [while he's in the hospital] and I just want to look him straight in the face and ask him why he did this. So I went in there and he said that those stories are wrong, that he was set up. He was trying to tell me so many times that he was set up and had to go to jail. Please forgive him. He just knew that I wouldn't understand until he had all the evidence in front of him.

GOFFARD: All a big misunderstanding?

DEBRA: All a big misunderstanding and he had an answer for everything; and it was so convincing that I thought, "Okay." He, literally, had convinced me, at this point, that he is not this person.

GOFFARD: Despite all of the paperwork?

DEBRA: Yes. All the facts were right there in front of me and he is that convincing. . . . I was also in love with him. It's so hard, when you're in love, to listen. You're listening to your heart, not your head.

GOFFARD: Did you ask about his nickname, Dirty John?

DEBRA: He said it wasn't true. He said, "I don't know where you got that from." It was as if everything . . . He was able to convince me. He was so good at it, it could be a cold day out and he could convince me that it's 95 degrees, that's how good he was. To where you questioned yourself.

GOFFARD: It's almost like he convinced you that all the facts about his life were some kind of hallucination on your part?

DEBRA: Yes, he made me out to be the one . . . That he was this great guy and that everyone else had done him wrong is what he had said. . . . He always, again, he always had a story. He told me that he had lied because he thought he'd lose me, that he feels so lucky that I'm such a forgiving person who, hell, I'm the love of his life, that I've made him a better person. Just all this kind of stuff. . . . I felt guilty, to some degree, that I'd married him and that he's in the hospital, but at the same time, I feared . . .

GOFFARD: Explain that to me. Guilty why?

DEBRA: Because I made a commitment. I made a commitment to marriage—for better, for worse.

As this exchange brings out, making someone question their own rationality, or think they're positively crazy, is only one way to achieve the kind of epistemic domination that I've argued gaslighting aims at.[25] (Though, even so, it may well be a knock-on *effect* of such treatment; Debra did question her own judgments, though not her own sanity.) Sometimes, as here, the gaslighter may manage to make believing his story and forgiving his extant sins into a moral imperative for his victim.[26] He may depict himself as the victim of other people or of his victim herself, and as vulnerable in myriad other ways—here, with John claiming to be suffering from multiple sclerosis (which there's no evidence he had) and to be potentially suicidal, rather than (as was in fact the case) a homicidal maniac.

Plying someone into submission by appealing to her sense of loyalty or sympathy—such that she won't question his story about himself, however implausible, out of a misplaced sense of guilt—can have much the same effect as making her doubt her rational capacities. The intended implication being that, if she questions him, there's something fundamentally wrong with her—either epistemically (she's "crazy," delusional, paranoid) or morally (she's a heartless bitch, incapable of trust, cruelly unforgiving, or similar). And the result will be much the same as well: someone who will not, cannot, challenge him.[27]

Gaslighting thus results in a victim who feels a false sense of obligation to believe *his* story over her own. She has been epistemically dominated—colonized, even. It's not hard to see how evil this is. It goes beyond harming someone. When successful, gaslighting robs the victim of the ability to *name* the harm done to her—and, equally, who did it.

The tactics John Meehan employed to win back Debra Newell and make her buy his thinly veiled lies and excuses were by no means an anomaly. He used them again and again, even after she had filed for a divorce from him. (He then claimed to be dying from cancer. "I'm dying, Deb. Slowly dying. Please, just come up with something so we can move on," he texted her. "I'm not doing well, Deb. I'm doing horrible without you. I need you.") And, according to Christopher Goffard, these plaintive self-depictions were entirely consistent with "John's master narrative of his life in which he was the perpetual victim." In reality, John had victimized at least eight other women in Laguna Beach, for starters, using many of the same techniques he employed with Debra Newell. Part of what he wanted was their money, to be sure. Goffard interviewed the attorney, Michael R. O'Neil, who tried to help Debra Newell extricate herself from this terrible situation:

> GOFFARD: His goal was to get into people's lives, marry them, and then take half their stuff, right?
> O'NEIL: No, to take *all* their stuff. . . . He believed, after all, he was entitled to it. He was entitled to it.

But John Meehan's sense of entitlement, as we've seen, went far beyond the fiscal. In fact, fleecing his female victims may have been merely a means to an end—a financial form of the domination over women for which his appetite seemed insatiable. That was what made him so frightening, and so dangerous. Goffard:

> Running through the stories [about John Meehan's victimization of women] was a streak of sadism and single-minded vindictiveness. They showed a man taking pleasure in the mechanics of a dark craft he had mastered. It seemed to go beyond just [extorting their] money. He seemed obsessed with humiliating anyone who defied his will.

Setting aside his preferred gaslighting tactics, Dirty John was in many ways a real-life Mr. Manningham. And in some respects at least his motives were even clearer. Though he also wanted money, "his endgame, it was the game," as Michael O'Neil put it. He was determined to win (over) these women, and he couldn't abide the possibility of losing in his mind games of seduction, deception, and domination. Gaslighting thus represented a unique solution to the problem he would have faced, given his warped perspective: how to maintain the *illusion* of having a partner and interlocutor in these women, someone with an independent perspective, while simultaneously destroying their ability to oppose him. That he had no compunction about literally destroying a victim, and thereby erasing her perspective, emerged in the final episode of the podcast—which detailed how he tried to kidnap and, in all likelihood, murder Debra's daughter Terra.[28] But by gaslighting the majority of his victims, rather than resorting to cruder methods of obliteration, he could also feel that he was attracting, charming, convincing them, while simultaneously precluding the possibility of challenge.

As Kate Abramson has argued, gaslighting someone is typically a long-term project. Manufacturing the sense of epistemic obligation to go along with the gaslighter's story takes time and, typically, quite a bit of effort (though that effort need not be consciously aimed at the end that gaslighting tries to achieve, of epistemic domination).[29] But epistemic entitlement can also result in a mistaken sense that others are *not* entitled to issue a contrary or threatening point of view, even if they in fact have every right to do so. This can lead to a man's systematic attempts to shut a woman up forever, or just his momentary outrage over her expressing her opinion. But even in the latter sort of case, the moments of outrage often exhibit a violent or threatening undercurrent. It's not for nothing that, as Rebecca Solnit observes, her classic essay on mansplaining began with a relatively benign-seeming incident and ended with rape and murder—a woman trying to testify to sexual assault and being permanently silenced.[30]

Examples of men becoming enraged at women for expressing their views online are not hard to come by, to put it mildly. I have experienced such anger myself, on many occasions, and have gradually learned to expect, and to live with, such misogyny. Even so, men's vitriol toward me and other girls and women threatens to take my breath away, on occasion.[31] When I was writing this chapter, a right-wing radio host in Australia, Alan Jones, who has a long history of misogynistic comments,[32] took exception to the views expressed about climate change by Jacinda Ardern, the female prime minister of New Zealand. During a Pacific Islands Forum attended by international leaders, Ardern stated, correctly, that Australia will "have to answer to the Pacific [Islands]," which will be devastatingly affected by rising sea levels, given Australia's current inaction on climate change. She also reiterated her commitment to have New Zealand do its bit to reduce carbon emissions to zero by 2050.[33] It wasn't surprising that these comments provoked Alan Jones's ire: studies have shown that, when it comes to climate change, conservative white men feel particularly entitled to their opinion, however incorrect, to the effect that what is happening is not happening.[34] (Such denial of basic realities is in some respects the attempted gaslighting of the planet.)

So Jones's anger may have been predictable.[35] But the way he chose to express it nevertheless made headlines. "Here she is preaching on global warming and saying we've got to do something about climate change," Jones said with outrage on his radio show. "I just wonder whether [Australian prime minister] Scott Morrison is going to be fully briefed to shove a sock down her throat."[36] In response to widespread condemnation of these threatening remarks—which veritably reveled in the prospect of Ardern's being silenced by a man in a position of comparable authority to her—Alan Jones initially refused to apologize. He merely tried to deflect in the most implausible way. Critics had willfully misconstrued his words, he said; he had actually meant that Ardern ought to shove her *own* sock down her *own* throat. Which is little better, and just not credible.[37]

There is a certain kind of man who is unable or unwilling to cope with others expressing views that threaten his own sense of what has happened, or ought to happen. Such men cannot abide girls and women, in particular, evincing their own, legitimate sense of epistemic entitlement to state what is happening in the world, or what has to change, going forward. They do not react merely by strenuously disagreeing with a girl or woman in this position. Indeed, they often seem to lack the wherewithal—or, again, the willingness—to disagree with her whatsoever. They instead want to shut her up, or to head off the very possibility of disagreement, by denying that her word has any meaning or merit whatsoever (she's crazy, or she's evil—so, either way, anything she says is beneath consideration). Or such a man instead imaginatively conjures up a world in which he and his ilk have the power to *make* her eat her words—in this case, by shoving something down her throat, thus silencing her forever. Strikingly, he is liable throughout this to feel like the justified, or even aggrieved, party.

As *The Guardian* reported, the CEO of the anti–domestic violence body Our Watch, Patty Kinnersly, voiced her concern over Jones's "verbal threat of violence"—pointing to the "power of words [to] create an environment where violence against women is seen as acceptable or can be justified." "You can disagree with someone without wanting to silence them," Kinnersly added, sensibly.[38]

Well, I assume *you* can, dear reader. But not everyone is so capable.

NINE

Unelectable—
On the Entitlement to Power

Following Hillary Clinton's surprise loss to Donald Trump in the 2016 U.S. presidential election, questions about women's electability in this country have been widely, and understandably, regarded as pressing.[1] An abundance of research shows that these questions are far from silly—though, as we'll see here eventually, the answers are vulnerable to manipulation and misinterpretation. But when it comes to the question of who is deemed entitled to hold power, women are subject to marked disadvantages under many (though not all) circumstances. And given that defeating Donald Trump in the 2020 election is, for many of us, a maximally urgent political imperative, it would be reckless to disregard the evidence about the difficulties women face in getting elected, at least as compared with their privileged male counterparts. We need to establish how strong this evidence is, and to ask whether or not these difficulties are likely to be insuperable. We should also ask who the "electability" framework tends to work in favor of—but that'll come later.

In a landmark study, Madeline Heilman and her collaborators asked participants to evaluate a hypothetical man versus a hypothetical woman—named "James" and "Andrea," respectively—based on information in a personnel file.[2] Both James and Andrea were described as holding down the same male-coded leadership position as an assistant vice president at an aircraft company. By swapping the names on the personnel files (such that the names on each file were switched for every second participant), the researchers were able to ensure that there was no substantive difference in the information participants received, on average, about the two people to be evaluated. Yet participants showed a marked, consistent bias toward the male leader. Specifically, when information about their competence was equivocal, participants judged "James" to be more competent than "Andrea" in some 86 percent of cases—though there was no significant difference between how the participants judged the candidates in terms of their likability. When the file contained information that made their high degree of competence unambiguous (by stating that each was in the top 5 percent of all employees at that level), the results shifted. This time, "James" was judged to be more likable than "Andrea" 83 percent of the time (though there were no significant differences in rankings of their relative competence). Interestingly, breaking the results down by participant gender made no difference to these findings: men and women exhibited the same biased tendencies.[3]

The upshot: regardless of their own gender, people tend to assume that men in historically male-dominated positions of power are more competent than women, unless this assumption is explicitly contradicted by further information. And when it is so contradicted, women are liable to be disliked and regarded, in particular, as "interpersonally hostile," a measure that, in this study, encompassed being perceived as conniving, pushy, selfish, abrasive, manipulative, and untrustworthy. The researchers described this effect as "dramatic"—and, they might well have added, depressing. How could a woman win, given the prevalence of these biases?

Further evidence of this difficulty comes in the form of a study that canvassed likely voters two years prior to the 2008 presidential election. The researchers, David Paul and Jessi Smith, had participants consider three Republicans—Rudy Giuliani, John McCain, and Elizabeth Dole—and two Democrats—John Edwards and Hillary Clinton. A female candidate lost to a male one in every single head-to-head matchup (both intraparty and interparty). Perhaps most strikingly, a substantial number of voters defected to a candidate from another party to avoid voting for a woman from their own—for example, Democratic voters chose a male Republican over Hillary Clinton. Given the strength of the tendency in recent decades for Americans to vote for their own party's candidates, this study provides some naturalistic support for the "women can't win" hypothesis, at least when it comes to women running for the presidency.[4] Further (and similarly depressing) evidence for this hypothesis comes from recent findings showing that many Americans (including a slim majority of American men) are still not "very comfortable" with the idea of a female president.[5]

Of course, we also have ample evidence that women *can* win elections, including against male rivals: the 2018 U.S. midterm election saw a record number of female politicians elected to Congress, just for one example.[6] But social psychologists have speculated that there's something about women who seek the highest positions of power and the most masculine-coded authority positions that people continue to find off-putting. In one study, hypothetical female politicians who were described as running for the Senate experienced little gender bias until they were explicitly portrayed as power-seeking—in which case the gendered backlash effects were striking. Further, as the researchers note, it doesn't take much to be perceived as power-seeking: It may be enough simply to run for the presidency. As they put it, "Backlash may occur more often in political roles requiring more of a commanding, decisive, and authoritative style (e.g., president of the United States, speaker of the House of Representatives)."[7] They speculate that similar penalties may apply to women seeking more humdrum positions of power—for example, as a boss or a manager—that are also perceived as highly masculine-coded.

So we can't just satisfy ourselves with the fact that large numbers of women are being elected to Congress or even to the Senate. We have to ask: What, if any, are the conditions under which the least palatable forms of female power become easier to swallow?

Further research by Heilman sheds crucial light on how and why women's power can sometimes be well tolerated. Heilman, together with her colleague Tyler Okimoto, set out to investigate the basis of the bias against women who occupy historically male-dominated power positions. They wanted to know why, "even when unequivocal evidence exists that a woman is successful in male gender–typed work, she faces career-hindering problems in work settings—problems of being disliked and interpersonally derogated."[8] The researchers hypothesized that such problems stem from a perception that a woman who succeeds in such a position must be lacking in "communality": the quality of being nurturing and prosocial, a deficit for which women tend to be harshly punished. For, as Heilman and Okimoto point out, there are widespread prescriptions that "specify that women should behave communally, exhibiting nurturing and socially sensitive attributes that demonstrate concern for others, such as being kind, sympathetic, and understanding."[9] Such social norms tend to be far more stringently enforced for women than for their male counterparts, as I have argued throughout this book. The researchers also noted that women don't have to *actively* demonstrate uncaring attributes in order to be perceived as uncommunal, and punished accordingly. Such a deficit will often be inferred or assumed, based simply on a woman's success in a male-coded leadership role. Heilman and Okimoto write:

> Several investigations have found that when research participants were told only that female managers had been successful (with no additional behavioral information supplied), they characterized these managers as lacking the prescribed favorable interpersonal qualities related to communality and as instead possessing traits such as selfishness, deceitfulness, deviousness, coldness, and manipulativeness. . . . It thus appears to take little more than knowledge that a woman is successful at male

sex–typed work to instigate interpersonally negative reactions to her.[10]

But can such inferences be blocked? Can such assumptions
be canceled?

They can. Heilman and Okimoto decided to investigate this
question using a research paradigm similar to the setup in the
opening study, with one crucial difference: in the experimental condition, they included information that implied that both
"James" and "Andrea" had a communal mind-set. (In the control condition, their mind-sets were not mentioned, and both
were portrayed as highly competent.) The results? Bias against
Andrea, and toward James, remained in full force in the control
condition (thus replicating the results of the previous study). But
when participants were explicitly told that Andrea had been described by her subordinates as someone who is "understanding
and concerned about others," that she "encourages cooperation
and helpful behavior," and that she "has worked to increase her
employees' sense of belonging," this pattern was reversed: participants were significantly more likely to choose Andrea as the
more desirable boss, the more likable of the pair, and judged her
as no more interpersonally hostile than James. And remember,
this held even though James was similarly described in this condition as having communal attributes.[11] Perceived communality
made an enormous difference for female but not male appli-
cants. When it comes to demonstrable niceness, it's an imperative for powerful women—and seemingly inconsequential for
their male rivals.[12]

So it would be a mistake to assume that male presidential
candidates will inevitably have an easier time garnering support

over similarly or even more qualified women.[13] The above research reveals that, under specific conditions, women can be perceived as entitled to wield power in such male-dominated domains—as much as, or even more than, the men they're up against. That is the good news. The bad news? These specific conditions will often go unmet. Being perceived as communal in presidential races turns out to be an uphill battle for many female candidates.

"SALAD FIEND AMY KLOBUCHAR ONCE BERATED AN AIDE FOR FORGETTING A FORK," read one headline, breathlessly.[14] The story had broken in a *New York Times* article titled, more soberly, "How Amy Klobuchar Treats Her Staff." That report combined valid concerns about the Minnesota senator—who had announced her presidential bid less than two weeks prior—with anecdotes that bordered on prurient in their framing. Most notably, this one:

> Senator Amy Klobuchar was hungry, forkless and losing patience.
>
> An aide, joining her on a trip to South Carolina in 2008, had procured a salad for his boss while hauling their bags through an airport terminal. But once on-board, he delivered the grim news: He had fumbled the plastic eating utensils before reaching the gate, and the crew did not have any forks on such a short flight.
>
> What happened next was typical: Ms. Klobuchar berated her aide instantly for the slip-up. What happened after that was not: She pulled a comb from her

bag and began eating the salad with it, according to four people familiar with the episode.

Then she handed the comb to her staff member with a directive: Clean it.[15]

It's telling that the article opened with this (now more than ten-year-old) incident, recounted from the perspective of the aide, and seemingly written so as to maximize embarrassment to the senator—rather than starting with behavior of hers detailed later in the story that was, to my mind, considerably more worrisome: throwing objects at aides and assigning them inappropriate tasks, such as regularly washing her dishes. And while concerns about Klobuchar's being positively abusive toward staffers certainly deserved to be taken seriously, there's no doubt that the story also raised the hackles of people who simply couldn't abide a female boss who displayed moments of anger, however understandable or human. More to the point, perhaps, even for those who think that all of these stories about Klobuchar were of direct public concern and appropriately framed, there are comparable reports about male politicians that received relatively little uptake. According to one story, for instance:

Joe Biden's outward appearance of geniality and good humor belie a fierce temper behind the scenes, with the former vice president routinely lashing out at staff, a new report says. . . . "Everyone who works for him has been screamed at," a former adviser told the magazine. . . .

The revelation about Biden echo those reported about 2020 rival Amy Klobuchar, a Minnesota senator, shortly before she announced her presidential run in February.[16]

The echoes may have been there, but the reverberations were very different. When it came to Biden, essentially, there were crickets.

Bernie Sanders has also been described as "unbelievably abusive" by a former subordinate. In an article entitled "Anger Management: Sanders Fights for Employees, Except His Own," published during his 2016 presidential bid, Paul Heintz disputed the grandfatherly image of Sanders:

> According to some who have worked closely with Sanders over the years, "grumpy grandpa" doesn't even begin to describe it. They characterize the senator as rude, short-tempered and, occasionally, downright hostile. Though Sanders has spent much of his life fighting for working Vermonters, they say he mistreats the people working for him.
>
> "As a supervisor, he was unbelievably abusive," says one former campaign staffer, who claims to have endured frequent verbal assaults. The double standard was clear: "He did things that, if he found out that another supervisor was doing in a workplace, he would go after them. You can't treat employees that way." . . . Others echoed the former employee's story, saying the senator is prone to fits of anger. "Bernie was an asshole," says a Democratic insider who worked with Sanders on the campaign trail. "Just unnecessarily an asshole."[17]

Yet another male presidential hopeful, Beto O'Rourke, behaved like an "asshole" to staffers too, by his own admission. In a documentary called *Running for Beto,* which followed his unsuccessful bid for the U.S. Senate in Texas, O'Rourke was shown "dropping f-bombs . . . complaining about having to 'dance' for the press, and snapping at his staff. . . . 'I know I was a giant asshole to be around sometimes,' O'Rourke acknowledges at one point in the documentary to his top aides, who do not dispute him on the point," read one news story, released prior to O'Rourke's announcement that he had decided to run for president.[18]

Compared with the reports about Klobuchar's treatment of her staff, such stories about Biden, Sanders, and O'Rourke have attracted little interest, and even less consternation. This jibes well with the finding that a perceived lack of communality in a powerful woman will tend to be harshly punished, while the same trait in her male counterparts will remain a matter of relative indifference. And however seriously one thinks we *should* take such moral lapses in a presidential candidate, there is obviously no excuse for gendered double standards here.

Reasonable minds can disagree about how much more traction Klobuchar's presidential bid would likely have received, had these stories not been circulating.[19] But there's another female presidential candidate whose prospects were surely hindered by a perceived lack of communality: New York senator Kirsten Gillibrand.[20] Gillibrand's supposed non-communal sin was quite different from Klobuchar's, but it attracted at least as much outrage. Gillibrand was widely perceived to have "thrown Al Franken under the bus," following allegations of sexual misconduct against the Minnesota senator—hence showing her to be disloyal, treacherous, selfish, and opportunistic.[21] And though Gillibrand was only one of around thirty Democrats to call for Franken's resignation, which he gave voluntarily early in 2018, the fact that she was the first to do so was, for many people, unforgivable.[22] After Gillibrand announced that she was dropping out of the presidential race, in August 2019, a Politico article summarized the situation nicely:

> At one point, Gillibrand looked on paper like a legitimate, if not formidable, presidential candidate—one with flaws but also the pluses of a perfect electoral record and a distinctly feminist message that looked like a compelling counter to Donald Trump. But Gillibrand, dogged by criticism for pushing for Sen. Al Franken's resignation, never took flight. . . . Hours after Gillibrand's announcement Wednesday night, both she and Franken trended on Twitter together, seemingly inextricably linked.
>
> "Franken was definitely a problem in terms of fundraising," the person familiar with the Gillibrand campaign said. "He just kept coming up, over and over again." Jen Palmieri, Clinton's former communications director, said there was "no question" that the Franken ordeal had a "huge, outsized impact on her." "The sub-current of her entire candidacy was the Franken resignation and people unfairly pinning that on her," Palmieri said. "It's a crowded field, and it's hard for all the candidates, but that really hampered her."[23]

For some people, there are few worse sins for a female leader than thwarting the power to which a man is tacitly deemed entitled, even if there are multiple credible reports of his being sexually inappropriate, lecherous, or handsy.

In their investigation of the bias against powerful women, Heilman and Okimoto undertook two further experiments. In one of these, they again included information that "Andrea," as well as "James," had behaved in communal ways. But this time, they left the motivation for such behavior unclear, implying that it was part of a broader department or company-wide initiative, and therefore "might have been performed [merely] to fulfill a job responsibility."[24] In one of two such similar descriptions (which were again alternately applied to "James" and "Andrea"), participants read: "In his/her last year at [unnamed company], James/Andrea worked for a supervisor who was known for placing high importance on employee relations." For the other target of evaluation, participants read: "In recent years, [unnamed company] has updated their mission statement, placing greater importance on understanding the concerns of employees. As part of this company-wide initiative, James/Andrea . . ." After reading descriptions of both candidates' engagement in communal behavior, participants went on, as before, to complete the evaluation.

Would the fact that Andrea had demonstrated care and consideration toward her subordinates still be enough to overcome the tendency to dislike her and judge her to be interpersonally hostile? No. When participants had no way to tell that Andrea's communal behavior was due to her personal characteristics, they once again exhibited the marked gender bias evinced in the previous studies (and, again, replicating these findings).[25] Communal behavior seems to count in a woman's favor only if it can be attributed to stable traits of character, or her own authentic nature.

This isn't particularly surprising. But it has troubling implications in the political arena, where it's difficult for prominent female politicians to be perceived as authentically anything. Accusations of being "fake," inauthentic, and merely trying to gain power have dogged several prominent female politicians— not only Hillary Clinton, but also Julia Gillard, the first female prime minister of Australia.[26] Clinton's approval rating was sky-high when she served as secretary of state, and it began to tank only when she initiated her bid for the presidency—which coincided with, and is partly explained by, her being portrayed in the media as cruelly indifferent to the fates of people in Benghazi, Libya, and to matters of national security (via the faux scandal of her emails). Julia Gillard was a fairly popular politician in Australia until she became prime minister—whereupon she was widely portrayed in the media as fake, selfish, opportunistic, cynical, and backstabbing (having toppled the former leader, Kevin Rudd, in an internal party challenge).[27]

Given the abundance of information about any person in the public eye, it is not too difficult to find a way to portray a prominent woman as having been, at some point in time, insufficiently caring, considerate, or cognizant of others. We should be wary not only of outright character assassinations and smear campaigns against her, but even of subtler, potentially valid concerns about her being accorded outsize importance.

The right way to take these points is a matter of some delicacy. Being communal *is* an important virtue. But there are many virtues we expect leaders to possess, and it is neither realistic nor fair to expect every person in a position of power to be *extraordinarily* communal (as opposed to reasonably kind, empathetic, considerate, and so on). There is also the simple point that, to the extent that our communal expectations of women *are* indeed reasonable, we often have a long way to go in holding men to the same warranted moral standards.

Another complexity worth pausing over is that perceptions about communality may differ radically depending on one's own political values. Congresswoman Alexandria Ocasio-Cortez, for example, is widely (and, I believe, quite rightly) perceived by people on the left as exceptionally communal. But to those on the right, she could hardly be considered less so, judging by the kind of consternation she attracts on Fox News and in other conservative outlets. The same goes for other prominent girls and women who are devoted to environmental causes, among other issues of social justice. Witness the polarized reaction to environmental activist Greta Thunberg's address to the United Nations, in which she resisted the feminine-coded pseudo-obligation to give hope to her audience. Instead, she righteously, and movingly, excoriated them:

> You have stolen my dreams and my childhood with your empty words. And yet I'm one of the lucky ones. People are suffering. People are dying. Entire ecosystems are collapsing. We are in the beginning of a mass extinction, and all you can talk about is money and fairy tales of eternal economic growth. How dare you!"[28]

The power dynamics explored in this chapter help explain the misogyny to which Ocasio-Cortez and Thunberg are disproportionately subject, even relative to the rather grim standards for female public figures.[29] The more the Left loves them (partly on the grounds of their extraordinary communality in fighting for future generations), the more the Right resents it— especially in view of their sense that this girl or woman is actually hurting people's (read: their own) interests and impugning their good character.[30]

There are also tricky issues about how perceptions of communality may interact with various kinds of marginalization, along with gender biases. Someone who is neuro-atypical or highly introverted, for example, may not be comfortable showing that they care via prolonged or extensive interpersonal interactions. They may nevertheless be deeply oriented to moral matters, and staunchly committed to social justice. We must make room for different ways of manifesting communal moral virtues.

And we must not let our vision of a communal leader devolve into a vision of bland niceness. There is a genuine entitlement under some circumstances to exhibit anger or even rage, as has been persuasively argued by the philosophers Myisha Cherry and Amia Srinivasan, the political theorist Brittney Cooper, and the political commentators and writers Soraya Chemaly and Rebecca Traister.[31] A nuanced understanding of communality should allow for such emotions to be freely expressed— especially on behalf of people who are wronged, oppressed, or marginalized. "I am angry and I own it," read the subject line of a recent email from Elizabeth Warren to her supporters, in response to Joe Biden's insinuation that she was excessively up in arms about things. In light of the injustices occurring in the wealthiest country in the world, we ought to be incensed, she wrote. Yet "over and over we are told that women are not allowed to be angry," she pointed out. "It makes us unattractive to powerful men who want us to be quiet."[32]

So there are several reasons why it may be difficult for an aspiring female political leader to improve the public's perception of her—even if she is a genuinely caring, kind, considerate person who should, in theory, be benefitting from the sort of communality boost Heilman and Okimoto found in their study. And there is also the point that having to show oneself to be authentically communal may present special difficulties for almost anyone, regardless of their gender. How do you show that you really care, and are not simply kissing babies for the photo opportunity? For that matter, is it reasonable to expect that kissing the baby will always *be* more than a photo opportunity? Given the number of demands on a politician's time and energy, expecting deep human engagement with each and every person who she meets on the campaign trail might seem tantamount to expecting her to be socially superhuman—a kind of female unicorn.

Enter Elizabeth Warren, who became well-known for making personal phone calls to minor donors, and who had taken some one hundred thousand selfies with individual voters by early in 2020.[33] The comedian and actor Ashley Nicole Black asked, in jest, on Twitter, whether Warren had a plan to fix her love life. "DM me and let's figure this out," Warren responded, before arranging a phone call that was apparently very helpful.[34]

When Warren's main rival on the left, Bernie Sanders, had a heart attack on the campaign trail, she not only sent him kind get-well messages (as did many presidential candidates). Warren went one better, and sent his staffers dinner and cookies while Sanders was in the hospital recovering.[35]

"Elizabeth Warren always knows exactly what she wants when she gets to the front of the Starbucks line and never holds everyone else up."[36] "Elizabeth Warren has never asked a bartender 'What whiskeys do you have?' She's already checked the shelf."[37] "Elizabeth Warren never takes up too much space on the sidewalk or the subway. She checks her own privilege and shares public space."[38]

Tweets of this sort, which briefly became a popular meme on Twitter, reflected a widespread perception that Elizabeth Warren is exceptionally communal: kind, caring, compassionate, attentive to others' needs, and so on. And in light of the empirical evidence canvassed in this chapter, this perception helps to explain Warren's moment of great popularity during her bid for the presidency, with her becoming the frontrunner in the race by October 2019.[39] It also helps to explain her rapid, dramatic downfall—with her coming in no better than third in any of the early primaries, including in Warren's home state of Massachusetts.[40]

This was despite the fact that, in addition to her communal virtues, Warren was arguably the most experienced, prepared, poised, and smartest of any of the Democratic candidates. She was famous for her comprehensive plans, from tackling climate change to the coronavirus pandemic. And when she made mistakes, such as undergoing DNA testing to confirm her (negligible) Native ancestry, she not only apologized, but learned from her missteps.[41] As Kimberlé W. Crenshaw put it, on Twitter:

> I voted for @ewarren today [because] she listens to Black women, understands that "Economic justice has not ever been sufficient to ensure racial justice," admits mistakes, is a tough broad, and [because] we now see how not having a leader [with] a plan costs lives.[42]

I couldn't agree more with this. And, in the interests of full disclosure, I write what follows as an avid Warren supporter. She had my vote from the outset.[43] I think she would have made an outstanding president, and I am gutted that, on the day of writing, her campaign has been suspended.

But while there is reasonable disagreement over whether Warren deserved to win the nomination, there has been considerable surprise and consternation that she didn't at least do *better* than she did—losing contests to various white men, in the form of Bernie Sanders, Joe Biden, and sometimes even Pete Buttigieg or Mike Bloomberg—especially given her erstwhile popularity.[44] The studies canvassed in this chapter shed light on this puzzling outcome.

For the problem with perceptions of communality is that they are likely to be volatile. They hence constitute a dangerous—if, as we have seen, necessary—facet of a female politician's appeal. A potent double bind presents itself to women in this position: embrace the hope that you're exceptionally communal and risk flaming out, when people are inevitably disappointed by some aspect of your history, views, or platform. *Don't* present yourself as exceptionally communal, and run a greater risk that your campaign will never go anywhere, like Klobuchar and Gillibrand.[45]

Of course, Warren also faced straight-up misogyny and the associated gender biases during her presidential campaign. Her righteous anger was off-putting and even unsettling to some people. ("Mean and angry Warren is not a good look," tweeted conservative writer Jennifer Rubin.[46]) Warren's professorial background, when instantiated in a woman, was an anathema to others.[47] Still others may have liked her well enough to embrace Warren as their *second* choice, but preferred a male candidate, at least when the moment of truth came at the voting booth. Sometimes this was likely an expression of the aforementioned gender biases (which is not to deny, of course, that some people had legitimate reasons, relative to their own values, for preferring Biden or Sanders).[48] Such biases are often unconscious, and subject to post hoc rationalization—including via the common trope that women are unelectable. (To which an apt response, emblazoned on a T-shirt, was: "She's electable if you f★★★ing vote for her." The shirt is also happily available in an uncensored version.[49]) And remember that, as this chapter has shown, such biases have been empirically demonstrated in women as much as men, as well as in people who are still young, as millennials.[50]

But subtler forms of misogyny would likely have afflicted Warren's chances too.[51] When she was pressed for details—far more strenuously than was her progressive rival, Sanders—about how she would implement Medicare for All, Warren eventually announced a comprehensive plan to expand the coverage provided under the Affordable Care Act, before passing a sweeping healthcare bill implementing a single-payer system during her third year in the White House.[52] Whatever one thought of this plan (and, for my own part, I am inclined toward a good dose of epistemic humility when it comes to exactly how to realize key progressive values), Warren was roundly and, to my mind, disproportionately condemned for supposedly backpedaling. The fact that it was a perceived failure vis-à-vis *care* that cost her so dearly does not seem likely to have been accidental. People tend to unwittingly demand caring perfection from a female leader—while forgiving similar and worse lapses in her male counterparts.[53]

Similarly, Warren plausibly lost a significant amount of support in some progressive quarters due to her decision, during the death throes of her campaign, to accept super-PAC money. Whether one agrees with this decision or not, it's at least unclear that, for a would-be Warren supporter, it should have been a deal-breaker. But, again, women are held to gendered double standards, when it comes to both their steadfastness and their purity: any supported lapse on this front tends to be seized on mercilessly.[54] And of course their trustworthiness is often doubted for *no* legitimate reason.[55]

We expect too much from women. And when a woman we like or respect disappoints us, even in minor and forgivable ways, she is liable to be punished—often by people who think they have the moral high ground, and are merely reacting to her as she deserves, rather than helping to enact misogyny via moralism. Meanwhile, no such perfection is demanded of her male rivals. Sanders paid essentially no penalty for flipping his 2016 position on whether the candidate with a plurality of delegates should automatically become the Democratic nominee, when that outcome stood to his potential advantage in 2020.[56] Nor did Biden face much criticism for his hazy public-option health plan, or for the embellished stories he told on the campaign trail—not to mention, his history of plagiarism.[57]

But perhaps the most important occasion of lost support during Warren's campaign was a rare moment of conflict between her and Sanders. This was following leaked details of their meeting during December 2018, when Warren told Sanders she was planning to run for president. According to Warren insiders, and later confirmed by Warren, Sanders said he didn't think a woman could win against Trump. Sanders, meanwhile, vehemently denies having said this. Rather, he maintains, he said that sexism would be weaponized by Trump against a female candidate.[58]

Whatever transpired—and it's not clear that the two candidates' versions of events are ultimately incompatible—Warren's role in the conflict likely did her far more damage than Sanders' did.[59] When a woman challenges the epistemic and moral authority of a trusted male figure, she is likely to be the one who comes off as incorrect or immoral, all else being equal. And in this instance, to make matters worse, she was also perceived as *whiney:* as accusing Sanders of sexism, despite her never having made this accusation. This, together with perceptions of Warren as betraying the progressive cause by failing to "play nice" with Sanders, likely cost her dearly. And that's despite the fact that, by and large, this was a *symmetrical* disagreement: each held that the other was failing to tell, or perhaps simply to remember, the full story. But when he says she's lying, people tend to believe him. When she says that *he* is, she's perceived as attacking him cruelly. Following this incident, a meme depicting Warren as a snake proliferated on Twitter. The symbolism is obvious: When a man and a woman clash, she is the one who is venomous and sneaky.

All of this reflects the widespread—and, yes—misogynistic sense that, unlike their male rivals, women are not entitled to make mistakes, especially when it comes to supposed communal values. They are not entitled to accept money. They are not entitled to challenge the narrative put forward by their male counterparts. And while they may be entitled to *have* power under certain conditions, they are not entitled to actively seek it, nor to take it away from the men they're up against. Until we face these facts, we will not have a female president.

Yet this isn't to endorse the narrative that Warren was unelectable in retrospect. The future remained open until the relevant votes were cast, in the primaries. And the electability framework had several decisive drawbacks.

For one thing, it is a self-fulfilling prophecy: the more voters are told that a certain candidate won't win, the less likely that they'll triumph. After all, electability isn't a static social fact; it's a social fact that we're constantly, and collectively, in the process of constructing.[60] A June 2019 poll showed that, when voters were asked who they would vote for in an election held that day, Joe Biden was the frontrunner, followed by Bernie Sanders. But when they were asked who they would *want* to be president if they could wave a magic wand, Elizabeth Warren emerged as the narrow favorite.[61]

So concerns about electability plausibly led some people to give up on Warren prematurely, despite her being their favored Democratic candidate. This was especially true for women. As Nate Silver of the election forecasting website 538 put it, "There are a lot of women who might not vote for a woman because they're worried that other voters won't vote for her. But if everyone just voted for who they actually wanted to be president, the woman would win!"[62]

The electability narrative also served as a convenient rationalization for other people's biased, unfair preferences. And it obscured the fact that *other* candidates may have equally or more potent barriers to their being elected, albeit for different reasons.

There is something deeply troubling about the degree to which concerns about electability emerged with unprecedented force during this election cycle, with such promising female candidates in the running (as well as male candidates of color[63]). There always seems to be *something* that fills in the lacuna in the sentence "I'd vote for her, but she's just not . . ." Whether the sentence continues by airing worries about her competence, her likability, or—now—her electability, this will often serve as a pretext for a foregone conclusion: voting for yet another white male candidate. In some cases, that is a reflection of the person's own unconscious gender biases. In others, it involves kowtowing to the imagined biases of others.[64] Either way, this is a recipe for conservatism writ large. And hence, as such, it constitutes a collective action problem. If we all give up on women prematurely under such conditions, because they are women, then they will never get anywhere. Effectively, moreover, they will be subject to misogyny: a barrier they face as women in a man's world, whatever the good intentions of at least some of those killing their prospects.

Perhaps most perniciously of all, the electability narrative framed voting for a woman in the 2020 Democratic primary as a selfish choice—as a political liability, given the existential threat of Trump being returned to the White House. As such, it preyed on the conscience of some of the people most likely to be attracted to Warren's politics: those who value communality, and who therefore might have been willing to sacrifice their voting preference for the sake of the supposedly bigger picture.

But the bigger picture is surely partly this: we are entitled in such contexts to vote for the person we think would be the best person for the job. For my money, that was not a man who recently defended working with segregationists and who lecherously sniffed the hair of a young Latina politician, nor a man who had a heart attack during his campaign and who subsequently refused to release his health records.[65] It was a woman who is whip-smart, truly compassionate, and who seemed to have a plan for everything.

TEN

Undespairing—
On the Entitlement of Girls

I finished my first book, *Down Girl,* in a spirit of despair. "I give up," I wrote. "I wish I could offer a more hopeful message." Instead, I concluded by offering a postmortem—a grim overview of the reasons I was pessimistic about getting people to take the problem of misogyny seriously, or even to face it as a problem whatsoever.

Although I am still far from hopeful, I am not so despairing anymore. In part, that's because I think I made an intellectual mistake the first time around: I confused the intransigence of *some* people with the unwillingness of *most* people to think soberly and deeply about the problems facing girls and women. In the interim, I have been pleasantly surprised—shocked, even—to hear from many readers who *have* been prepared, even eager, to think through these problems with me, with the aim of combating them. There is still an enormous amount of energy that goes into denying and minimizing misogyny, of course, as this book has sadly made all too clear. But there is also a lot of momentum—extant and building—in the efforts to resist it.

Another reason I'm no longer as despairing is more personal. I wrote much of this book while pregnant with my first child, and I came to feel that my previous despair had been something of a luxury—a luxury I can now ill afford to indulge in. I am still pessimistic about the possibility of making much-needed feminist social progress without incurring destructive, toxic backlash.[1] But giving up no longer feels like a viable option. I increasingly feel the need to keep fighting, regardless of the outcome. Hope, to me, is a belief that the future will be brighter, which I continue not to set much store in. But the idea of fighting for a better world—and, equally importantly, fighting against backsliding—is not a belief; it's a political *commitment* that I can get on board with.[2]

These sentiments were further fueled when my husband and I were told we were having a girl. We were delighted—and terrified. It is difficult to reconcile the desires we naturally have for our child with a sober acknowledgment of the realities of misogyny and the male entitlement that often gives rise to it. As we've seen throughout this book, girls and women are all too frequently punished for not giving a man what he is tacitly deemed entitled to—and not just because of his own overblown sense of what he deserves, but by dint of the social structures that work to enable, foster, and sustain male privilege. Clearly, as parents, we want better for our daughter.

At the same time, I must admit that the news that we were having a girl—or, more accurately, a child who's provisionally a girl[3]—came as a slight relief to me. The prospect of raising a boy to be confident and joyful, yet appropriately mindful of his own privilege, seemed like a particularly daunting moral challenge. It's obvious that *no* child should grow up with the grim sense of himself as a potential villain haunting his childhood. That would be unproductive, unethical, and even abusive, if taken to extremes. So when it comes to how to strike the right balance here, my husband and I look forward to learning from others with the requisite wisdom and experience.[4] The same goes for endless parenting questions, most of which apply regardless of a child's gender. I do not want to present myself in what follows as being any kind of expert; indeed, at this point in my life, I could hardly be less so.

But over the course of writing this book, I did find myself with some thoughts about what I want our daughter to feel entitled to. These are goods that *all* people are entitled to, whatever their gender; yet girls and women are often socialized to feel not only less important than or inferior to boys and men, but also less entitled to certain forms of basic humanity and common decency. Entitlement, as I've written about it in these pages, has most often referred to some people's undue sense of what they deserve or are owed by others. But, for all that, entitlement is *not* a dirty word: entitlements can be genuine, valid, justified.

And I think the prospective parental lens is conceptually helpful here, for at least two reasons. One is that when it comes to what women truly deserve or are owed, it's all too easy to fall into the trap of victim blaming. In the unjust social world we occupy, I will rarely fault a woman for not being in touch with what she is morally entitled to, or for being reticent about claiming it. But there's a difference between stating—retrospectively, and often judgmentally—that a woman ought to have asserted herself in some way, versus hoping that my daughter and her cohort will be empowered to do so in a forward-looking manner. That doesn't mean, of course, that it will always be feasible or safe for her to lay claim to what she has a right to: that's part of what misogyny polices and prohibits. But I want her to at least be clear about her entitlements, and to be prepared to assert them when conditions make that possible. And when they do not, I want her to feel lucid anger, and to push for structural changes, on behalf of herself as well as those who are less privileged.

So it helps to keep the emphasis here on the future: on moral *development*. It's also helpful, I believe, to emphasize these efforts as a facet of *moral* development. Learning what one is entitled to is—or at least should be—inextricably connected with learning what one owes to others. Among many other things, it is vital that our daughter become aware of her own privilege, as a white girl born to two highly educated, comparatively wealthy, middle-class, cisgender, heterosexual, and largely non-disabled parents. This goes beyond the admittedly crucial task of teaching her to understand and embrace human difference, diversity, and various kinds of vulnerability. It will also involve teaching her that she has special obligations to defend and support people subject to forms of marginalization and oppression from which she will be spared. She will be obligated not to tolerate, let alone participate in, the legal and extralegal policing practices that oppress Black and brown bodies in our society, for one obvious example. Similarly, she will be obligated not to "lean down" exploitatively on the emotional and material labor of women of color, as have so many white women before her. And her sense of warranted entitlement must always be tempered with a knowledge of what she is *not* entitled to do, to say, or to rely on, as a person who will be born into privilege, along multiple axes.

So what do I want my daughter to know, when it comes to what she is entitled to? I want my daughter to know that she is entitled to feel pain—be it physical or emotional—and that she is subsequently entitled to cry out or ask for help, and to be cared for, soothed, nurtured. I want her to know that she is entitled to be believed about her physical and emotional needs, and that she is as worthy of care—medical and otherwise—as any other person.

I want her to know that she is entitled to bodily autonomy—to choose whether, when, and how she is touched by anyone who expresses a desire to do so (and yes, they must ask for, rather than just assuming, her consent). I want her to know that hugs and kisses, however well-meaning, are always optional. I want her to feel no guilt or shame in saying "no" to anyone's potential encroachment upon her body. When the time comes, I want her to know that she is entitled to full control over her reproductive capacities, and that the decision about whether or not to bear children is her own and no one else's.

I want her to know that her presumed gender is just that, a presumption, on our part—which she is entirely entitled to tell us we've been wrong about. I want our child to know that being a boy or being non-binary are not only viable options but will be positively embraced and supported within our household—and that we will fight at every turn to make the world a place in which all trans and non-binary children and adults can flourish.

I want my daughter to know that women, as much as men, along with non-binary people, are entitled to support from others in fulfilling adult responsibilities. I am relieved that she will grow up in a household where she is just as likely (if not likelier) to see her father as her mother making meals, doing the dishes, or putting in a load of laundry. Studies show that the school-aged daughters of fathers tend to be more ambitious when he does his fair share of housework—saying they want to be a lawyer or a doctor, for example, rather than that they want to follow a specifically feminine-coded path, as a teacher, a nurse, or staying at home with children.[5] And this pattern holds even if both parents in a household where the mother does more of the housework explicitly espouse gender egalitarian beliefs: actions speak louder than words here, seemingly. Whether or not this translates into long-term life goals and career choices, it shows that children pick up more than one might think, in terms of gendered divisions of labor.

I want my daughter to know that she is entitled to use and enjoy her body in a huge variety of ways: to play sports, to play music, to dance, to stim, to express joy or grief or fear or sheer silliness. I want her to know that she is entitled to eat heartily, to take up space, to be loud, and to enjoy the kind of lack of bodily self-consciousness I can only dream of. Even during my pregnancy, I can anticipate being willing to cheerfully *kill* anyone who makes her feel ashamed of her body, whatever its shape, size, disabilities, typicality, and so on. (To be clear, I am perfectly well aware that I am not entitled to do this.)

I want my daughter to know that human sexuality comes in so many different forms—that she is entitled to be straight, queer, bisexual, asexual, and so on. As she grows older, I want her to know that she is entitled to thoroughly enjoy her sexuality, whatever that turns out to be, without the slightest shame or stigma. I want her to know that she is entitled to say no to sex, without the slightest shame or stigma, either. I also want her to know—and this is hard to write—that any abuse, harassment, or assault she may face, sexual or otherwise, is a moral abomination. I have not yet figured out how, or how much, to tell her about the realities of male sexual entitlement and violence that have so occupied my consciousness over the past several years, including while pregnant with her, in writing the book you've been reading. Here, words fail me.[6]

I want my daughter to know that she is entitled—and sometimes obligated—to speak her mind and to speak out against injustice, even if it makes some of the people around her uncomfortable. I want her to know that she is entitled to speak, *period*. Studies show that in the classroom, boys continue to be called on vastly more than girls—a pattern that is particularly entrenched in STEM fields.[7] I want her to know that this is deeply unjust, if typically unintentional, and to understand that, if it happens, the fault lies not with her but with the system. I want her to know that she is entitled to know things and to explain them to other people, without the prospect of subsequent backlash or peremptory mansplaining. Obviously, I also want her to be a good listener—cognizant and alive to the knowledge of those more expert than she is.

I want her to know that it's not her job to tailor truths about her body or mind to suit other people's feelings—including ours, as her parents. Indeed, I believe that one reason why gaslighting is such an insidious phenomenon, and liable to occur even in loving, well-meaning, and apparently well-functioning families, is that children are not given the scope by their parents to experience and air their feelings fully. "You *can't* feel that" and "You *mustn't* say that" are expressions that can easily be used to make a child feel crazy or guilty, unless she buries her true emotions. I want my daughter to know that she is entitled to be angry, sad, anxious, or simply uncertain.

I want my daughter to know that she is entitled to be powerful and, on occasion, to compete with other people, including privileged boys and men. I want her to know that if she does end up winning or otherwise outranking them, she may well be entitled to occupy a position of power or authority over them. I want her to be a kind and fearless leader. I want her, of course, to be a graceful loser. I want her to be communally minded and altruistic. At the same time, I want her to feel entitled to make mistakes, moral mistakes included. I want her to know, unlike so many girls and women, that she is lovable and forgivable, even if and when she falters. I want her to be prepared to make amends and admit to her mistakes, fully and freely, when she inevitably makes them.

And I want my daughter to know that her own entitlements in these respects are crucially connected with some of her most important moral obligations: the obligation *all* of us share, regardless of our gender, to make this world one in which structural injustices are actively being rectified. Together, we must fight for a world in which girls and women are valued, cared for, and believed, within our social, legal, and medical institutions. Together, we must fight for a world in which the bodies of girls and women are not routinely controlled, sexualized, harassed, assaulted, and injured—or even destroyed altogether. Together, we must fight for a world in which every girl or woman is safe and free to be her own person, rather than consigned to be predominantly a human giver of the sex, care, and love to which privileged boys and men are tacitly deemed entitled. These are only a fraction of the structural changes that desperately need to happen, of course, in order to achieve justice for all members of our moral community; even so, they are radical. Indeed, at the time of writing, they are difficult to envision.

So, as I write this, I can't imagine successfully teaching my daughter all of these things. There is so much counter-messaging in our culture; and there is so much here to teach her that I never learned myself—not properly, not fully. I still have tremendous difficulty picturing a world in which girls and women can reliably lay claim to what they are entitled to, let alone one in which they get it. It will be a long, perhaps interminable fight. But, for her, I can say: I am in it.

ACKNOWLEDGMENTS

So many people helped me with this book—which was nearly six years in the making, though a shorter time in the writing—that I despair of giving everyone the thanks I surely owe them. But, for an incomplete and inadequate beginning: I'm deeply indebted to my editor at Crown, Amanda Cook, for her brilliant insights and editorial vision, as well as for her unfailing support and belief in me during this project. I'm also tremendously grateful to my editor at Penguin UK, Casiana Ionita, for astute comments that improved this book tremendously—and, again, for the kind of support that is every author's dream come true. And although we didn't work together on this particular project, I would never have been able to even conceive of it without my editor for my first book, Peter Ohlin at Oxford University Press, who oversaw the writing of *Down Girl* with extraordinary patience, kindness, and insight.

Huge thanks to my agent, Lucy Cleland, who has been yet another amazing source of ideas and support throughout the execution of this book. I'm also grateful to Stephanie Steiker for crucial help during the development stages.

I owe thanks to audiences at Fordham University, the University of Michigan, the University of North Carolina–Chapel Hill, MIT, the University of Indiana–Bloomington, RIT, the University of Alabama–Birmingham, the Brooklyn Public Library, Wooster College, Nassau Community College, Princeton University, CUNY, the University of Buffalo, Amherst College, the University of Connecticut, Wellesley College, the Society for the Humanities at Cornell University, Southern Illinois University Edwardsville, the University of Puget Sound, Grinnell College, and the University of Southern California, for their generous and astute feedback on various portions of the material contained herein. I'm also deeply indebted to my faculty and graduate student colleagues at the Sage School of Philosophy at Cornell for providing such a wonderful intellectual atmosphere in which to do the work I do.

On a more personal note, I owe so much to my parents, Anne and Robert, as well as my sister, Lucy, for being the most wonderful family imaginable, and for providing the kind of "secure base" from which to spend a lifetime pursuing controversial, and sometimes divisive, ideas. I am so grateful to each of them both for their support, and for being who they are.

Finally, I couldn't do any of this without my amazing husband, Daniel. He is my rock. He is my safe place. He is the person who supports me every day—intellectually, materially, and emotionally—and who I can always count on. He is my first reader, my best friend, and, now, my co-parent. I can only hope to someday go some way toward deserving him.

ONE Indelible—On the Entitlement of Privileged Men

1. Kavanaugh was also accused of sexual assault or misconduct by three other women: Deborah Ramirez, Julie Swetnick, and an anonymous complainant. See Christine Hauser, "The Women Who Have Accused Brett Kavanaugh," *The New York Times,* September 26, 2018, https://www.nytimes.com/2018/09/26 /us/politics/brett-kavanaugh-accusers-women.html. However, I'll focus on Dr. Christine Blasey Ford's allegations for the purposes of this introductory chapter.

2. For example, "As much as I admired Dr. Ford's courage and found her personally to be convincing and sympathetic, it does not change my conviction that uncorroborated and un-investigable accusations from a pre-adult time in a man or woman's life shouldn't derail a demonstrably exceptional career," wrote Anneke E. Green in an article entitled "We Can Believe Ford and Confirm Kavanaugh," RealClearPolitics, October 3, 2018, https:// www.realclearpolitics.com/articles/2018/10/03/we_can_believe _ford_and_confirm_kavanaugh_138240.html.

3. For an example of someone who insinuated she was lying, see Cheryl K. Chumley, who wrote: "If Ford has anything, anything at all that could show her claims against Kavanaugh are rooted in fact and truth, she needs to cough it up and cough it up quick. It's not incumbent on Kavanaugh to prove his innocence. It is,

however, incumbent on Ford to prove his guilt—to prove she's not lying and using a shameful, despicable tactic to disrupt the Supreme Court proceedings and kill Kavanaugh's nomination." "Christine Blasey Ford Could Indeed be Lying," *Washington Times*, September 22, 2018, https://www.washingtontimes.com/news /2018/sep/22/christine-blasey-ford-could-indeed-be-lying/.

Susan Collins, on the other hand, held that Ford's testimony was unreliable due to a case of mistaken identity. Following her casting of the deciding vote to confirm Kavanaugh, she put it this way, during a TV interview: "[Christine Blasey Ford] was clearly terrified, traumatized, and I believed that a sexual assault had happened to her. What I think she is mistaken about is who the perpetrator was. I do not believe her assailant was Brett Kavanaugh." Jaclyn Reiss, "Susan Collins Says She Thinks Brett Kavanaugh's Accuser Was 'Mistaken,'" *The Boston Globe*, October 8, 2018, https://www.bostonglobe.com/news/politics/2018/10/07 /susan-collins-says-she-thinks-christine-blasey-ford-was-mistaken -about-identity-perpetrator-being-brett-kavanaugh/JD3AyfW6tly 9KfUZjJxNwJ/story.html.

4. It's worth noting that male privilege—like privilege of other forms, e.g., white privilege—has many dimensions aside from entitlement. And while one can and should of course aim as a privileged person (like me, for the record, in every respect bar gender) not to act in objectionably entitled ways, there is often a limit to how much one can feasibly renounce (as opposed to recognizing and mitigating) one's privilege. For a classic treatment of (white) privilege, see Peggy McIntosh, "White Privilege: Unpacking the Invisible Knapsack," *Peace and Freedom Magazine* (1989): 10–12. For a state-of-the-art treatment, see Rachel McKinnon and Adam Sennet's "Survey Article: On the Nature of the Political Concept of Privilege," *Journal of Political Philosophy* 25, no. 4 (2017): 487–507.

As will emerge throughout this book, white women's privilege and sense of entitlement is an important topic in its own right. However, my focus here for the most part is male privilege, which constitutes a set of phenomena that cluster together in ways that are salutary to study together, systematically and intersectionally.

5. Sam Brodey, "'The Most Telling Moment': Sen. Amy Klobuchar in National Spotlight After Brett Kavanaugh Hearings," *Minnesota*

Post, September 28, 2018, https://www.minnpost.com/national /2018/09/the-most-telling-moment-sen-amy-klobuchar-in -national-spotlight-after-brett-kavanaugh-hearings/.

6. Billy Perrigo, "Sen. Lindsey Graham Says Christine Blasey Ford 'Has Got a Problem' as He Continues Attack on Democrats," *Time,* September 28, 2018, https://time.com/5409636/lindsey -graham-christine-blasey-ford-problem/.

7. Compare Donald Trump's himpathetic remarks, as canvassed in my article "Brett Kavanaugh and America's 'Himpathy' Reckoning," *The New York Times,* September 26, 2018, https://www .nytimes.com/2018/09/26/opinion/brett-kavanaugh-hearing -himpathy.html.

8. See the (variously inflected) naysaying from notes 2 and 3 in this chapter, as well as the letter from sixty-five women who knew Kavanaugh in high school, defending him largely on the basis of their never having known him to commit sexual assault toward them, personally. But, as is often the case, absence of (direct, firsthand) evidence is not decisive evidence of absence here. In other words, the fact that these women could testify to not having been assaulted by Brett Kavanaugh themselves hardly casts doubt on Ford's testimony. See Tara Golshan, "65 Women Who Knew Brett Kavanaugh in High School Defend His Character," Vox, September 14, 2018, https://www.vox.com/2018/9/14 /17860488/brett-kavanaugh-sexual-assault-georgetown-prep -defense.

9. Obviously the law enforcement metaphor is meant to be exactly that: metaphorical. I'm certainly not arguing for a restriction of misogyny to *formal* policing and enforcement mechanisms, as will become clear shortly.

10. According to recent statistics, girls comprise 82 percent of all juvenile rape victims, and women comprise 90 percent of all adult rape victims. Moreover, girls and women aged sixteen to nineteen are four times more likely to be the victims of rape, attempted rape, or sexual assault than are members of the general population. See RAINN, "Victims of Sexual Violence: Statistics," https:// www.rainn.org/statistics/victims-sexual-violence.

11. A small sample of these messages: "No one believes you. Karma is a bitch and it will be visiting you very very soon"; "From what I've heard, you have six months to live, you disgusting slime." Erin Durkin, "Christine Blasey Ford's Life 'Turned Upside Down'

After Accusing Kavanaugh," *The Guardian,* September 19, 2018, https://www.theguardian.com/us-news/2018/sep/19/christine -blasey-ford-brett-kavanaugh-sexual-assault-accuser-threats.

12. I originally used this metaphor in an interview for *Guernica* with Regan Penaluna. "Kate Manne: The Shock Collar That Is Misogyny," February 7, 2018, https://www.guernicamag.com /kate-manne-why-misogyny-isnt-really-about-hating-women/.

13. Kavanaugh said, in his opening remarks at the hearings: "A majority of my 48 law clerks over the last 12 years have been women. In a letter to this committee, my women law clerks said I was one of the strongest advocates in the federal judiciary for women lawyers, and they wrote that the legal profession is fairer and more equal because of me. In my time on the bench, no federal judge, not a single one in the country has sent more women law clerks to clerk on the Supreme Court than I have." "Brett Kavanaugh's Opening Statement: Full Transcript," *The New York Times,* September 26, 2018, https://www.nytimes.com/2018 /09/26/us/politics/read-brett-kavanaughs-complete-opening -statement.html.

14. In chapter 6, for example, I argue that the anti-abortion move-ment in the United States is deeply misogynistic, without that necessarily impugning all of the individuals who subscribe to its tenets as being so.

15. Note that this isn't to deny, by any means, the possibility or concrete reality of feminist social progress in the United States and other contexts. It's to say that historically patriarchal social norms still linger and have an influence on our behavior, often unwit-tingly, even when counteracted by egalitarian social mores.

16. As someone who practices cultural analysis, I generally focus on social contexts where I can count myself as an insider—leaving questions about how other cultural contexts may be similar or different for other, more suitably positioned readers to consider. This is not to say that this is the only way to avoid moral imperial-ism, however. See Serene Khader's *Decolonizing Universalism: A Transnational Feminist Ethic* (New York: Oxford University Press, 2018) for a state-of-the-art discussion of these issues.

17. For two classic and groundbreaking pieces on intersectionality by Crenshaw, see her "Mapping the Margins: Intersectionality, Identity Politics, and Violence Against Women of Color," *Stanford*

Law Review 43, no. 6 (1991): 1241–99, and her "Beyond Race and Misogyny: Black Feminism and 2 Live Crew," in *Words That Wound,* edited by Mari J. Matsuda, Charles Lawrence III, Richard Delgado, and Kimberlé Williams Crenshaw (Boulder: Westview Press, 1993), pp. 111–132.

18. Hopefully, needless to say, these questions and the others I try to answer throughout these pages don't constitute a comprehensive list of topics when it comes to male privilege and entitlement, but merely some of the central ones, and the ones that I found myself in a reasonably good position to comment on.

19. Ewan Palmer, "Christine Blasey Ford Can't Return Home for 'Quite Some Time' Due to Continuous Death Threats: Lawyer," *Newsweek,* October 8, 2018, https://www.newsweek.com /christine-blasey-ford-cant-return-home-continuous-death -threats-1157262.

20. Chris Riotta, "Trump Accused of 26 New Cases of 'Unwanted Sexual Contact,'" *Independent,* October 9, 2019, https://www .independent.co.uk/news/world/americas/trump-sexual-assault -allegations-harassment-groping-women-karen-johnson-book -a9149021.html.

TWO Involuntary—On the Entitlement to Admiration

1. "Timeline of Murder Spree in Isla Vista," CBS News, May 26, 2014, http://www.cbsnews.com/news/timeline-of-murder -spree-in-isla-vista/.

2. Fortunately, the video was quickly removed from YouTube. But a transcript of it can be found here: http://www.democratic underground.com/10024994525 (last accessed October 5, 2019). Rodger had also previously uploaded other, similar videos to YouTube, resulting in his mother alerting the police to his activities. Officers questioned Rodger outside his apartment, but they did not take the matter further.

3. I discuss the case of Elliot Rodger at length in my book *Down Girl: The Logic of Misogyny* (New York: Oxford University Press, 2018), chapters 1–2. For some remarks on Rodger's mental health history—which is notable largely for his *lack* of any concrete diagnoses, despite having received extensive therapy, thanks to his conscientious parents—see my replies to critics, *The APA Newsletter in Feminism and Philosophy* 8, no. 2 (2019): 28–29.

4. I draw here on the following piece by Steve Hendrix, who also credits Julie Tate for her contributions to the story: "He Always Hated Women. Then He Decided to Kill Them," *The Washington Post*, June 7, 2019, https://www.washingtonpost.com/graphics/2019/local/yoga-shooting-incel-attack-fueled-by-male-supremacy/.

5. Nikolas Cruz, the nineteen-year-old who in 2018 killed seventeen people at Marjory Stoneman Douglas High School in Parkland, Florida, had also made comments lauding Rodger on YouTube.

6. For an excellent history of incel culture, from these early and (by all reports) ostensibly benign beginnings to the present-day misogynistic horror show, see Zack Beauchamp's article "Our Incel Problem: How a Support Group for the Dateless Became One of the Internet's Most Dangerous Subcultures," Vox, April 23, 2019, https://www.vox.com/the-highlight/2019/4/16/18287446/incel-definition-reddit.

7. Alana (who prefers not to give her surname) has recently tried to come up with more productive alternatives, after having seen the incel community devolve and degenerate over the past few decades. Her new project, Love Not Anger, attempts to revive her website's original spirit: supporting those who consider themselves unlucky in love, without being resentful—much as she once did. Alana told *Vox* writer Zack Beauchamp:

   > "The aim is to help people be less lonely, by researching why some people—of all genders and orientations—have difficulty with dating and creating effective support services. The project doesn't have ways to reduce violence directly. A lonely person who is not too far gone into their own hatred might benefit from whatever hope Love Not Anger can offer."

   Ibid.

   This reminder that women as much as men, and queer people as well as straight, can be lonely and feel loveless or be sexually dissatisfied will presumably do little to persuade the committed incel. But it may be a helpful reality check for those who might otherwise eventually be radicalized. There is a world of difference between simply wanting something badly and wrongly feeling entitled to (and hence unfairly deprived of) it.

8. As Zack Beauchamp writes:

[Incels] are overwhelmingly young men and boys with a history of isolation and rejection; they turn to the internet to make sense of their pain. . . .

While there is no rigorous scientific study on incel demographics—the community is deeply hostile to outsiders, particularly researchers and journalists—their forums have conducted informal surveys on the demographics of their users. . . .

An informal poll of 1,267 Braincels [a once-popular incel forum on Reddit that has subsequently been quarantined] users found that about 90 percent of forum participants were under the age of 30. The users are almost all men—women are banned on sight, but a handful do sneak in—and roughly 80 percent live in Europe or North America.

Ibid.

9. Alice Hines, "How Many Bones Would You Break to Get Laid? 'Incels' Are Going Under the Knife to Reshape Their Faces, and Their Dating Prospects," *The Cut,* May 28, 2019, https://www.thecut.com/2019/05/incel-plastic-surgery.html.

10. See, e.g., Ross Douthat, who opined:

The sexual revolution created new winners and losers, new hierarchies to replace the old ones, privileging the beautiful and rich and socially adept in new ways and relegating others to new forms of loneliness and frustration. Our widespread isolation and unhappiness and sterility might be dealt with by reviving or adapting older ideas about the virtues of monogamy and chastity and permanence and the special respect owed to the celibate.

From "The Redistribution of Sex," *The New York Times,* May 2, 2018, https://www.nytimes.com/2018/05/02/opinion/incels-sex-robots-redistribution.html.

Similarly, Jordan Peterson was quoted by reporter Nellie Bowles in *The New York Times* opining that the solution to the problem of incels is "enforced monogamy." Bowles writes:

Violent attacks are what happens when men do not have partners, Mr. Peterson says, and society needs to work to make sure those men are married.

"He was angry at God because women were rejecting him," Mr. Peterson says of the Toronto killer [Alek Minassian]. "The cure for that is enforced monogamy. That's actually why monogamy emerges."

Mr. Peterson does not pause when he says this. Enforced monogamy is, to him, simply a rational solution. Otherwise women will all only go for the most high-status men, he explains, and that couldn't make either gender happy in the end.

"Half the men fail. And no one cares about the men who fail," Peterson added, himpathetically.

Nellie Bowles, "Jordan Peterson, Custodian of the Patriarchy," *The New York Times,* May 18, 2018, https://www.nytimes.com /2018/05/18/style/jordan-peterson-12-rules-for-life.html.

11. Other, similar incidents involving Beierle are detailed by Hendrix (in collaboration with Tate), in "He Always Hated Women," *The Washington Post.*

There are also serious questions about the prevalence of sexual assault within the incel community, as Zack Beauchamp has detailed in his investigative reporting. He writes:

The most chilling incel stories are about outright sexual assault. . . .

One user claims to serially assault women on public transit. "I do it all the time, rub my dick on their back/ass until I cum," he writes. A second says that he injected his semen into chocolate bars at his office to "punish" a woman who he thought was flirting with him but actually had a boyfriend. A third claims to have "groped so many women," estimating his total at between 50 and 70—and claimed he wanted to escalate to violent rape. . . .

There's no way to know how true any of this is. But even assuming a fraction of it is, what you've got is a community where men who target women are celebrated and incentivized to escalate.

From "Our Incel Problem," Vox.

12. I owe the phrase "aggrieved entitlement" to the sociologist Michael Kimmel; see his *Angry White Men: American Masculinity at*

the End of an Era (New York: National Books, 2013), pp. 18–25 and chapter 1.

13. As Zack Beauchamp notes:

> Despite drawing users largely from majority-white countries, Braincels [a subsequently quarantined forum for incels on Reddit] has an ethnically diverse set of contributors; 55 percent of the site's user base is white, with significant percentages of posters who self-identify as East Asian, South Asian, Black, and Latino. A poll that ran on incels.co, the largest incel site outside of Reddit, came out with similar numbers on their user base's age, race, and geographic distribution.
>
> From "Our Incel Problem," Vox.

14. This quote comes from Rodger's "My Twisted World," his "manifesto" that was released publicly following the incident. A copy of it is available here: http://s3.documentcloud.org /documents/1173619/rodger-manifesto.pdf (last accessed October 5, 2019).

15. "Timeline of Murder Spree in Isla Vista," CBS News, http:// www.cbsnews.com/news/timeline-of-murder-spree-in-isla-vista/.

16. Rodger went on:

> Females truly have something mentally wrong with them. Their minds are flawed, and at this point in my life I was beginning to see it. The more I explored my college town of Isla Vista, the more ridiculousness I witnessed. All of the hot, beautiful girls walked around with obnoxious, tough jock-type men who partied all the time and acted crazy. They should be going for intelligent gentlemen such as myself. Women are sexually attracted to the wrong type of man. This is a major flaw in the very foundation of humanity. It is completely and utterly *wrong,* in every sense of the word. As these truths fully dawned on me, I became deeply disturbed by them. Deeply disturbed, offended, and traumatized.
>
> See my subsequent remarks in this chapter on Rodger's frequent complaints of having been traumatized, rather than merely disappointed, by women.

17. All of Beierle's videos, including this one and another entitled *The Plight of the Adolescent Male*—addressed to teenage incels—are

available here: https://www.youtube.com/watch?v=8Ca00hc
OND8 (last accessed October 5, 2019). The quoted passage (my
own transcription) is taken from approximately one and a half to
two minutes into this compilation.

18. The aforementioned incel who committed his murders at an
Oregon community college, Chris Harper-Mercer, also wrote a
similar racist screed in which he bemoaned his lack of a girlfriend
and his status as a virgin.

19. Closely echoing Rodger's rhetoric, Alek Minassian commented in
a police interrogation after his attacks (footage of which was
released on September 26, 2019): "Sometimes I am a bit upset
[with women] that they choose to date obnoxious men instead of
a gentleman." He identified a pivotal episode of being rejected at a
Halloween party in 2013:

> I walked in and attempted to socialize with some girls,
> however they all laughed at me and held the arms of the big
> guys instead. . . . I felt very angry . . . because I considered
> myself a supreme gentleman, I was angry that they would give
> their love and affection to obnoxious brutes.

Minassian also spoke with great admiration of Elliot Rodger
and claimed to have met him online—calling him the "founding
forefather" who started "the movement of angry incels such as
myself" to "overthrow the Chads which would force the Staceys
to reproduce with the incels." As for the "involuntary" in "incel,"
he said that incels like him were "thrown into true forced loneliness, and unable to lose [our] virginity." The video from which I
took these remarks is available here: https://www.youtube.com
/watch?v=S_zSdw1nShk.

20. According to a source who had known Beierle at the time, the
characters in the manuscript were Beierle's real classmates, with
their names slightly altered. "This is basically his school journal,"
said the man, who spoke to *The Washington Post*'s reporters on
condition of anonymity. See Hendrix (in collaboration with Tate),
"He Always Hated Women," *The Washington Post*.

21. For a discussion of the complex relationship between objectification and misogyny, according to my definition of the latter, see my
book *Down Girl,* "Misogyny and Sexual Objectification," in
chapter 3.

22. For further discussion of this point, see ibid., chapter 5.

23. Compare these remarks by an incel forum user on why he began to stalk women:

> I once approached a teenage girl (around 14 years old) by asking her for directions at first. Then I proceeded to ask for her name. She became afraid and started walking away. I followed her, and then she went from walking briskly to running. Her gait was peculiar, because she ran like a new-born fawn, turning around every so often, trying to see if I am still following. (Now, I want to make clear that I absolutely abhor rape and did not have any intention in that direction, not molestation not any of that.)
>
> She had no reason to be frightened. I wasn't going to do anything. But the feeling when you follow a girl and she notices you, and she tries to lose you or picks up the pace. That is kind of a good feeling. You become important to her. You are no longer some random insignificant face in the crowd.
>
> I know it is kind of low-level behavior. But I do enjoy doing that. I go to another city, look for a girl walking by herself and start following her. After a while they notice you. . . . I recommend you lonely incels try it some time.

"Incel Creeper: It's Fun to Follow 14-Year-Old Girls Down the Street and Scare Them to Death," *We Hunted the Mammoth,* April 20, 2018, http://www.wehuntedthemammoth.com/2018 /04/30/incel-creeper-its-fun-to-follow-14-year-old-girls-down -the-street-and-scare-them-to-death/.

24. Pace Amia Srinivasan in her essay "Does Anyone Have the Right to Sex?" *London Review of Books,* March 22, 2018, https://www .lrb.co.uk/v40/n06/amia-srinivasan/does-anyone-have-the-right -to-sex.

25. As Zack Beauchamp remarks of two incels he interviewed, Abe and John:

> It's hard not to feel for people like Abe or John. All of us have, at one point, experienced our share of rejection or loneliness. What makes the incel world scary is that it takes these universal experiences and transmutes the pain they cause into unbridled, misogynistic rage.

From "Our Incel Problem," Vox.

26. It may also be worth noting that not only does the act of ministering to the pain do a potentially grave disservice to others—by effectively validating the incel's sense that the world, in general, and women, in particular, owe him certain favors—but it may not even help the incel, at least in the long term. It may only *increase* his pain and feed a vicious cycle, since his pain has its ultimate source in wrongheaded views about the degree to which he *deserves* to be attended to, pacified, soothed, nurtured, babied.

27. Patrick Lohmann, "Bianca Devins: Lies, Scams, Misogyny Explode Online Before Facts; Grieving Family Debunks Rumors," *Syracuse,* July 15, 2019, https://www.syracuse.com/crime /2019/07/bianca-devins-lies-scams-misogyny-explode-online -before-facts-emerge-grieving-family-debunks-rumors.html.

28. Alia E. Dastagir, "Bianca Devins' Murder Is 'Not an Instagram Story,' Domestic Violence Expert Says," *USA Today,* July 17, 2019, https://www.usatoday.com/story/news/nation/2019/07/17 /bianca-devins-death-posted-instagram-thats-not-story /1748601001/.

29. In New York, charges of first-degree murder are reserved for premeditated killings that meet certain special conditions—e.g., killing a law enforcement officer, firefighter, judge, or crime witness; mass killings; killing someone while committing a felony; and killing someone in a particularly heinous way, such as by torturing them.

30. Dastagir, "Bianca Devins' Murder Is 'Not An Instagram Story,'" *USA Today.*

31. Ibid.

32. Ibid.

33. See Mary Emily O'Hara, "Domestic Violence: Nearly Three U.S. Women Killed Every Day by Intimate Partners," NBC News, April 11, 2017, https://www.nbcnews.com/news/us-news /domestic-violence-nearly-three-u-s-women-killed-every-day -n745166, for one representative recent piece on this well-established statistic.

34. See *Down Girl,* Introduction and chapter 4—especially the section on the notion of entitled shame and the phenomenon of family annihilators. These are men who murder not only their female intimate partner or ex-partner but also their children (before killing themselves, typically). They strike once per week in the

United States, on average. Yet family annihilators have attracted far less attention than incels on the Internet.

35. Dastagir, "Bianca Devins' Murder Is 'Not An Instagram Story,'" *USA Today*.

THREE Unexceptional—On the Entitlement to Sex

1. The following account owes heavily to the collection of first-person testimony and subsequent investigative reporting by Bernice Yeung of ProPublica, Mark Greenblatt of Newsy, and Mark Fahey of Newsy, in collaboration with the *Reveal* podcast about this case: "Case Cleared: Part 2," *Reveal,* November 17, 2018, https://www.revealnews.org/episodes/case-cleared-part-2/.

2. However, it's worth noting that in Minnesota, rape committed by someone with whom the victim is in "an ongoing voluntary relationship" was still prosecuted under a different code at the time. This led to some successful deployments of the "voluntary relationship defense," which entailed a de facto marital rape exception—including in a case of a woman raped by her ex-husband, while their divorce was still pending. He made a video of the rape, filmed while their four-year-old child slept nearby. He was sentenced to just forty-five days in jail, for "invasion of privacy." Fortunately, this statute was repealed in May 2019, following a public outcry. See Amir Vera, "Marital Rape Is No Longer Legal in Minnesota with New Law," CNN, May 3, 2019, https://www.cnn.com/2019/05/03/us/minnesota-marital-rape -repeal/index.html.

3. For another case that highlights the intersection of disability, sexual violence, and—in this case—racism, consider the Native woman who was raped and subsequently became pregnant and gave birth, all while being in a comatose state in a nursing facility. Amanda Sakuma, "A Woman in a Vegetative State Suddenly Gave Birth. Her Alleged Assault Is a #MeToo Wake-Up Call," Vox, January 7, 2019, https://www.vox.com/2019/1/7/18171012 /arizona-woman-birth-coma-sexual-assault-metoo.

4. There are general psychological mechanisms that help explain this tendency. Research has shown that when someone is made sympathetic to one party, A, by being told a hard-luck story about A, that person will tend to become aggressive and hostile to A's rival, B, during a simple competitive game in which A and B are

engaged. Psychologists established this by showing that participants gave B more hot sauce to ingest (a standard clinical measure
of aggression) when A had been described in a sympathetic light,
as compared with the control condition, where no such backstory
was given. Note that this aggression was shown toward B despite
the facts that B had done nothing objectionable to A, that B
might have had an equally or *more* sympathetic backstory, and that
punishing B would not help A in the slightest. See Paul Bloom,
"The Dark Side of Empathy," *The Atlantic,* September 25, 2015,
https://www.theatlantic.com/science/archive/2015/09/the
-violence-of-empathy/407155/ for discussion; for the original
study, see Anneke E. K. Buffone and Michael J. Poulin, "Empathy,
Target Distress, and Neurohormone Genes Interact to Predict
Aggression for Others—Even Without Provocation," *Personality
and Social Psychology Bulletin* 40, no. 11 (2014): 1406–22.

5. The crime took place in January 2015, with the trial in March
2016. Miller was known for years only as Emily Doe, via her
moving victim-impact statement. Shortly before this book went
into production, she released an extraordinary memoir, *Know My
Name,* recounting her experience of the assault and its aftermath.
A chilling coincidence emerges in it: Miller was a student at the
University of California, Santa Barbara, when Elliot Rodger
struck, and she was deeply affected by his violence. She writes:

> Six classmates had been stolen from us, Elliot the seventh. I
> do not include the victims' names here, for names are sacred,
> and I do not want them identified solely by what he did to
> them.

> From *Know My Name* (New York: Viking, 2019), p. 89. This
crystallizes my own inchoate thinking on these matters, and is
why I've chosen to continue my practice in this book of not
listing their names in connection with Rodger's rampage.

6. I draw here on my book *Down Girl: The Logic of Misogyny* (New
York: Oxford University Press, 2018), from the section "Himpathy," in chapter 6. Another crucial factor to subsequently emerge,
via Miller's memoir: she is Chinese American, making Turner's
whiteness (and, hence, comparative privilege) plausibly all the
more relevant to the outcome.

7. See Malcolm Gladwell's analysis of this case, in his most recent
book, where he writes:

A young woman and a young man meet at a party, then proceed to tragically misunderstand each other's intentions— and they're drunk. . . . The entire case turned on the degree of Emily Doe's drunkenness. . . .

The challenge in these kinds of cases is reconstructing the encounter. Did both parties consent? Did one party object, and the other party ignore that objection? Or misunderstand it? . . .

The outcome of *People v. Brock Turner* brought a measure of justice to Emily Doe. But so long as we refuse to acknowledge what alcohol does to the interaction between strangers, that evening at Kappa Alpha will be repeated again. And again.

From *Talking to Strangers* (New York: Little, Brown, 2019), chapter 8.

But as Chanel Miller aptly and succinctly put it in a *60 Minutes* interview: "Rape is not a punishment for getting drunk." Bill Whitaker, "*Know My Name:* Author and Sexual Assault Survivor Chanel Miller's Full *60 Minutes* Interview," CBS News, September 22, 2019, https://www.cbsnews.com/news/chanel-miller-full-60 -minutes-interview-know-my-name-author-brock-turner-sexual -assault-survivor-2019-09-22/.

8. Miller, *Know My Name,* p. 285.
9. Gabriella Paiella, "Report: Brock Turner Creeped Out Members of the Stanford Women's Swim Team," *The Cut,* June 16, 2016, https://www.thecut.com/2016/06/report-brock-turner-creeped -women-out.html.
10. Miller, *Know My Name,* p. 284.
11. Sam Levin, "Stanford Sexual Assault: Read the Full Text of the Judge's Controversial Decision," *The Guardian,* June 14, 2016, https://www.theguardian.com/us-news/2016/jun/14/stanford -sexual-assault-read-sentence-judge-aaron-persky.
12. ABC did eventually change the headline, however. See Donte Gibson, "Maryland Teen Demanded That ABC News Change Its Maryland School Shooter Headline," A Plus, March 26, 2018, https://articles.aplus.com/a/great-mills-high-school-shooting -lovesick-teen-headline.
13. Olly Hennessy-Fiske, Matt Pearce, and Jenny Jarvie, "Must Reads: Texas School Shooter Killed Girl Who Turned Down His

Advances and Embarrassed Him in Class, Her Mother Says," *The Los Angeles Times*, May 19, 2018, https://www.latimes.com /nation/la-na-texas-shooter-20180519-story.html.

14. Ibid.

15. Ibid.

16. After outraged reactions on social media, the headline was subsequently amended to read: "Wife Dies Hours After Her Children Were Killed in Car Inferno Lit by League Player Father," *Fox Sports Australia,* February 19, 2020, https://www.foxsports .com.au/nrl/nrl-premiership/teams/warriors/exnrl-star-rowan -baxter-dies-alongside-three-kids-in-brisbane-car-fire-tragedy /news-story/e1b715cb015ff853a4c8ccf115637e30.

17. Kelsey Wilkie, "From Trips to the Beach to Loving Bedtime Stories: How an Ex-Footy Star Portrayed Himself as a Loving Dad Who Would Do Anything for his Three Kids—Before Killing Them All in Car Fire Horror," *Daily Mail,* February 18, 2020, https://www.dailymail.co.uk/news/article-8018989/Rowan -Baxter-died-three-children-car-set-alight-Brisbane.html.

18. https://twitter.com/thebettinaarndt/status/1230623373232787456 ?lang=en (accessed February 29, 2020).

19. Arndt's Twitter handle reads: "Once it was sex that was taboo, now it's men's issues. Help Bettina achieve gender equity through advocacy for men. #MenToo," https://twitter.com/thebettinaarndt (accessed February 29, 2020). Well, *some* men; Arndt is on the record as having defended a scoutmaster who allegedly abused boys as a "good bloke," adding that "such minor abuse rarely has lasting consequences." See Samantha Maiden, "Independent Board to Consider Rescinding Bettina Arndt's Order of Australia Honour," *The New Daily,* February 24, 2020, https://thenewdaily .com.au/news/national/2020/02/24/bettina-arndt-david-hurley/. This piece also details the subsequent efforts to have Arndt's honor rescinded.

20. On the phenomenon of family annihilators, see the penultimate note from the previous chapter.

21. Note that the latter does not follow from the former: in Minnesota, people can be prosecuted without ever being arrested.

22. A standard definition of "probable cause" is "a reasonable amount of suspicion, supported by circumstances sufficiently strong to justify a prudent and cautious person's belief that certain facts are probably true"; whereas "proof beyond a reasonable doubt" means

that the proposition presented by the prosecution must be proven to the extent that there could be no reasonable doubt in the mind of a reasonable person about its veracity. See https://www .lawfirms.com/resources/criminal-defense/defendants-rights /defining-probable-cause.htm.

23. Itasca County (where Rae Florek lived) has charged more than forty suspects with rape over the past five years. These cases nearly all involved child victims. In the very few exceptions—i.e., rape cases involving adult victims—the suspect used force or explicit coercion. And prosecutors rejected around 60 percent of the 170 sex crime cases brought to them by law enforcement.

24. "Case Cleared: Part 1," *Reveal,* November 10, 2018, https://www .revealnews.org/episodes/case-cleared-part-1/. See also Mark Fahey, "How We Analyzed Rape Clearance Rates," ProPublica, November 15, 2018, https://www.propublica.org/article/how -we-analyzed-rape-clearance-rates.

25. More precisely:

> In the FBI's Uniform Crime Reporting (UCR) Program, law enforcement agencies can clear, or "close," offenses in one of two ways: by arrest or by exceptional means. . . .
>
> CLEARED BY EXCEPTIONAL MEANS
> In certain situations, elements beyond law enforcement's control prevent the agency from arresting and formally charging the offender. When this occurs, the agency can clear the offense *exceptionally.* Law enforcement agencies must meet the following four conditions in order to clear an offense by exceptional means. The agency must have:
>
> • Identified the offender.
> • Gathered enough evidence to support an arrest, make a charge, and turn over the offender to the court for prosecution.
> • Identified the offender's exact location so that the suspect could be taken into custody immediately.
> • Encountered a circumstance outside the control of law enforcement that prohibits the agency from arresting, charging, and prosecuting the offender.
>
> Examples of exceptional clearances include, but are not limited to, the death of the offender (e.g., suicide or justifiably

killed by police or citizen); the victim's refusal to cooperate with the prosecution after the offender has been identified; or the denial of extradition because the offender committed a crime in another jurisdiction and is being prosecuted for that offense. In the UCR Program, the recovery of property alone does not clear an offense.

See: FBI, "2107: Crime in the United States," https://ucr.fbi .gov/crime-in-the-u.s/2017/crime-in-the-u.s.-2017/topic-pages /clearances.

26. Note that even in rape cases where the victim initially comes forward, but later ceases to cooperate with the investigation, this is not—or ought not to be—a decisive barrier to the police pursuing the case further, and eventual prosecution. As Tom McDevitt told reporters, they can, for example, search the suspect's computer and phone, as well as interview the suspect (since confessions under these circumstances are not uncommon). They can also, of course, try harder to win the trust and cooperation of the victim—whose participation in the prosecution is, in any case, not essential. Compare the practice of building so-called evidence-based cases (which do not rely on the victim's testimony in court) against the perpetrators of crimes where victims are reliably reluctant to press charges—e.g., nonfatal manual strangulation, which I discuss in the Introduction of *Down Girl*.

27. For two representative studies that bear out this estimate, see: Marc Riedel and John G. Boulahanis, "Homicides Exceptionally Cleared and Cleared by Arrest: An Exploratory Study of Police/ Prosecutor Outcomes," *Homicide Studies* 11, no. 2 (2007): 151–64, and John P. Jarvis and Wendy C. Regoeczi, "Homicides Clearances: An Analysis of Arrest Versus Exceptional Outcomes," *Homicide Studies* 13, no. 2 (2009): 174–88.

After this, data collected by *The Washington Post* also showed around a 10 percent exceptional clearance rate, on average, for homicide cases in fifty-five major cities between 2007 and 2017. See Dan Bier, "Why Are Unsolved Murders on the Rise?" Freethink, October 18, 2018, https://www.freethink.com/articles /why-don-t-we-solve-murder-anymore for a summary.

28. It's worth noting that the police said that in this case they failed to obtain DNA evidence from the victim's rape kit. However, given

that the man accused by the victim had been identified by them and had admitted to having sex with her that night (which he said was consensual), this is far from a decisive barrier to eventual prosecution—especially given that the initial exam provided evidence that the encounter had been violent. See "Case Cleared: Part 1," Reveal.

29. Nancy Kaffer, "Kaffer: 8 Years into Tests of Abandoned Rape Kits, Worthy Works for Justice," *Detroit Free Press,* December 17, 2017, https://www.freep.com/story/opinion/columnists/nancy -kaffer/2017/12/17/rape-kit-detroit/953083001/.

30. Ibid.

31. Consider, too, the phenomenon of police officers perpetrating sexual assault—and, often, getting away with it. See Jonathan Blanks, "The Police Who Prey on Victims," *Democracy Journal,* November 1, 2017, https://democracyjournal.org/arguments /the-police-who-prey-on-victims/; and see, in chapter 6 of *Down Girl,* "Misogynoir in Action: The Daniel Holtzclaw Case," for further relevant discussion.

32. Eliza Relman, "The 24 Women Who Have Accused Trump of Sexual Misconduct," Business Insider, June 21, 2019, https:// www.businessinsider.com/women-accused-trump-sexual -misconduct-list-2017-12.

33. Up until this point, Epstein had served just thirteen months in a private wing of a Palm Beach county jail for these crimes. He was granted work release to go to an office described as comfortable for some twelve hours a day, six days a week. This despite the fact that work release is not permitted for sex offenders in this jurisdiction. These exceptions were made for Epstein due to a plea deal he made in 2008 with Alexander Acosta, then Miami U.S. Attorney and now Trump's labor secretary. The non-prosecution agreement also granted immunity to "any potential co-conspirators" and even concealed the plea deal from thirty of the victims—many of whom did not know, until recently, about Epstein's shockingly lenient sentence. Thanks to the particular victims selected in the plea deal arranged by Acosta—the youngest of whom was sixteen at the time of the alleged sexual abuse, whereas many victims were significantly younger—Epstein was even able to avoid having to register as a sex offender in any of the states in which he had a residence, Florida included.

Were it not for the trenchant efforts of one journalist, Julie K. Brown, Epstein would likely have continued to get away with his crimes having faced only these minimal consequences. As it was, he was arrested on sex trafficking charges in July 2019, before committing suicide in jail in August. See Tiffany Hsu, "The Jeffrey Epstein Case Was Cold, Until a *Miami Herald* Reporter Got Accusers to Talk," *The New York Times,* July 9, 2019, https:// www.nytimes.com/2019/07/09/business/media/miami-herald -epstein.html.

34. Jennifer Peltz, "Over 1,000 Arrests Nationwide After Authorities Test Backlogged Rape Kits," *HuffPost,* March 13, 2019, https:// www.huffpost.com/entry/new-york-feds-join-to-get-100k-rape -kits-tested-around-us_n_5c88f54fe4b0fbd7661f8840?ncid =engmodushpmg00000006.

35. I am in fact sympathetic, without being committed, to prison abolitionism. But this is another issue, and one I won't weigh in on here.

36. Andrew Van Dam, "Less Than 1% of Rapes Lead to Felony Convictions. At Least 89% of Victims Face Emotional and Physical Consequences," *The Washington Post,* October 6, 2018, https://www.washingtonpost.com/business/2018/10/06/less-than -percent-rapes-lead-felony-convictions-least-percent-victims -face-emotional-physical-consequences/. For a compelling first-hand account of rape and its aftermath, see the philosopher Susan J. Brison's book, *Aftermath: Violence and the Remaking of a Self* (Princeton: Princeton University Press, 2002).

37. See RAINN, "The Criminal Justice System: Statistics," https:// www.rainn.org/statistics/criminal-justice-system.

38. In this section, I draw on a group blog post for The Daily Nous I contributed to, which was convened by Justin Weinberg: "Philosophers on the Art of Morally Troubling Artists," November 21, 2017, http://dailynous.com/2017/11/21/philosophers-art -morally-troubling-artists/.

39. Roxane Gay, *Hunger: A Memoir of (My) Body* (New York: HarperCollins, 2017), p. 44.

40. Tara Culp-Ressler, "Five Important Takeaways from a New National Study on U.S. Teens and Sexual Violence," Think Progress, 2013, https://thinkprogress.org/five-important-take aways-from-a-new-national-study-on-u-s-teens-and-sexual -violence-9d454f54cea1/amp/.

41. See, e.g., David Finkelhor, Richard Ormrod, and Mark Chaffin, "Juveniles Who Commit Sex Offenses Against Minors," *OJJDP Bulletin,* December 2009, https://www.ncjrs.gov/pdffiles1/ojjdp /227763.pdf.

42. See the discussions of testimonial injustice, quieting, and smothering in chapters 5 and 8.

43. T. Christian Miller and Ken Armstrong, "An Unbelievable Story of Rape," ProPublica, December 16, 2015, https://www .propublica.org/article/false-rape-accusations-an-unbelievable -story; the case has subsequently been dramatized in the TV series *Unbelievable.*

44. Ibrahim's mother, Sandra Allen, commented:

> We found out that within days of her reporting the attack the police started investigating [her]. . . . The police trot out these words that victims will be believed but I don't think they ever bothered investigating what Layla was saying from the beginning. I will fight for her innocence to my dying day. What happened to her was beyond horrific, she suffered that night, she suffered in prison and she is still suffering.

Ibrahim's lawyer, Nigel Richardson, added:

> These cases seem to be pursued with a particular vehemence by the police and CPS [Crown Prosecution Service]. It's as though lying to the police, as they would see it, demands a really heavy reaction. There comes a moment when the woman goes from being a victim in the eyes of the police to a suspect. She may not even know that has happened.

From Sandra Laville, "109 Women Prosecuted for False Rape Claims in Five Years, Say Campaigners," *The Guardian,* December 1, 2014, https://www.theguardian.com/law/2014/dec/01 /109-women-prosecuted-false-rape-allegations.

45. As Richard Ackland wrote in *The Guardian:*

> In every instance, the judge preferred the applicant's evidence. [Rush's witness] Armfield didn't see any of the inappropriate behaviour, nor did Buday; some of the allegations were not put to Winter; things Norvill said in evidence were not in her original prepared statement; and she sent Rush friendly

greetings and text messages even after he had allegedly behaved "inappropriately" towards her.

The judgment does not adequately explore why this may have been so. There was no explicit judicial recognition of the close friendship between Rush's main theatre witnesses, an aspect that should have been considered and carefully weighed.

It is also entirely possible that . . . even though Norvill had an unhappy time during the *King Lear* production she still wanted to keep a good relationship with a significant star like Rush. None of that was sufficiently explored in the judgment. . . .

Norvill gave evidence that . . . she had a conversation with Nevin in which she said Rush had harassed her. She told the court that Nevin's response was, "I didn't think Geoffrey was doing that anymore."

[The judge] did not accept that Norvill had taken her concerns to Nevin.

He rejected the accusation that Rush consciously stroked her right breast: "How could Mr. Rush maintain the focus and state of mind which he considered necessary to properly perform this difficult scene, and yet engage in such a base and crude action as intentionally stroking Ms. Norvill's breast?"

As for the "socially inappropriate thoughts" with the panting emoji this too went nowhere. While many might regard this as suggestive of an older man salivating at the thought of a younger woman, Justice Wigney arrived at an entirely different conclusion—it was a throwaway line, a joke, and it simply meant the actor was sorry for missing the opening night of a play in which Norvill was performing.

It was not believable that Rush was "putting it out there."

From Richard Ackland, "The Geoffrey Rush Trial Shows Defamation Can Make Victims Become Victims All Over Again," *The Guardian,* April 17, 2019, https://www.theguardian.com /commentisfree/2019/apr/18/the-geoffrey-rush-trial-shows -defamation-can-make-victims-become-victims-all-over-again.

46. Rush was initially awarded AUD$850,000 in damages from *The Daily Telegraph,* which published stories detailing Norvill's accusations. For details about the eventual, much larger defama-

tion payout, see Clarissa Sebag-Montefiore, "Geoffrey Rush Awarded $2 Million in Defamation Case, a Record for Australia," *The New York Times,* May 23, 2019, https://www.nytimes. com/2019/05/23/world/australia/geoffrey-rush-defamation.html.

47. Nicole Pasulka, "How 4 Gay Black Women Fought Back Against Sexual Harassment—and Landed in Jail," *Code Switch,* NPR, June 30, 2015, https://www.npr.org/sections/codeswitch/2015 /06/30/418634390/how-4-gay-black-women-fought-back -against-a-sexual-harasser-and-landed-in-jail.

48. As with many of the themes of this book, I strongly suspect the same holds, and worse, for non-binary people.

49. A far more accurate term is "nonconsensual pornography," since many of the perpetrators are not motivated by revenge—and, in any case, their motivations are not what primarily matters here. For a compelling treatment of this phenomenon, together with its gendered nature and legal ramifications, see Danielle Keats Citron, *Hate Crimes in Cyberspace* (Cambridge, Mass.: Harvard University Press, 2014).

FOUR Unwanted—On the Entitlement to Consent

1. Kristen Roupenian, "Cat Person," *The New Yorker,* December 4, 2017, https://www.newyorker.com/magazine/2017/12/11/cat -person.

2. Bari Weiss, "Aziz Ansari Is Guilty. Of Not Being a Mind Reader," *The New York Times,* January 15, 2018, https://www.nytimes.com /2018/01/15/opinion/aziz-ansari-babe-sexual-harassment.html.

3. Katie Way, "I Went on a Date with Aziz Ansari. It Turned into the Worst Night of My Life," Babe, January 13, 2018, https:// babe.net/2018/01/13/aziz-ansari-28355.

4. Compare the notorious scene from *It's Always Sunny in Philadel-phia* (Episode: "The Guys Buy a Boat") where a man opines to his friend that persuading a woman to have sex would be easier on a boat, because of the implication that if she refuses, harm may come to her—and her body could then be conveniently disposed of at sea. This man doesn't intend to harm women, personally— merely to benefit from "the implication."

5. Jennifer Van Evra, "Sarah Silverman's Response to a Twitter Troll Is a Master Class in Compassion," CBC, January 3, 2018, https:// www.cbc.ca/radio/q/blog/sarah-silverman-s-response-to-a-twitter -troll-is-a-master-class-in-compassion-1.4471337.

6. Caitlin Flanagan, "The Humiliation of Aziz Ansari," *The Atlantic,* January 14, 2018, https://www.theatlantic.com/entertainment /archive/2018/01/the-humiliation-of-aziz-ansari/550541/.

7. Not to mention hypocritical, given Ansari's having built much of his career on a reputation for wokeness vis-à-vis "modern romance": the phrase serves as the title of his 2015 book and is one of the main themes of *Master of None,* his popular TV show on Netflix.

8. Daniel Holloway, "Netflix Wants Aziz Ansari's *Master of None* to Return for Season 3, Originals Chief Says," *Variety,* July 29, 2018, https://variety.com/2018/tv/news/netflix-aziz-ansari-master-of -none-1202889434/.

9. Stanley Milgram, *Obedience to Authority: An Experimental View* (New York: Harper & Row, 1974).

10. Ibid., p. 6.

11. Matthew Hollander, "The Repertoire of Resistance: Non-Compliance with Directives in Milgram's 'Obedience' Experiments," *British Journal of Social Psychology* 54, no. 3 (2015): 425–44.

12. Milgram, *Obedience to Authority,* p. 9.

13. Ibid., p. 6.

14. Somewhat reduced (but still significant) rates of obedience were obtained by varying the original condition on this score—e.g., by having the experimenter operate out of a shady basement in Connecticut, with no ostensible affiliation with the famous university. Milgram implemented many other conditions, some of which significantly affected the results of the experiment—e.g., having an experimenter deliver his instructions by phone (which markedly reduced rates of obedience) and having two experimenters, who argued with one another (which massively reduced rates of obedience). Ibid., chapters 6 and 8. Another interesting condition would have been varying the experimenter's gender, by running the experiment with a female authority figure. But as far as I have been able to tell, this was never attempted.

15. Ibid., p. 21.

16. It's also possible that all the participants who were given the fourth prompt were on their way out of there already. However, the interpretation in the text also fits with other findings in social psychology—e.g., a study that showed that when asked for bus fare by a stranger at a bus stop, people gave twice the amount of money on average if they were explicitly told "But you are free to

agree or refuse" by the person asking. See Christopher Carpenter, "A Meta-Analysis of the Effectiveness of the 'But You Are Free' Compliance-Gaining Technique," *Communication Studies* 64, no. 1 (2013): 6–17.

17. In a more general discussion of results in social psychology that include, but are not exhausted by, the Milgram experiments, John Sabini and Maury Silver write:

> We suggest, then, that there is a single thread that runs through social psychology's discoveries of people acting in surprising and demoralizing ways: people's understandings of the world— . . . the moral world in the case of the obedience experiments . . . —are strongly influenced by what they take to be other people's perceptions of those worlds. We smugly assume that we stick to our guns when no one challenges us, but it turns out that it is harder than we think to do this when we must face (without allies) a confrontation with other people's apparent views.
>
> And, the theme continues, the emotional price people pay when they face a situation in which they must act by their own lights contrary to what they think are others' lights is embarrassment. People who must act in such circumstances are confused and inhibited by the anticipation of embarrassment, and that we argue is the lesson to be drawn from social psychological research. People are also, we suggest, unaware of how potent fear of embarrassment is as a motivation for behavior.

From John Sabini and Maury Silver, "Lack of Character? Situationism Critiqued," *Ethics* 115, no. 3 (2005): 559.

18. See "Harvey Weinstein: Full Transcript of the 'Horrifying' Exchange with Ambra Gutierrez," ABC News, October 10, 2017, https://www.abc.net.au/news/2017-10-11/harvey-weinstein-full -transcript-of-audio-with-ambra-gutierrez/9037268.

19. Ronan Farrow, "From Aggressive Overtures to Sexual Assault: Harvey Weinstein's Accusers Tell Their Stories," *The New Yorker,* October 10, 2017, https://www.newyorker.com/news/news-desk /from-aggressive-overtures-to-sexual-assault-harvey-weinsteins -accusers-tell-their-stories. Of course, my discussion of Weinstein in the context of this chapter, which focuses on the "soft" side of sexual coercion, in connection with a male sense of entitlement

not only to sex but also to consent, should not distract readers from the highly credible evidence of Weinstein's outright sexual assaults against multiple victims—in view of which he was convicted of rape and a criminal sex act in February 2020.

20. Anonymous, "We Need to Talk About Sexual Assault in Marriage," Vox, March 8, 2018, https://www.vox.com/first -person/2018/3/8/17087628/sexual-assault-marriage-metoo.

21. The author of the Vox piece cited in note 20, just above, mentions not only how difficult it was to speak about her experiences with her husband but how "nearly every woman with whom I have broached this subject has shared stories—her own, a friend's, or both—about suffering unwanted sex in marriage." And yet, as she rightly points out, such accounts are hard to come by (and even hers is understandably anonymous).

22. Salma Hayek, "Harvey Weinstein Is My Monster Too," *The New York Times,* December 12, 2017, https://www.nytimes.com /interactive/2017/12/13/opinion/contributors/salma-hayek -harvey-weinstein.html.

23. I draw here on my piece "Salma Hayek Was Destroyed by the Same Shame That Protected Harvey Weinstein," *Newsweek,* December 14, 2017, https://www.newsweek.com/salma-hayek -shame-harvey-weinstein-748377.

24. Although these are fictional cases, they establish what I need for present purposes—the *intelligibility* of the social-sexual dynamics in question, regardless of how often they are instantiated in reality. (As a matter of fact, I do suspect that many people will recognize their own experiences in these portraits; but, admittedly, this is speculative.)

25. I draw here on my piece "Good Girls: How Powerful Men Get Away with Sexual Predation," *HuffPost,* March 24, 2017, https:// www.huffpost.com/entry/good-girls-or-why-powerful-men-get -to-keep-on-behaving_b_58d5b420e4b0f633072b37c3.

26. J. M. Coetzee, *Disgrace* (New York: Penguin, 1999), p. 23.

27. Ibid.

28. Ibid., p. 28.

29. Ibid., p. 53.

FIVE Incompetent—On the Entitlement to Medical Care

1. Tressie McMillan Cottom, *Thick: And Other Essays* (New York: New Press, 2019), p. 82.

2. Ibid.
3. Ibid., p. 83.
4. Ibid.
5. Ibid., pp. 83–84.
6. Ibid., pp. 84–85.
7. Ibid., p. 85.
8. Centers for Disease Control and Prevention, Pregnancy Mortality Surveillance System, https://www.cdc.gov/reproductivehealth/maternalinfanthealth/pregnancy-mortality-surveillance-system.htm.
9. A recent analysis of births in New York City found that "Black college-educated mothers who gave birth in local hospitals were more likely to suffer severe complications of pregnancy or childbirth than white women who never graduated from high school"—noting that highest educational level attained is a fairly reliable proxy for income. See New York City Department of Health and Mental Hygiene, *Severe Maternal Morbidity in New York City, 2008–2012* (New York, 2016), https://www1.nyc.gov/assets/doh/downloads/pdf/data/maternal-morbidity-report-08-12.pdf.
10. See Linda Villarosa, "Why America's Black Mothers and Babies Are in a Life-or-Death Crisis," *The New York Times,* April 11, 2018, https://www.nytimes.com/2018/04/11/magazine/black-mothers-babies-death-maternal-mortality.html.
11. Maya Salam, "For Serena Williams, Childbirth Was a Harrowing Ordeal. She's Not Alone," *The New York Times,* January 11, 2018, https://www.nytimes.com/2018/01/11/sports/tennis/serena-williams-baby-vogue.html.
12. Cottom, *Thick,* pp. 85–86.
13. By the time women were referred to this specialty pain clinic, they had experienced pain for longer, and were older, than their male counterparts. In another study of a pain clinic, women were more likely to have been referred to the clinic by a specialist; men, by a general practitioner. As Hoffmann and Tarzian point out, "the results suggest that women experience disbelief or other obstacles at their initial encounters with health-care providers." Diane E. Hoffmann and Anita J. Tarzian, "The Girl Who Cried Pain: A Bias Against Women in the Treatment of Pain," *Journal of Law, Medicine and Ethics* 29 (2001), p. 17.
14. Of course, receiving opiates for pain relief is, in some cases, at best a mixed blessing, given the opioid crisis in this country. However,

the point here is just that the prescription of opiates to boys and men, rather than non-narcotic pain medication that's widely available over the counter, indicates that male pain is being taken more seriously than female pain—regardless of what constitutes best clinical practices, bearing in mind the risk of dependency.

15. Hoffmann and Tarzian, "The Girl Who Cried Pain," p. 19.

16. Ibid., p. 20.

17. Anke Samulowitz, Ida Gremyr, Erik Eriksson, and Gunnel Hensing, "'Brave Men' and 'Emotional Women': A Theory-Guided Literature Review on Gender Bias in Health Care and Gendered Norms Towards Patients with Chronic Pain," *Pain Research and Management* 2018 (2018), p. 10.

Similarly, when it came to emergency room treatment, Caroline Criado Perez writes: "A US Institute of Medicine publication on chronic pain released in 2011 suggested that not much has changed [since the 1990s and 2000s], reporting that women in pain face 'delays in correct diagnosis, improper and unproven treatments,' and 'neglect, dismissal and discrimination' from the healthcare system." Caroline Criado Perez, *Invisible Women: Data Bias in a World Designed for Men* (New York: Abrams, 2019), p. 228.

18. Samulowitz et al., p. 8.

19. In one study, many providers interviewed about patients with fibromyalgia held them to be time-consuming and frustrating malingerers. Some patients were even held accountable for their own pain by clinicians. Ibid., p. 5.

20. Ibid., p. 7.

21. Ibid., p. 5.

22. Kate Hunt, Joy Adamson, Catherine Hewitt, and Irwin Nazareth, "Do Women Consult More Than Men? A Review of Gender and Consultation for Back Pain and Headache," *Journal of Health Services Research and Policy* 16, no. 2 (2011): 108–13.

23. Ibid., p. 109.

24. Ibid., p. 116.

25. Ibid., p. 109.

26. Ibid., p. 116.

27. See Lindsey L. Cohen, Jean Cobb, and Sarah R. Martin, "Gender Biases in Adult Ratings of Pediatric Pain," *Children's Health Care* 43, no. 2 (2014): 87–95, and Brian D. Earp, Joshua T. Monrad, Marianne LaFrance, John A. Bargh, Lindsey L. Cohen, and

Jennifer A. Richeson, "Gender Bias in Pediatric Pain Assessment," *Journal of Pediatric Psychology* 44, no. 4 (2019): 403–14.

28. Interestingly, the most recent replication of this study, by Earp et al. (ibid.), produced a significant effect for female but not male participants viewing the footage. The explanation for this is unclear, but it jibes with the fact that many gender biases hold just as much for women as for men—or perhaps, in this case, more so. See chapter 9 in this book for a discussion of some such biases.

29. This is as opposed to a trait (supposedly) being hardwired due to differences that emerge later—e.g., hormonal factors that kick in in adolescence.

30. Samulowitz et. al., " 'Brave Men' and 'Emotional Women,' " p. 10.

31. I say "privileged" partly because racism as well as misogyny—together with their toxic intersection, misogynoir, of which more shortly—undoubtedly plays a crucial role in inadequate pain treatment. In 2016, a landmark study shed light on the reason why, as the researchers note, "Black Americans are systematically undertreated for pain relative to white Americans." They investigated the prevalence of false beliefs about biological differences between Black and white people (e.g., "Black people's skin is thicker than white people's skin"), and found that a full half of their sample of white medical students and residents harbored such false beliefs. These participants were also significantly more likely to believe that a Black patient was experiencing less pain than a white counterpart, and made less accurate recommendations when it came to their pain management. See Kelly M. Hoffman, Sophie Trawalter, Jordan R. Axt, and M. Norman Oliver, "Racial Bias in Pain Assessment," *Proceedings of the National Academy of Sciences* 113, no. 16 (2016): 4296–4301.

32. Kristie Dotson, "Tracking Epistemic Violence, Tracking Practices of Silencing," *Hypatia* 26, no. 2 (2011): 242. A discussion of Dotson's concept of testimonial smothering, a kind of coerced self-silencing, will follow in chapter 8, "Unassuming."

33. Miranda Fricker, *Epistemic Injustice: Power and the Ethics of Knowing* (Oxford: Oxford University Press, 2007), chapters 1–2.

34. For a history of the term, coined by Bailey in 2008 and written about online since 2010 by Bailey and Trudy (a.k.a. @thetrudz), see their coauthored article: Moya Bailey and Trudy, "On Misogynoir: Citation, Erasure, and Plagiarism," *Feminist Media Studies* 18, no. 4 (2018): 762–68.

35. Jazmine Joyner, "Nobody Believes That Black Women Are in Pain, and It's Killing Us," *Wear Your Voice Magazine*, May 25, 2018, https://wearyourvoicemag.com/race/black-women-are-in-pain.

36. Compare the experiences of Rachel, who also suffered from a twisted fallopian tube, as written about by her husband. See Joe Fassler, "How Doctors Take Women's Pain Less Seriously," *The Atlantic*, October 15, 2015, https://www.theatlantic.com/health/archive/2015/10/emergency-room-wait-times-sexism/410515/. But without wishing to detract one iota from the terrible suffering and injustice Rachel experienced, it is striking that her story received far more uptake (and appeared in a premier venue), in contrast to Joyner's. For, often, misogynoir partly *consists* in the hostile indifference toward Black women's suffering and the injustices they face—in contrast to Rachel, a presumptively white woman. There is also the fact that Rachel's story was told by her husband, and thus plausibly benefited from the weight of his (male) testimony.

37. Jazmine Joyner, "Nobody Believes That Black Women Are in Pain," *Wear Your Voice Magazine*.

38. Valuable conversations with Tammy Nyden helped me recognize the extent to which mothers of mentally ill children are disproportionately punished within the U.S. medical system—stigmatized as "bad" women and blamed for their children's struggles.

39. Patricia Hill Collins, *Black Feminist Thought: Knowledge, Consciousness, and the Politics of Empowerment*, 2nd ed. (New York: Routledge, 2000), p. 72.

40. Similarly, when women testify against powerful men, e.g., about their sexual and other abuses, there is a marked tendency to discount their word—as opposed to when they testify in these men's *favor*, whereupon testimonial injustice becomes much less of an issue. So, again, such dismissals are neither random nor universal for speakers who belong to a particular social category. Instead, they often work to uphold and sustain existing social hierarchies. See my book *Down Girl: The Logic of Misogyny* (New York: Oxford University Press, 2018), Introduction and chapter 6, for discussion. And more on these issues follows here, in chapter 8, "Unassuming."

41. Angela Garbes, *Like a Mother: A Feminist Journey Through the Science and Culture of Pregnancy* (New York: HarperCollins, 2018), p. 28.

42. I say "actually" because, as recent Pew statistics show, white women have among the lowest rates of interracial marriage of any other group. See "Intermarriage in the U.S., 50 Years After *Loving v. Virginia*," May 18, 2017, https://www.pewsocialtrends.org/2017/05/18/1-trends-and-patterns-in-intermarriage/.

43. Criado Perez, *Invisible Women*, p. 234.

44. Ibid.

45. Ibid., p. 196.

46. Even nonhuman animal studies exhibit this prevalent bias: a 2014 survey found that some 80 percent of the studies that specified sex used only male animals, despite the somewhat *greater* variability of, e.g., male rats than female rats. Ibid., p. 205.

47. Ibid., p. 209.

48. Ibid., p. 228.

49. Ibid., pp. 212–18.

50. Ibid., pp. 204–05.

51. Ibid., p. 222.

52. Cory Doctorow, "Women Are Much More Likely to Be Injured in Car Crashes, Probably Because Crash-Test Dummies Are Mostly Male-Shaped," *Boing Boing*, July 23, 2019, https://boingboing.net/2019/07/23/in-every-dreamhome-a-heartache.html.

53. Criado Perez, *Invisible Women*, p. 233.

54. Ibid., p. 233

55. Ibid., p. 234.

SIX Unruly—On the Entitlement to Bodily Control

1. Six Democrats, including two female Democrats, voted no on the bill; three state senators (one female Democrat and two male Republicans) did not vote for the bill; and one female Democrat abstained from voting.

2. The bill, dubbed the "Human Life Protection Act," also reclassified abortion as a class A felony, punishable by up to ninety-nine years in prison for doctors who perform abortions. For details on how the law was subsequently frozen, see Alice Miranda, "Federal Judge Blocks Alabama's Near-Total Abortion Ban," Politico, October 29, 2019, https://www.politico.com/news/2019/10/29/federal-judge-blocks-alabamas-near-total-abortion-ban-061069.

3. Constitutionally protected at the time of writing—although, given Brett Kavanaugh's well-known anti-abortion stance and his

position on the Supreme Court, this may not be true for much longer.

4. Jessica Glenza, "The Anti-Gay Extremist Behind America's Fiercely Strict Abortion Bans," *The Guardian,* April 25, 2019, https://www.theguardian.com/world/2019/apr/25/the-anti-abortion-crusader-hopes-her-heartbeat-law-will-test-roe-v-wade.

    Such bills have been signed into law (if only to be subsequently struck down) in seven states at the time of writing: Iowa, Kentucky, Mississippi, North Dakota, Ohio, Georgia, and Missouri. The Alabama law with which I opened is even stricter.

5. Anti-abortion activism has also, for many years, whittled away access to clinics, many of which have shut down as a result of this. See my book *Down Girl: The Logic of Misogyny* (New York: Oxford University Press, 2018), chapter 3, for discussion.

6. Katie Heaney, "Embryos Don't Have Hearts," *The Cut,* May 24, 2019, https://www.thecut.com/2019/05/embryos-dont-have-hearts.html.

7. Lydia O'Connor, "The Lawmakers Behind 'Fetal Heartbeat' Abortion Bans Are Lying to You," *HuffPost,* May 22, 2019, https://www.huffpost.com/entry/six-week-fetal-heartbeat-abortion-ban-lies_n_5ce42ccae4b075a35a2e6fb0.

8. Kate Smith, "A Pregnant 11-Year-Old Rape Victim in Ohio Would No Longer Be Allowed to Have an Abortion Under New State Law," CBS News, May 14, 2019, https://www.cbsnews.com/news/ohio-abortion-heartbeat-bill-pregnant-11-year-old-rape-victim-barred-abortion-after-new-ohio-abortion-bill-2019-05-13/.

9. Jonathan Stempel, "U.S. Judge Blocks Ohio 'Heartbeat' Law to End Most Abortions," Reuters, July 3, 2019, https://www.reuters.com/article/us-usa-abortion-ohio/u-s-judge-blocks-ohio-heartbeat-law-to-end-most-abortions-idUSKCN1TY2PK.

10. Laurie Penny, "The Criminalization of Women's Bodies Is All About Conservative Male Power," *The New Republic,* May 17, 2019, https://newrepublic.com/article/153942/criminalization-womens-bodies-conservative-male-power.

11. Daniel Politi, "Trump: After Birth, Baby Is 'Wrapped' in a Blanket and Mother, Doctor Decide Whether to 'Execute the Baby,'" *Slate,* April 28, 2019, https://slate.com/news-and-politics/2019/04/trump-abortion-baby-wrapped-blanket-execute-baby.html.

And compare Vice President Mike Pence's tweet, in reference to an anti-abortion protest in Times Square in May 2019, which featured a live ultrasound of a fetus in the third trimester projected onto a giant screen: "As Democrat Governors in NY & VA advocate for late term abortion & even infanticide—& Democrats in Congress refuse to allow a vote on the Born-Alive bill— TODAY in Times Square an ultrasound will be shown for all to see, demonstrating the miracle of life" (https://twitter.com/vp /status/1124742840184201216?lang=en).

12. Anti-abortion activists have hijacked the expression "late-term," which is a medical expression used to describe pregnancies that extend past forty weeks. See Pam Belluck, "What Is Late-Term Abortion? Trump Got It Wrong," *The New York Times,* February 6, 2019, https://www.nytimes.com/2019/02/06/health/late -term-abortion-trump.html.

13. Jia Tolentino, "Interview with a Woman Who Recently Had an Abortion at 32 Weeks," Jezebel, June 15, 2016, https://jezebel .com/interview-with-a-woman-who-recently-had-an-abortion -at-1781972395.

14. The procedure then involved giving Elizabeth a shot to prevent labor until she could fly back to New York, where she delivered the baby—vaginally, but without pushing, with the doctor using forceps and sheer muscle to extract the fetus manually (a tremendously painful procedure, and not one they could have ethically performed had the fetus still been alive).

    Full abortion procedures at that Colorado clinic cost $25,000. And the clinic is barely keeping its head above water, partly due to the danger pay needed to retain staff. At the time Tolentino's interview was published, the roof was in fact leaking.

15. Lori Mooreaug, "Rep. Todd Akin: The Statement and the Reaction," *The New York Times,* August 20, 2012, https://www .nytimes.com/2012/08/21/us/politics/rep-todd-akin-legitimate -rape-statement-and-reaction.html.

16. Susan Milligan, "Go Back to Health Class," *U.S. News & World Report,* February 24, 2015, https://www.usnews.com/opinion /blogs/susan-milligan/2015/02/24/idaho-lawmaker-asks-about -swallowing-cameras-to-get-pregnancy-pictures.

17. The lawmaker in question was advocating insurance coverage for a nonexistent procedure. See Kayla Epstein, "A Sponsor of an Ohio Abortion Bill Thinks You Can Reimplant Ectopic Pregnancies.

You Can't," *The Washington Post,* May 10, 2019, https://www
.washingtonpost.com/health/2019/05/10/sponsor-an-ohio
-abortion-bill-thinks-you-can-reimplant-ectopic-pregnancies
-you-cant/.

18. Occasionally an ectopic pregnancy that has implanted somewhere
    other than the fallopian tube (e.g., in the abdomen) has been
    viable. But this is an extremely rare occurrence.

19. According to recent data, bleeding from an ectopic pregnancy is
    responsible for 4–10 percent of all pregnancy-related deaths and is
    the leading cause of death in the first trimester in the United
    States. See Krissi Danielsson, "Ectopic Pregnancy Statistics,"
    Verywell Family, published August 1, 2019, updated October 29,
    2019, https://www.verywellfamily.com/what-do-statistics-look
    -like-for-ectopic-pregnancy-2371730.

20. Georgi Boorman, "Is Abortion Really Necessary for Treating
    Ectopic Pregnancies?" *The Federalist,* September 9, 2019, https://
    thefederalist.com/2019/09/09/is-abortion-really-necessary-for
    -treating-ectopic-pregnancies/.

21. https://twitter.com/DrJenGunter/status/1171167907834806272
    (accessed September 18, 2019).

22. In response to widespread condemnation from the medical com-
    munity, Boorman eventually apologized for her article, saying it
    no longer expresses her opinion. See "I Was Wrong: Sometimes
    It's Necessary to Remove Ectopic Babies to Save Their Mother's
    Life," *The Federalist,* September 19, 2019, https://thefederalist.
    com/2019/09/19/i-was-wrong-sometimes-its-necessary-to
    -remove-ectopic-babies-to-save-their-mothers-life/. But the
    original article is still available on *The Federalist* at the time of
    writing (September 23, 2019), albeit with a link to Boorman's
    subsequent apology and recanting.

    Notably, the mortality rate for ectopic pregnancies is vastly
    (nearly seven times) higher for Black women as compared with
    white ones—part of a pattern of dismal healthcare for Black
    women that was a major focus in the previous chapter.

23. Jess Morales Rocketto, "Seven Children Have Died in Immigra-
    tion Custody. Remember Their Names," BuzzFeed News,
    September 30, 2019, https://www.buzzfeednews.com/article
    /jessmoralesrocketto/remember-their-names.

24. Jay Parini, "Alabama's 'Pro-Life' Governor Is a Hypocrite," *CNN,*

May 17, 2019, https://www.cnn.com/2019/05/16/opinions
/alabama-kay-ivey-hypocrisy-parini/index.html.

25. Roni Caryn Rabin, "Huge Racial Disparities Found in Deaths
Linked to Pregnancy," *The New York Times,* May 7, 2019, https://
www.nytimes.com/2019/05/07/health/pregnancy-deaths-.html.

26. Nor are they prone to raise much of a fuss about a vast swathe of
vulnerable beings with heartbeats who are brutally slaughtered by
the billions every year in the U.S. alone: the non-human animals
subject to factory farming. Consider also the non-human animals
subject to unnecessary and cruel forms of experimentation and
testing.

27. Maggie Fox, "Abortion Rates Go Down When Countries Make
It Legal: Report," NBC News, May 20, 2018, https://www
.nbcnews.com/health/health-care/abortion-rates-go-down-when
-countries-make-it-legal-report-n858476.

28. Reva B. Siegel and Linda Greenhouse, "Before (and After) *Roe v.
Wade*: New Questions About Backlash," *Faculty Scholarship Series*
4135 (2011): 2056–2057. https://digitalcommons.law.yale.edu
/cgi/viewcontent.cgi?article=5151&context=fss_papers.

29. Ibid., p. 2057.

30. Linda Greenhouse and Reva B. Siegel, *Before Roe v. Wade: Voices
that Shaped the Abortion Debate Before the Supreme Court's Ruling*
(New York: Kaplan, 2010), p. 257.

As Greenhouse and Siegel go on to show in their article,
though, Nixon's anti-abortion stance had limited efficacy in the
end:

> The Nixon campaign saw the strategic benefit in invoking
> abortion for its power in signaling social conservatism; staking
> out a position on abortion itself appeared to offer little
> benefit. On August 28, 1972, campaign strategists sent John
> Ehrlichman "data showing 'a sizeable majority of Americans,
> including Roman Catholics, now favoring liberal abortion
> laws,'" and "the president decided to leave [the] matter to the
> states, . . . privately affirm[ing] that 'abortion reform' was 'not
> proper ground for Federal action'" and that he " 'would never
> take action as President.'" Only three days before, the mid-
> 1972 Gallup poll published in newspapers around the country
> showed that "a record high of 64 percent support full liberal-

ization of abortion laws," a sharp increase from the preceding January. In contrast to the doctrinal message being preached with increasing vigor by the Church hierarchy, the new poll showed that substantial numbers of Catholics in fact supported liberalizing access to abortion: "Fifty-six per cent of Catholics believe that abortion should be decided by a woman and her doctor." . . . In November 1972, two months before the Supreme Court handed down *Roe v. Wade,* Nixon won reelection with the support of a majority of the Catholic voters, although abortion was not a significant determinant in attracting votes. Soon after, when the Court handed down *Roe,* Nixon "directed his aides to 'keep out' of the case."

From Greenhouse and Siegel, "Before (and After) *Roe v. Wade,* p. 2058.

31. Greenhouse and Siegel, *Before Roe v. Wade,* p. 257.
32. Michelle Oberman and W. David Ball, "When We Talk About Abortion, Let's Talk About Men," *The New York Times,* June 2, 2019, https://www.nytimes.com/2019/06/02/opinion/abortion-laws-men.html.
33. Jill Filipovic, "Alabama's Abortion Bill Is Immoral, Inhumane, and Wildly Inconsistent," *Vanity Fair,* May 15, 2019, https://www.vanityfair.com/style/2019/05/alabamas-abortion-bill-is-immoral-inhumane-and-wildly-inconsistent.
34. Although many trans boys and men, as well as non-binary people who can become pregnant, are just as much affected by the resulting policies.
35. Pace Laurie Penny, when she writes that the anti-abortion laws canvassed in this chapter "are about women as things." "The Criminalization of Women's Bodies," https://newrepublic.com/article/153942/criminalization-womens-bodies-conservative-male-power.
36. Some of the many anti-choice Republican men who are known to have enabled or actively pressured their female sexual partners to have abortions include Scott Lloyd, Elliott Broidy, Tim Murphy, and Scott DesJarlais. The former two even paid (in full or in part) for the procedure. See Arwa Mahdawi, "A Republican Theme on Abortions: 'It's OK for Me, Evil for Thee,'" *The Guardian,* August 25, 2018, https://www.theguardian.com/world

/2018/aug/25/a-republican-theme-on-abortions-its-ok-for-me
-evil-for-thee.

37. Emily Oster, *Expecting Better: Why the Conventional Pregnancy Wisdom Is Wrong—and What You Really Need to Know* (New York: Penguin, 2018), pp. 40–52.

38. This isn't to deny that these benefits exist, of course—just that they must be rationally weighed against the risks, difficulty, or impossibility of a vaginal birth for many patients. And see the obstetrician-gynecologist Amy Tuteur's book, *Push Back: Guilt in the Age of Natural Parenting* (New York: Dey Street, 2016), for a fascinating account of how anything other than so-called natural childbirth came to be a source of intense, needless guilt for birth parents. And for a compelling, more general, account of the policing of gestation, see Quill R Kukla, writing as Rebecca Kukla, *Mass Hysteria: Medicine, Culture, and Mothers' Bodies* (Lanham, MD: Rowman & Littlefield, 2005).

39. Emily Oster, *Cribsheet: A Data-Driven Guide to Better, More Relaxed Parenting, from Birth to Preschool* (New York: Penguin, 2019), chapter 4.

40. The same lack of consideration of the costs and benefits will often apply to chestfeeding, for trans male birth parents—although transphobic and exclusionary views may conspire to make this an even more fraught site of bodily control, guilting, shaming, and so on.

41. Kirsten Powers, "Kevin Williamson Is Wrong. Hanging Women Who Have an Abortion Is Not Pro-Life," *USA Today*, April 6, 2018, https://www.usatoday.com/story/opinion/2018/04/06 /kevin-williamson-atlantic-fired-hanging-women-who-have -abortion-column/491590002/. And see *Down Girl*, pp. 96–98, for further discussion of such views.

42. Ronald Brownstein, "White Women Are Helping States Pass Abortion Restrictions," *The Atlantic*, May 23, 2019, https://www .theatlantic.com/politics/archive/2019/05/white-women-and -support-restrictive-abortion-laws/590101/.

43. Moreover,

> In most cases pregnancy provided a "but for" factor, meaning that but for the pregnancy, the action taken against the woman would not have occurred. In seven cases, efforts to

deny women their liberty also included allegations related to actions a woman took after she had delivered a baby and was no longer pregnant.

From Lynne M. Paltrow and Jeanne Flavin. "Arrests of and Forced Interventions on Pregnant Women in the United States, 1973–2005: Implications for Women's Legal Status and Public Health," *Journal of Health Politics, Policy and Law* 38, no. 2 (2013): 301.

Another brutal and common practice is forcing pregnant people who are incarcerated to give birth while in shackles. See "Shackling Pregnant Inmates Is Still a Practice in Many States," CBS News, March 13, 2019, https://www.cbsnews.com/news /shackling-pregnant-inmates-is-still-a-practice-in-many-states/.

There are many other travesties of reproductive justice, including forced sterilization, forced abortion, and the "removal" (or, more accurately, stealing) of children from their parents. These crimes—to which poor, nonwhite, Indigenous, and disabled girls and women have been massively disproportionately vulnerable— are a topic of deep importance, but further discussion would take me beyond the scope of this chapter. For a useful primer and set of resources on this subject, see Amanda Manes, "Reproductive Justice and Violence Against Women: Understanding the Intersec- tions," VAWnet, February 28, 2017, https://vawnet.org/sc /reproductive-justice-violence-against-women-understanding -intersections.

44. Paltrow and Flavin, "Arrests of and Forced Interventions on Pregnant Women in the United States," p. 311.

45. Paltrow and Flavin explain:

In 2008, as a result of post-conviction relief proceedings, the South Carolina Supreme Court unanimously overturned her conviction, concluding that she had received ineffective assistance of counsel at her trial. The court described the research that the state had relied on as "outdated" and found that McKnight's trial counsel had failed to call experts who would have testified about "recent studies showing that cocaine is no more harmful to a fetus than nicotine use, poor nutrition, lack of prenatal care, or other conditions commonly associated with the urban poor." To avoid being retried and possibly sentenced to an even longer term, McKnight pleaded guilty to manslaughter and was released from prison.

From Paltrow and Flavin, p. 306.
Note, then, that McKnight will still be classified as a felon.

46. See "'Bathroom Bill' Legislative Tracking," http://www.ncsl.org /research/education/-bathroom-bill-legislative-tracking635951130 .aspx.

47. Brian Barnett, "Anti-Trans 'Bathroom Bills' Are Based on Lies. Here's the Research to Show It," *HuffPost*, September 11, 2019, https://www.huffpost.com/entry/opinion-transgender-bathroom -crime_n_5b96c5b0e4b0511db3e52825.

48. Another parallel with the anti-abortion movement is the role white cis women have often played in such moral policing, sometimes under the aegis of so-called radical feminism. See Katelyn Burns, "The Rise of Anti-Trans 'Radical' Feminists, Explained," Vox, September 5, 2019, https://www.vox.com /identities/2019/9/5/20840101/terfs-radical-feminists-gender -critical, for a primer on this subject.

49. Barnett, "Anti-Trans 'Bathroom Bills' Are Based on Lies," Huff- post, https://www.huffpost.com/entry/opinion-transgender -bathroom-crime_n_5b96c5b0e4b0511db3e52825.

50. As well as the work by Bettcher to be discussed shortly, see the following works by Robin Dembroff, Emi Koyama, Rachel V. McKinnon, and Julia Serano for illuminating feminist discussions of transgender identity and transphobia:

Robin Dembroff, "Real Talk on the Metaphysics of Gender," in *Gendered Oppression and its Intersections,* a special issue of *Philosophical Topics,* edited by Bianka Takaoka and Kate Manne, forthcoming.
Robin Dembroff, "Trans Women Are Victims of Misogyny, Too—and All Feminists Must Recognize This," *The Guardian,* May 19, 2019, https://www.theguardian.com/commentisfree /2019/may/19/valerie-jackson-trans-women-misogyny -feminism.
Emi Koyama, "The Transfeminist Manifesto," in *Catching a Wave: Reclaiming Feminism for the 21st Century,* edited by Rory Dicker and Alison Piepmeier (Boston: Northeastern Univer- sity Press, 2003), pp. 244–59.

Rachel V. McKinnon, "Stereotype Threat and Attributional Ambiguity for Trans Women," *Hypatia* 29, no. 4 (2014): 857–72.

Rachel V. McKinnon, "Trans*formative Experiences," *Res Philosophica* 92, no. 2 (2015): 419–40.

Julia Serano, *Whipping Girl: A Transsexual Woman on Sexism and the Scapegoating of Femininity,* 2nd ed. (2007; repr., Berkeley, Calif.: Seal Press, 2016).

51. Talia Mae Bettcher, "Full-Frontal Morality: The Naked Truth About Gender," *Hypatia* 27, no. 2 (2012): 320. Here she draws on the work of Harold Garfinkel.

52. Talia Mae Bettcher, "Evil Deceivers and Make-Believers: On Transphobic Violence and the Politics of Illusion," *Hypatia* 22, no. 3 (2007): 43–65.

53. Bettcher, "Full-Frontal Morality," p. 332.

54. Another appallingly false pseudo-obligation in the vicinity that the law has nevertheless enshrined in many states: recognizing the parental rights of rapists. See Analyn Megison, "My Rapist Fought for Custody of My Daughter. States Can't Keep Survivors Tied to Rapists," *USA Today,* June 19, 2019, https://www.usatoday.com /story/opinion/voices/2019/06/19/abortion-laws-bans-rape -parental-rights-column/1432450001/.

55. Julie Euber, "American Medical Association: Transgender Deaths Are an Epidemic," *Non-Profit Quarterly,* October 2, 2019, https:// nonprofitquarterly.org/american-medical-association-transgender -deaths-are-an-epidemic/. For a useful recent estimation of the rates of homicide in the United States for trans women versus cis men, see the data scientist Emily Gorcenski's "Transgender Murders: By the Numbers," January 13, 2019, https://emilygor-censki.com/post/transgender-murders-by-the-numbers/. And note that the risks here are particularly high for trans girls and women of color. See Rick Rojas and Vanessa Swales, "18 Trans-gender Killings This Year Raise Fears of an 'Epidemic,'" *The New York Times,* September 27, 2019, https://www.nytimes.com/2019 /09/27/us/transgender-women-deaths.html.

56. Bettcher, "Evil Deceivers and Make-Believers," pp. 43–45.

57. Following a mistrial, Magidson and Merel were eventually convicted of second-degree murder, without hate-crime enhance-ment. Nabors pleaded guilty during the first trial to voluntary

manslaughter. Cazares ultimately pleaded no-contest to voluntary manslaughter.

58. For a nuanced discussion of the connection here between trans-phobia and homophobia, see Bettcher, "Evil Deceivers and Make-Believers," p. 47.

59. This is hence a paradigm case of himpathy, a concept explained and explored in earlier chapters.

SEVEN Insupportable—On the Entitlement to Domestic Labor

1. Darcy Lockman, *All the Rage: Mothers, Fathers, and the Myth of Equal Partnership* (New York: HarperCollins, 2019), p. 205.

2. Jill E. Yavorsky, Claire M. Kamp Dush, and Sarah J. Schoppe-Sullivan, "The Production of Inequality: The Gender Division of Labor Across the Transition to Parenthood," *Journal of Marriage and Family* 77, no. 3 (2015): 662–79.

3. "Time Spent in Primary Activities by Married Mothers and Fathers by Employment Status of Self and Spouse . . . 2011–15," Bureau of Labor Statistics, https://www.bls.gov/tus/tables/a7_1115.pdf.

4. "Why the Majority of the World's Poor Are Women," Oxfam International, accessed July 15, 2019, https://www.oxfam.org/en/even-it/why-majority-worlds-poor-are-women.

5. See "Men Taking on 50 Percent of the World's Childcare and Domestic Work Requires Global Goal and Immediate Action, Reveals State of the World's Fathers Report," https://men-care.org/2017/06/09/men-taking-on-50-percent-of-the-worlds-childcare-and-domestic-work-requires-global-goal-and-immediate-action-reveals-state-of-the-worlds-fathers-report/, and International Labour Organization, *A Quantum Leap for Gender Equality: For a Better Future of Work for All* (Geneva, Switzerland: International Labour Office, 2019), https://www.ilo.org/wcmsp5/groups/public/---dgreports/---dcomm/---publ/documents/publication/wcms_674831.pdf.

6. Sara Raley, Suzanne M. Bianchi, and Wendy Wang, "When Do Fathers Care? Mothers' Economic Contribution and Fathers' Involvement in Childcare," *American Journal of Sociology* 117, no. 5 (2005): 1422–59.

7. Lockman, *All the Rage,* p. 16.

8. "Sharing Chores at Home: Houses Divided," *Economist,* October 5, 2017, https://www.economist.com/international/2017/10/05/houses-divided.

9. Scott Coltrane, "Research on Household Labor: Modeling and Measuring the Social Embeddedness of Routine Family Work," *Journal of Marriage and Family* 62, no. 4 (2000): 1210.

10. Claire Kamp Dush, "Men Share Housework Equally—Until the First Baby," *Newsweek,* May 10, 2015, https://www.newsweek.com/men-share-housework-equally-until-first-baby-330347.

11. Lockman, *All the Rage,* p. 3.

12. Tracy Moore, "The Stupid-Easy Guide to Emotional Labor," *Mel Magazine,* 2018, https://melmagazine.com/en-us/story/the-stupid-easy-guide-to-emotional-labor.

13. In a recent interview, Hochschild said:

    Emotional labor, as I introduced the term in *The Managed Heart,* is the work, for which you're paid, which centrally involves trying to feel the right feeling for the job. This involves evoking and suppressing feelings. Some jobs require a lot of it, some a little of it. From the flight attendant whose job it is to be nicer than natural to the bill collector whose job it is to be, if necessary, harsher than natural, there are a variety of jobs that call for this. Teachers, nursing-home attendants, and child-care workers are examples. The point is that while you may also be doing physical labor and mental labor, you are crucially being hired and monitored for your capacity to manage and produce a feeling.

    From Julie Beck, "The Concept Creep of 'Emotional Labor,'" *The Atlantic,* November 26, 2018, https://www.theatlantic.com/family/archive/2018/11/arlie-hochschild-housework-isnt-emotional-labor/576637/.

14. Gemma Hartley, *Fed Up: Emotional Labor, Women, and the Way Forward* (New York: HarperCollins, 2018), pp. 3–4.

15. Ibid., p. 4.

16. Ibid., p. 1.

17. Ibid., p. 5.

18. See, for example, Eyal Abraham, Talma Hendler, Irit Shapira-Lichter, Yaniv Kanat-Maymon, Orna Zagoory-Sharon, and Ruth Feldman, "Father's Brain Is Sensitive to Childcare Experiences," *Proceedings of the National Academy of Sciences* 111, no. 27 (2014): 9792–97. For a more general discussion of such sexist hypotheses, which play a role in rationalizing and naturalizing a patriarchal

social order, see my book *Down Girl: The Logic of Misogyny* (New York: Oxford University Press, 2018), chapter 3.

19. See Arlie Russell Hochschild (with Anne Machung), *The Second Shift: Working Families and the Revolution at Home* (London: Penguin, 1989), pp. 5–6, and Lockman, *All the Rage*, p. 17.

20. And it's worth noting that even when privileged women *do* obtain paid help with housework and child-rearing responsibilities, they often have the added emotional burden of having to single-handedly manage the relationships with those they hire to help them.

21. Susan Chira, "Men Don't Want to Be Nurses. Their Wives Agree," *The New York Times*, June 24, 2017, https://www.nytimes .com/2017/06/24/opinion/sunday/men-dont-want-to-be-nurses -their-wives-agree.html.

22. Ibid. Admittedly, this study didn't speak to the question of whether these men's wives disapprove of this work inherently and deem it beneath the dignity of their husbands or, alternatively, anticipate intolerable emotional fallout if their husbands do take low-status and lower-paying work than that to which they've been accustomed.

23. N. Gregory Mankiw, "Why Aren't More Men Working?" *The New York Times*, June 15, 2018, https://www.nytimes.com/2018 /06/15/business/men-unemployment-jobs.html. Note that the percentage of women out of the labor force has decreased dramatically during the same time period: from nearly two-thirds in 1950 to 43 percent today.

24. The quote is taken from Lockman's *Atlantic* piece "Don't Be Grateful That Dad Does His Share," May 7, 2019, https://www .theatlantic.com/ideas/archive/2019/05/mothers-shouldnt-be -grateful-their-husbands-help/588787/.

For the research Lockman is drawing on here, see, for example, Suzanne M. Bianchi, John P. Robinson, and Melissa A. Milkie, *Changing Rhythms of American Life* (New York: Russell Sage Foundation, 2006), pp. 121–22; Andrea Doucet, "Can Parenting Be Equal? Rethinking Equality and Gender Differences in Parenting," in *What Is Parenthood?*, edited by Linda C. McClain and Daniel Cere (New York: NYU Press, 2013), pp. 251–75; and Claire M. Kamp Dush, Jill E. Yavorsky, and Sarah J. Schoppe-Sullivan, "What Are Men Doing While Women Perform Extra

Unpaid Labor? Leisure and Specialization at the Transitions to Parenthood," *Sex Roles* 78, no. 11–12 (2018): 715–30.

25. Hartley, *Fed Up,* pp. 27–28.

26. Jancee Dunn, *How Not to Hate Your Husband After Kids* (New York: Little, Brown, 2017), p. 8.

27. Ibid., p. 58.

28. Ibid., p. 60.

29. Claire Cain Miller, "Why Women, but Not Men, Are Judged for a Messy House," *The New York Times,* June 11, 2019, https://www .nytimes.com/2019/06/11/upshot/why-women-but-not-men-are -judged-for-a-messy-house.html. Notwithstanding the article's headline, the research findings are somewhat more equivocal:

> When participants were told that a woman occupied the clean room, it was judged as less clean than when a man occupied it, and she was thought to be less likely to be viewed positively by visitors and less comfortable with visitors.
>
> Both men and women were penalized for having a messy room. When respondents were told it was occupied by a man, they said that it was in more urgent need of cleaning and that the men were less responsible and hardworking than messy women. The mess seemed to play into a stereotype of men as lazy slobs, the researchers said.
>
> But there was a key difference: Unlike for women, participants said messy men were not likely to be judged by visitors or feel uncomfortable having visitors over.

30. Note, though, that the hypothesis that women are better than men at *noticing* household disorder or at multitasking or task switching has been thoroughly debunked. See Leah Ruppanner, "Women Are Not Better at Multitasking. They Just Do More Work, Studies Show," *Science Alert,* August 15, 2019, https://www .sciencealert.com/women-aren-t-better-multitaskers-than-men -they-re-just-doing-more-work.

31. Lockman, *All the Rage,* p. 25.

32. According to recent reports, in the U.S., over 40 percent of mothers were the sole or primary breadwinners for their families, with just under a quarter of mothers being "co-breadwinners"— defined as married people "whose wages comprise at least 25 percent of their total household earnings." Moreover, in U.S. families with children at home, over two-thirds of married

mothers do paid work outside the home. Sarah Jane Glynn, "Breadwinning Mothers Continue to Be the U.S. Norm," *Centre for American Progress,* May 10, 2019, https://www.americanprogress.org/issues/women/reports/2019/05/10/469739/breadwinning-mothers-continue-u-s-norm/.

33. Dunn, *How Not to Hate Your Husband,* p. 64.
34. Ibid., p. 58.
35. Lockman, "Don't Be Grateful," *The Atlantic.*
36. Dunn, *How Not to Hate Your Husband,* p. 250.
37. At the same time, as noted above, it is in general vital to be aware—particularly as a comparatively wealthy white woman—of the dangers of "leaning down" on more vulnerable women: the women of color and poor women who wealthy white women often end up exploiting for care labor, rather than insisting upon the involvement of a male partner.
38. Dunn, *How Not to Hate Your Husband,* p. 257.
39. Ibid., p. 256.
40. Ibid., p. 247.
41. Ibid., p. 272.

EIGHT Unassuming—On the Entitlement to Knowledge

1. Laura Dodsworth, interviewed by Liv Little, "Me and My Vulva: 100 Women Reveal All," *The Guardian,* February 9, 2019, https://www.theguardian.com/lifeandstyle/2019/feb/09/me-and-my-vulva-100-women-reveal-all-photographs.
2. See, e.g., Dr. Jen Gunter's apt intervention: https://twitter.com/DrJenGunter/status/1094831250945191936 (accessed July 5, 2019).
3. Julie Scagell, "Guy Mansplains 'Vulva' vs. 'Vagina' to Women and It Goes About as Well as Expected," Scary Mommy, February 12, 2019, https://www.scarymommy.com/vulva-versus-vagina-twitter/.
4. Some of his subsequent comments veered into incoherence: "You are begging the question in as much is [*sic*] if I thought it were a dumbing down and I wouldn't be supporting it. I'm taking issue with that sort of position." This was in response to the (at that point, one might have thought welcome) suggestion that his mistake was due to a more widespread "dumbing down" of the correct anatomical terminology, substituting "vagina" for "vulva," incorrectly.

5. For an argument in favor of such "ameliorative" approaches to definitional questions, pioneered by Sally Haslanger, see my book *Down Girl: The Logic of Misogyny* (New York: Oxford University Press, 2018), chapters 1–2. For Haslanger's original, groundbreaking analysis, see her article "Gender and Race: (What) Are They? (What) Do We Want Them to Be?" *Noûs* 34, no. 1 (2000): 31–55, reprinted in her book *Resisting Reality: Social Construction and Social Critique* (New York: Oxford University Press, 2012).

6. As usual, by "attitude," I don't mean something deeply psychological—the kind of thing that is between an individual agent and their psychologist to figure out. I'm interested in attitudes as gestured toward by the common question "What's with the attitude?" As in, here, what's up with a common kind of bad behavior, in terms of the general social expectations or assumptions it reflects and perpetuates?

7. This was not the first time that a man tried to correct a woman about a body part that she possessed, and he did not, on Twitter. In October 2016, after the release of hot-mike footage of Donald Trump boasting about grabbing women "by the pussy," a male user named @DaveBussone mistook the fact that the vagina is indeed an internal organ for the impossibility of being sexually assaulted by being forcibly touched, or "grabbed," in that area. He tweeted to political commentator Kirsten Powers, who had reported on the story: "Normally I give you a pass. Not this time. The vagina is internal. Check an anatomy book. It cannot be grabbed. #MAGA." Kirsten Powers tweeted back: "I know where my vagina is." See https://www.facebook.com/kirstenpowers10/posts/1070957156354394/.

8. I'm here implicitly construing "epistemic entitlement" as a pejorative term—to refer to an *unwarranted* and *overly* entitled attitude along these lines. Later, I'll have occasion to distinguish such an attitude from a *warranted* or *justified* sense of epistemic entitlement to, e.g., assert one's views, claim knowledge, or authoritatively impart information.

9. Another important distinction to be made here is *moral* in nature: whereas testimonial injustice is about an agent not meeting their epistemic obligations to listen to others, epistemic entitlement is about an agent's undue and overly entitled attitudes and behavior—in other words, their assuming too much about *another's obligations to listen to them*. See note 20 in this chapter.

10. Dotson's full definition of testimonial smothering is as follows:

> Testimonial smothering, ultimately, is the truncating of one's own testimony in order to insure that the testimony contains only content for which one's audience demonstrates testimonial competence. . . . Three circumstances . . . routinely exist in instances of testimonial smothering . . . : 1) the content of the testimony must be unsafe and risky; 2) the audience must demonstrate testimonial incompetence with respect to the content of the testimony to the speaker; and 3) testimonial incompetence must follow from, or appear to follow from, pernicious ignorance.

From "Tracking Epistemic Violence, Tracking Practices of Silencing," *Hypatia* 26, no. 2 (2011): 244.

11. Rebecca Solnit, "Men Explain Things to Me," reprinted in *Guernica* magazine, August 20, 2012, https://www.guernicamag.com/rebecca-solnit-men-explain-things-to-me/.

12. Tressie McMillan Cottom, *Thick: And Other Essays* (New York: New Press, 2019), p. 219.

13. Patrick Hamilton, *Angel Street: A Victorian Thriller in Three Acts* (copyrighted under the title *Gas Light*) (New York: Samuel French, 1939).

14. Ibid., p. 5.

15. This gets at part of the ableism of gaslighting: the idea that mental illness is something to be shamed and stigmatized, rather than treated in a humane, effective, and nonjudgmental manner. Thanks in particular to Bobbi Cohn and Nicholas Tilmes, as well as other members of my spring 2019 "(Un)following" seminar at the Society for the Humanities at Cornell, for discussion on this point.

16. As the philosopher Kate Abramson has argued, isolation is a key tactic employed by gaslighters, so that the victim or target won't have people she can easily consult to vindicate or at least support her own perceptions. See Abramson's "Turning Up the Lights on Gaslighting," *Philosophical Perspectives* 28 (2014): 2.

17. Hamilton, *Gas Light,* pp. 34–35.

18. Ibid., pp. 10–11.

19. It's worth noting here that although gaslighting is not *necessarily* gendered, it frequently exploits and perpetuates gendered dynamics, in ways illuminated by Kate Abramson. As she points out:

To begin with (1) women are more frequently the targets of gaslighting than men, and (2) men more often engage in gaslighting. More importantly, gaslighting is frequently, though again, not necessarily, sexist in the following ways: (3) it frequently takes place in the context of, and in response to, a woman's protestation against sexist (or otherwise discriminatory) conduct; (4) some of the forms of emotional manipulation that are employed in gaslighting frequently rely on the target's internalization of sexist norms, (5) when gaslighting is successful—when it actually undermines the target in the ways it is designed to do—it can reinforce the very sexist norms which the target was trying to resist and/or those on which the gaslighter relies in his/her manipulation of the target, and (6) sometimes it is some subset of those very sexist norms which the gaslighter seeks to preserve through his/her gaslighting conduct.

From her "Turning Up the Lights," p. 3.

20. Earlier, I highlighted some differences between testimonial injustice and (an undue assumption of) epistemic entitlement. Another distinction worth highlighting can now be drawn between testimonial injustice and gaslighting (which, as I've argued, often stems from an extreme form of epistemic entitlement). Testimonial injustice involves the perpetrator not meeting their genuine moral obligation to treat their interlocutor as a knower or a potential knower. Gaslighting involves the perpetrator—the gaslighter—imposing a *spurious* moral obligation on their interlocutor to treat the *gaslighter* as the knower in the exchange, regardless of the potential superiority of the interlocutor's own epistemic position. So although gaslighting may be a form of testimonial injustice—as Rachel V. McKinnon has persuasively argued—it also goes beyond this and is particularly creepy. See Rachel V. McKinnon, "Allies Behaving Badly: Gaslighting as Epistemic Injustice," in *The Routledge Handbook of Epistemic Injustice,* edited by Gaile Polhaus, Jr., Ian James Kidd, and José Medina (New York: Routledge, 2017), pp. 167–75.

21. Abramson, "Turning up the Lights," p. 9.

22. Kyle Swenson, "Abuse Survivor Confronts Gymnastics Doctor: 'I Have Been Coming for You for a Long Time,'" *The Washington Post,* January 17, 2018, https://www.washingtonpost.com/news

/morning-mix/wp/2018/01/17/ive-been-coming-for-you-for-a
-long-time-abuse-survivor-confronts-gymnastics-doctor/.

23. John Meehan also sought to isolate Debra Newell from her
children and other relatives. Again, this is a common tactic
employed by gaslighters, as Kate Abramson has argued (see note
16 in this chapter).

24. For this quote and the following excerpts from the podcast *Dirty
John* see https://www.latimes.com/projects/la-me-dirty-john/.

25. Here my conception of gaslighting is somewhat more expansive
than Kate Abramson's, who writes that

> the phenomenon that's come to be picked out with [the term
> "gaslighting"] is a form of emotional manipulation in which
> the gaslighter tries (consciously or not) to induce in someone
> the sense that her reactions, perceptions, memories and/or
> beliefs are not just mistaken, but utterly without grounds—
> paradigmatically, so unfounded as to qualify as crazy. . . .
> Gaslighting is aimed at getting another not to take herself
> seriously as an interlocutor.

> She writes later:

> Gaslighters charge their targets with being crazy, oversensitive,
> paranoid. What these terms have in common in the context
> of gaslighting is that they are ways of charging someone not
> simply with being *wrong* or *mistaken,* but being in no condi-
> tion to judge whether she is wrong or mistaken. The accusa-
> tions are about the target's basic rational competence—her
> ability to get facts right, to deliberate, her basic evaluative
> competencies and ability to react appropriately: her indepen-
> dent standing as deliberator and moral agent. When gaslight-
> ing succeeds, it drives its targets crazy in the sense of deeply
> undermining just these aspects of a person's independent
> standing.

> From "Turning Up the Lights," p. 2 and p. 8 (respectively).

26. There was a dark reason lurking in Debra Newell's past as to why
she may have been prepared to forgive her husband and relinquish
her own perceptions. Her older sister, Cindi, had been murdered
by her husband, Billy Vickers, several decades prior. He shot her
in the back of the head, at point-blank range, after she filed for a
divorce from him. Yet Cindi and Debra's mother, Arlane Hart,

forgave Billy everything. She even came forward, at her own behest, to testify on his behalf at the murder trial. She practiced an extreme form of forgiveness—to the detriment of her daughter's memory, according to at least some of the people who witnessed her behavior. Christopher Goffard writes:

> Her testimony stunned the prosecutor, Thomas Avdeef, who regarded it as a cold-blooded execution. As he interpreted it, the mother's testimony . . . portrayed Cindi as having mistreated her husband.
>
> "They threw her under the bus," Avdeef says. "I don't know the dynamics of the family. I could never understand that. Why say bad things about the victim?"
>
> From https://www.latimes.com/projects/la-me-dirty-john/.

I hope that this book has helped answer that good question, by exploring a prevalent tendency to sympathize with a male perpetrator over his female victim—even, as here, when she is your own daughter. In a word, himpathy; it's responsible for a multitude.

27. Some may insist that gaslighting involves the *motive* on the part of the gaslighter of driving the victim crazy. But this, to my mind, makes gaslighting too dependent on psychological factors—both yielding too psychologistic a definition and requiring too much intentionality on the part of the perpetrator. I prefer a conception which would move to define gaslighting in terms of what *the act* tries to achieve (i.e., its purpose or "telos"), whether or not the gaslighter is consciously *aiming* at this end, and whether or not he is employing a crazy-making or, alternatively, moralizing tactic (or some combination of the two—or, perhaps, another tactic entirely, such as threatening behavior). But, of course, I don't pretend that these brief remarks here are more than suggestive. The best way to understand and define gaslighting is a much larger philosophical topic; interested readers would do well to read the illuminating pieces referenced in the notes above by Kate Abramson and Rachel V. McKinnon, among others.

28. Christopher Goffard commented that John Meehan "approved of the mob's way of doing business, particularly when it came to dealing with enemies. Over and over, he spoke approvingly of a cold-blooded ethos: A dead enemy couldn't suffer, so you went after their loved ones. You went after their families." And that is

plausibly why he went to Terra Newell's apartment one evening, armed with what police called a "kidnap kit"—including duct tape, cable ties, a set of kitchen knives, a vial of injectable testosterone, and his passport. John proceeded to stab Terra with a knife before she managed to fight back. Ultimately, she succeeded in disarming him, then stabbed him several times in self-defense. He died four days later, in the hospital. Goffard writes, "Detectives told the prosecutor, Matt Murphy, that it looked like a clear-cut case of self-defense. In such scenarios, the killer usually wound up on the run, the victim dead, dumped off a freeway or in the desert."

Terra was neither arrested nor prosecuted. From https://www.latimes.com/projects/la-me-dirty-john-terra/.

29. Abramson, "Turning Up the Lights," pp. 8–12.
30. Solnit, "Men Explain Things to Me," Guernica.
31. Of course, anyone can be the target of wrath on the Internet. But the point—and what makes it misogyny, by the lights of my analysis—is both that this targeting of women is demonstrably disproportionate (as compared with their male counterparts) and that it often involves distinctively gendered threats and insults. On the first score, see "The Dark Side of Internet Comments," *The Guardian,* April 12, 2016, https://www.theguardian.com/technology/2016/apr/12/the-dark-side-of-guardian-comments.
32. For example, in 2012, Jones said that Australia's first female prime minister, Julia Gillard, should be "shoved in a chaff bag" and drowned at sea. Later that year, when Gillard's father died, Jones opined that his shame toward his daughter must have been what killed him.
33. Ardern has subsequently made good on this commitment, with New Zealand enshrining this target into law. "New Zealand 'On the Right Side of History' with 2050 Carbon Emissions Target, Jacinda Ardern Says," ABC News, November 7, 2019, https://www.abc.net.au/news/2019-11-07/new-zealand-passes-leading-carbon-emissions-law/11683910.
34. Aaron M. McCright and Riley E. Dunlap, "Cool Dudes: The Denial of Climate Change Among Conservative White Males in the United States," *Global Environmental Change* 21, no. 4 (2011): 1163–72.
35. Compare some of the many put-downs of environmental activist Greta Thunberg, who—as a person on the Autism spectrum—is

also the subject of ableist stereotypes and the associated rhetoric. See, for example, Australian columnist Andrew Bolt's appalling attack on her: "I have never seen a girl so young and with so many mental disorders treated by so many adults as a guru," he wrote in an article entitled "The Disturbing Secret to the Cult of Greta Thunberg," *The Herald Sun,* August 1, 2019, https://www .heraldsun.com.au/blogs/andrew-bolt/the-disturbing-secret-to -the-cult-of-greta-thunberg/news-story/55822063e3589e02707 fbb5a9a75d4cc.

36. Kate Lyons, Naaman Zhou, and Adam Morton, "Scott Morrison Condemns Alan Jones's Call to 'Shove Sock Down Throat' of Jacinda Ardern," *The Guardian,* August 15, 2019, https://www .theguardian.com/media/2019/aug/15/alan-jones-scott-morrison -shove-sock-throat-jacinda-ardern.

37. Under considerable pressure (from companies pulling ads, as well as the displeased broadcasting network itself), Jones subsequently did issue a halfhearted apology—on the same day he called Jacinda Ardern "gormless" and a "hypocrite." "Alan Jones Writes to Jacinda Ardern to Apologise After Companies Pull Ads," *The Guardian,* August 16, 2019, https://www.theguardian.com/media /2019/aug/16/alan-jones-writes-to-jacinda-ardern-to-apologise -after-companies-pull-ads.

38. Lyons, Zhou, and Morton, "Scott Morrison Condemns Alan Jones's Call to 'Shove Sock Down Throat' of Jacinda Ardern," *The Guardian.*

NINE Unelectable—On the Entitlement to Power

1. Not fewer than seventeen thousand news stories mentioning elect- ability and the most popular female presidential hopeful, Elizabeth Warren, had been published at the time of writing (September 1, 2019, well over a year before the election). Of course, some of these stories could in theory have focused more on the electability of a male candidate or on electability in general. But scanning the relevant headlines suggests otherwise, in most cases. See, e.g., from a single week in August 2019:

> Aaron Blake, "Elizabeth Warren Is Surging, but This One Big Question [Electability] Looms Over Her," *The Washington Post,* August 8, 2019, https://www.washingtonpost.com

/politics/2019/08/08/elizabeth-warren-all-important
-electability-question/;
Jonathan Martin, "Many Democrats Love Elizabeth Warren.
They Also Worry About Her [Electability]," *The New York
Times,* August 15, 2019, https://www.nytimes.com/2019
/08/15/us/politics/elizabeth-warren-2020-campaign
.html; and
Nicole Goodkind, "Democrats Worry That a Female
Candidate Can't Beat Trump," *Newsweek,* August 15, 2019,
https://www.newsweek.com/2020-candidates-women-vote
-trump-electability-1454622.

2. Madeline E. Heilman, Aaron S. Wallen, Daniella Fuchs, and
    Melinda M. Tamkins, "Penalties for Success: Reactions to Women
    Who Succeed at Male Gender-Typed Tasks," *Journal of Applied
    Psychology* 89, no. 3 (2004): 416–27.
3. Note that one participant did not identify their gender, perhaps
    due to a simple omission, or perhaps due to being non-binary.
        Note too that while Heilman et al.'s study was published in
    2004, it has been widely replicated, as will emerge through the
    course of this chapter. Moreover, the participants were then
    college students, with a mean age of 20.5 years, thus making them
    millennials. This obviates facile dismissals of these results as merely
    a historical relic.
4. David Paul and Jessi L. Smith, "Subtle Sexism? Examining Vote
    Preferences When Women Run Against Men for the Presidency,"
    Journal of Women, Politics, and Policy 29, no. 4 (2008): 451–76.
        Again, disaggregating the results by gender made no differ-
    ence to the results here. I discuss this study at greater length, along
    with the one referenced in note 2 for this chapter, in my piece
    "It's the Sexism, Stupid," Politico, April 11, 2019, https://www
    .politico.com/magazine/story/2019/04/11/its-the-sexism-stupid
    -226620.
5. Emily Peck, "Half the Men in the U.S. Are Uncomfortable with
    Female Political Leaders," *HuffPost,* November 21, 2019, https://
    www.huffpost.com/entry/half-us-men-uncomfortable-with
    -female-political-leaders_n_5dd30b73e4b0263fbc993674.
6. As a result of that election, 117 women were sent to the 116th
    Congress, compared to 89 women elected in the 2016 cycle. Li

Zhou, "A Historic New Congress Will Be Sworn in Today," Vox, January 3, 2019, https://www.vox.com/2018/12/6/18119733/congress-diversity-women-election-good-news.

7. Tyler G. Okimoto and Victoria L. Brescoll, "The Price of Power: Power Seeking and Backlash Against Female Politicians," *Personality and Social Psychology Bulletin* 36, no. 7 (2010): 933.

8. Madeline Heilman and Tyler Okimoto, "Why Are Women Penalized for Success at Male Tasks?" *Journal of Applied Psychology* 92, no. 1 (2007): 81.

9. Ibid.

10. Ibid., p. 82.

11. If Andrea was described in the above way, James would be similarly described as "an involved manager who is caring and sensitive to the needs" of his subordinates, someone who "emphasizes the importance of having a supportive work environment," and as having been "commended for his efforts to promote a positive community." Ibid., p. 83. As usual, these two communal descriptions were switched for every second participant.

   Note that the researchers also added a condition where positive, *noncommunal* information about both targets of evaluation was added, to check that it was not merely the insertion of praise that made the difference for women but not men (it wasn't).

12. Yet again, participant gender made no difference to these findings—suggesting that one's *own* gender does not make a difference either to these biases, or to the way they can be ameliorated. Ibid., p. 84.

13. It's worth reminding the reader here that Clinton did win the popular vote. However, the force of this point is limited in the context of the dialectic. I believe reasonable minds can disagree widely about how good a president Clinton would have made. But that she would have made a *better* president than Trump seems to me to be scarcely questionable. Hence, as the vastly more qualified candidate, her 2016 election defeat remains a troubling—though not, as we'll see, remotely decisive—data point regarding women's electability in general.

14. Tina Nguyen, "Salad Fiend Amy Klobuchar Once Berated an Aide for Forgetting a Fork," *Vanity Fair*, February 22, 2019, https://www.vanityfair.com/news/2019/02/amy-klobuchar-comb-fork-salad. To be fair, the tone of the article itself was

more circumspect, and authors don't generally get to choose their headlines.

15. Matt Flegenheimer and Sydney Ember, "How Amy Klobuchar Treats Her Staff," *The New York Times,* February 22, 2019, https://www.nytimes.com/2019/02/22/us/politics/amy-klobuchar-staff.html.

16. Joseph Simonson, "Biden Aide: 'Everyone Who Has Worked for Him Has Been Screamed At,'" *Washington Examiner,* July 1, 2019, https://www.washingtonexaminer.com/news/biden-aide-everyone-who-has-worked-for-him-has-been-screamed-at.

17. Paul Heintz, "Anger Management: Sanders Fights for Employees, Except His Own," *Seven Days,* August 26, 2015, https://www.sevendaysvt.com/vermont/anger-management-sanders-fights-for-employees-except-his-own/.

   See also:

   Harry Jaffe, "Bernie Sanders Is Cold as Ice," *Boston Magazine,* September 29, 2015, https://www.bostonmagazine.com/news/2015/09/29/bernie-sanders/;
   Mickey Hirten, "The Trouble with Bernie," *Lansing City Pulse,* October 7, 2015, https://www.lansingcitypulse.com/stories/the-trouble-with-bernie,4622; and
   Graham Vyse, "10 Things Biographer Harry Jaffe Learned About Bernie Sanders," InsideSources, December 23, 2015, https://www.insidesources.com/10-things-biographer-harry-jaffe-learned-about-bernie-sanders/.

   Admittedly, some of these sources are much smaller and less prestigious than those that broke the Klobuchar story. But in a way, that's part of my point: such rumors about the female senator were deemed far more newsworthy from the outset.

18. Alex Seitz-Wald, "Beto O'Rourke Drops F-Bombs, Snaps at Staff, Stresses Out in Revealing New Documentary," NBC News, March 9, 2019, https://www.nbcnews.com/politics/2020-election/beto-o-rourke-drops-f-bombs-snaps-staff-stresses-out-n981421.

19. Politico began recording polling numbers on February 3, 2019. Klobuchar polled at 3–4 percent initially, in the weeks between February 10 and March 10, and then between 1 and 2 percent for most of the remainder of 2019, once falling out of the top ten

candidates recorded: https://www.politico.com/2020-election /democratic-presidential-candidates/polls/ (site accessed December 20, 2019). And despite a surprisingly strong third-place finish in the New Hampshire primary, Klobuchar dropped out of the race prior to Super Tuesday.

20. For a candidate who was widely expected to be a genuine contender for the presidency, Gillibrand's polling numbers were even more dismal than Klobuchar's. She initially polled at 1 percent consistently, and she broke 2 percent just once (in the week ending April 7). In July and August, she never made the top ten in Politico's rankings, before dropping out of the race on Wednesday, August 28, having not qualified for the third Democratic debate: https://www.politico.com/2020-election/democratic-presidential -candidates/polls/.

21. A few representative tweets, in response to Gillibrand's announcement that she was dropping out of the presidential race:

> "I am happy with the 10 chosen candidates, but still bitter . . . @alfranken would have been a formidable person to eliminate [Trump] which we will never see . . . but you knew that . . . right?" https://twitter.com/criteria681/status/1166879516 951797762;
>
> "The party thanks you. Also we will never forget the NRA and Al Franken," https://twitter.com/rmayemsinger/status /1166845231448256518; and
>
> "Bye girl . . . Signed, AL Franken," https://twitter.com /DCRobMan/status/1166827567040598018.

22. It is worth reminding the reader that, morally speaking, the responsibility for Franken's resignation lay solely with Franken— who is responsible, moreover, for his original bad behavior (about which I believe the complainants).

For more on this, see my piece "Gillibrand's Al Franken Problem Won't Die," *The Cut,* January 17, 2019, https://www .thecut.com/2019/01/kirsten-gillibrands-al-franken-problem -wont-die.html.

23. Elena Schneider, "Why Gillibrand Crashed and Burned," Politico, August 29, 2019, https://www.politico.com/story/2019/08/29 /kirsten-gillibrand-drops-out-2020-race-1477845.

24. Heilman and Okimoto, "Why Are Women Penalized for Success at Male Tasks?" p. 86.

25. The researchers showed one further way in which this gender bias could be overcome: including information that the target of the evaluation was a *parent*. Women were seen in a more favorable light when they were mothers; for men, again, this appeared to make no difference—that is, there was no appreciable "boost" in likability or boss desirability for fathers, as opposed to men without children. But, as Heilman and Okimoto note, this result is of somewhat limited applicability, since numerous studies have shown that women are subject to a potent motherhood bias, whereby mothers are often perceived as less competent and committed to the job than their child-free counterparts. The prospect of another unjust double bind hence glints grimly on the horizon.

26. Suspecting that this might be a distinctively gendered dynamic, I found evidence from aggregated ratemyprofessor.com student evaluations that female professors were also far more likely to be described in these terms—lending some modest evidence to the hypothesis that there's something about female authority that tends to read as inauthentic, at least in male-dominated positions. See my book *Down Girl: The Logic of Misogyny* (New York: Oxford University Press, 2018), chapter 8 (and the section "Faking It," in particular).

27. See *Down Girl,* chapter 8.

28. "Transcript: Greta Thunberg's Speech at the U.N. Climate Action Summit," NPR, September 23, 2019, https://www.npr.org/2019/09/23/763452863/transcript-greta-thunbergs-speech-at-the-u-n-climate-action-summit.

29. Compare the response to Jacinda Ardern, the female prime minister of New Zealand, who was widely lauded for her deeply empathetic response to the mosque shootings in Christchurch in March 2019. But see the end of chapter 8, "Unassuming," of this book for a discussion of the consternation Ardern has attracted from some quarters for addressing environmental causes.

    For an excellent analysis of the connection between misogyny and climate change denialism more broadly, see Martin Gelin's piece "The Misogyny of Climate Deniers," *The New Republic,* August 28, 2019, https://newrepublic.com/article/154879/misogyny-climate-deniers.

30. Being perceived as communal may be easier on the right than the left, given that one can thereby portray oneself as upholding

traditional, family values. This jibes with my prediction in *Down
Girl* that conservative women in politics will be subject to less
misogyny, all else equal, than left-wing and centrist women. See
Chapter 4, pp. 114–15.

31. See Myisha Cherry, "Love, Anger, and Racial Injustice," in *The
Routledge Handbook of Love in Philosophy,* edited by Adrienne
Martin (New York: Routledge, 2019), chapter 13; Amia Sriniva-
san, "The Aptness of Anger," *Journal of Political Philosophy* 26, no. 2
(2018): 123–44; Brittney Cooper, *Eloquent Rage: A Black Feminist
Discovers Her Superpower* (New York: St. Martin's, 2018); Soraya
Chemaly, *Rage Becomes Her: The Power of Women's Anger* (New
York: Atria, 2018); and Rebecca Traister, *Good and Mad: The
Revolutionary Power of Women's Anger* (New York: Simon &
Schuster, 2018).

32. Shannon Carlin, "Elizabeth Warren Doesn't Care If Joe Biden
Thinks She's Angry," Refinery 29, November 10, 2019, https://
www.refinery29.com/en-us/2019/11/8752565/elizabeth-warren
-angry-joe-biden-email-response.

33. Benjamin Fearnow, "Elizabeth Warren Celebrates Taking 100,000
'Selfies' with Supporters During 2020 Campaign," *Newsweek,*
January 5, 2020, https://www.newsweek.com/elizabeth-warren
-celebrates-taking-100000-selfies-supporters
-during-2020-campaign-1480473.

34. Lauren Strapagiel, "Elizabeth Warren Followed Through on
Giving This Woman Advice on Her Love Life," BuzzFeed News,
May 19, 2019, https://www.buzzfeednews.com/article/lauren
strapagiel/elizabeth-warren-followed-through-on-giving-this
-woman-love.

35. Aris Folley, "Warren's Campaign Team Sends Dinner, Cookies to
Sanders Staffers After Heart Procedure," The Hill, October 3,
2019, https://thehill.com/homenews/campaign/464253-warrens
-campaign-team-sends-dinner-cookies-to-sanders-staffers-after
-heart.

36. This tweet received 1.8K retweets and 22.8K likes (accessed
August 11, 2019), https://twitter.com/AlishaGrauso/status
/1144073941922832385.

37. This tweet received 3.1K retweets and 32.5K likes (accessed
August 11, 2019), https://twitter.com/MerrillBarr/status
/1144074388993499136.

38. This tweet received 3.8K retweets and 41.6K likes (accessed

August 11, 2019), https://twitter.com/ashleyn1cole/status
/1144125555438018560.

39. See Steve Peoples, "Analysis: Elizabeth Warren Growing into
Front-Runner Status," *AP News,* October 16, 2019, https://
apnews.com/43a868c4b91746f5a5a74df751a08df3.

40. Following Super Tuesday, as of March 4, 2020 at 1pm, Warren
had accrued just 47 delegates, compared to Biden, at 513, Sanders,
at 461 (with Buttigieg accruing 26, Bloomberg, 24, and Klobuchar, 7, before each of them suspended their campaigns. Tulsi
Gabbard also earned one delegate). https://twitter.com/NBC
News/status/1235264711136071680.

41. I say this given Warren's pledge not only to do better, but to make
the needs of Native community members a priority moving
forward. See, e.g., Thomas Kaplan, "Elizabeth Warren Apologizes
at Native American Forum: 'I Have Listened, and I Have
Learned,'" *The New York Times,* August 19, 2019, https://www
.nytimes.com/2019/08/19/us/politics/elizabeth-warren-native
-american.html.

42. https://twitter.com/sandylocks/status/1234924330040954880
(accessed March 4, 2020).

43. Nominally speaking—as an Australian citizen, and a permanent
resident of the U.S., I can't vote, as I write this.

44. See, e.g., Roxane Gay, who wrote on Twitter: "I am mystified by
this election cycle. I expect[ed] Sanders to do well but I also
expect[ed] Warren to do well. Her results are just baffling. Biden
cruising on through is so disappointing. If he is the nominee ugh.
He better make Beyoncé his VP." https://twitter.com/rgay/
status/1235081083038752768 (accessed March 4, 2020).

45. Kamala Harris is a trickier case here, for a number of reasons. For
one thing, before she dropped out, she enjoyed significantly more
support than either Klobuchar or Gillibrand, although significantly
less than Warren. For another, there were genuine concerns about
her record as a prosecutor—about which, I confess, I remain quite
ambivalent. Did this role, and some of the decisions of her office
regarding incarcerated trans women—for example, to deny them
gender-affirmation surgery—show her to be genuinely lacking in
communality and compassion? It seems to me that reasonable
minds differ even more widely on this score than when it comes
to what to think about Klobuchar with respect to the latter's
treatment of her staffers. Harris contributed to *institutional* racism,

transphobia, and other such structural problems. This, to my mind, is a more important issue. Finally, and on a different note, the comparison between the aforementioned white women has some epistemic advantages for the limited purposes of the discussion here, since Harris was doubtless subject to unique forms of bias as a Black woman aspiring to the presidency.

Thanks to Reginald Dwayne Betts for helping me think through these issues and prompting me to rethink some (though not all) of my original worries about Harris's prosecutorial record.

46. https://twitter.com/JRubinBlogger/status/123031799118054 6049 (accessed March 4, 2020).

47. For a good summary of such criticisms, see Susan J. Demas, "Nobody Likes a Smarty Pants: Why Warren and Obama Irk Pundits So Much," *Wisconsin Examiner,* February 20, 2020, https://wisconsinexaminer.com/2020/02/20/nobody-likes-a -smarty-pants-why-warren-and-obama-irk-pundits-so-much/.

48. Shortly before the primaries, Warren was in fact the *top* second choice among Democratic voters. See Philip Bump, "A New National Poll Answers a Critical Question: Who Is the Second Choice of Democratic Voters?" *The Washington Post,* January 28, 2020, https://www.washingtonpost.com/politics/2020/01/28 /new-national-poll-answers-critical-question-who-is-second -choice-democratic-voters/.

49. The T-shirts are available at: https://nextlevely.com/product/shes -electable-if-you-fucking-vote-for-her-elizabeth-warren-shirt/ (accessed March 4, 2020).

50. See note 3 in this chapter.

51. I draw here on my piece, "Warren Succeeded Because Voters Saw Her as Caring. That's Also Why She Failed," *The Washington Post,* March 6, 2020, https://www.washingtonpost.com/outlook /warren-succeeded-because-voters-saw-her-as-caring-thats-also -why-she-failed/2020/03/06/8064b7c2-5f0f-11ea-b014-4fafa 866bb81_story.html.

52. See Alex Thompson and Alice Miranda Ollstein, "Warren Details How She'd Transition Country to 'Medicare for All,'" Politico, November 15, 2019, https://www.politico.com/news/2019/11 /15/warren-medicare-for-all-071152.

53. For some evidence of Sanders' failures of compassion vis-à-vis a disabled Vermont constituent's health, see my "Unfeeling the Bern: Or, He Is the One Who Protests," https://www.academia

.edu/30041350/Unfeeling_the_Bern_or_He_is_the_One_Who
Protests--_Draft_of_June_2. For a more general discussion of
my reservations about Sanders' politics, see my "The Art of
Losing: Bernie Sanders' White Male Problem," https://www
.academia.edu/30040727/The_Art_of_Losing_Bernie_Sanders
_White_Male_Problem_Draft_of_May_24_2016_.

54. "It can't be stated enough that Elizabeth Warren, a rightwing
corporate lawyer who once faked her race to become Harvard's
1st "female professor of color," now has the largest super PAC in
the field despite her website saying she will "disavow any super
PAC formed to support her," read one representative tweet, by
Aren R. LeBrun @proustmalone (https://twitter.com/proust
malone/status/1235215120160219139, accessed March 4, 2020).

55. For an extensive discussion of the (I believe, largely false) perception that Hillary Clinton and Julia Gillard were particularly
untrustworthy politicians, see my *Down Girl,* Chapter 8.

56. Hope Yen, "AP Fact Check: Sanders' Shift on Delegates Needed
to Win," *AP News,* March 1, 2020, https://apnews.com/a5f8f2335
cf1b617dbb6626845b1c4a8.

57. On the first score, see Libby Watson, "Joe Biden's Individual
Mandate Madness," *The New Republic,* October 23, 2019, https://
newrepublic.com/article/155477/joe-bidens-individual-mandate
-madness; on the second, see Matt Flegenheimer, "Biden's First
Run for President Was a Calamity. Some Missteps Still Resonate,"
The New York Times, June 4, 2019, https://www.nytimes.com
/2019/06/03/us/politics/biden-1988-presidential-campaign.html.

58. MJ Lee, "Bernie Sanders Told Elizabeth Warren in Private 2018
Meeting That a Woman Can't Win, Sources Say," CNN, January 13, 2020, https://www.cnn.com/2020/01/13/politics
/bernie-sanders-elizabeth-warren-meeting/index.html.

59. Note that saying that sexism would be weaponized against a
female candidate by Trump in the general election carries a strong
implication, in the context of such a conversation, that a woman
would indeed be hard-pressed to win against him. (Otherwise,
why mention it? Especially since this would hardly have been
news to Warren.) However, there is reasonable disagreement about
whether Sanders having implied this would have itself been sexist,
or merely an undiplomatic way of recording a plausible—though
not, as we've seen, ultimately justified—hypothesis about the
insuperable barriers women face in being elected president.

60. I draw here on my interview with Ezra Klein, "Kate Manne on Why Female Candidates Get Ruled 'Unelectable' So Quickly," Vox, April 23, 2019, https://www.vox.com/policy-and -politics/2019/4/23/18512016/elizabeth-warren-electability -amy-klobuchar-2020-primary-female-candidates.

61. Biden secured 29 percent of people's votes in the "horse race" question, followed by Sanders at 17 percent, and Warren at 16 percent. But when asked the "magic wand" question, 21 per- cent of people favored Warren, compared to 19 percent who favored either Biden or Sanders. Max Greenwood, "Poll: Demo- crats Prefer Warren When Not Considering 'Electability,'" The Hill, June 19, 2019, https://thehill.com/homenews/ campaign/449315-poll-dems-prefer-warren-when-not -considering-electability.

62. Silver was quoted by Michelle Cottle in a piece in which she also canvassed the poll results discussed in the previous note: "Elizabeth Warren Had a Good Run. Maybe Next Time, Ladies," The New York Times, March 5, 2020, https://www.nytimes.com/2020/03 /04/opinion/democrats-super-tuesday-warren.html.

63. It is telling that, by Super Tuesday (when many states hold their primaries), the most diverse Democratic party field in history had been winnowed down to three white men in their late seventies, plus Elizabeth Warren hanging on, albeit barely.

64. For an excellent discussion of the concept of "sexism by proxy," see Moira Donegan's "Elizabeth Warren's Radical Idea," The Atlantic, August 26, 2019, https://www.theatlantic.com/ideas /archive/2019/08/sexism-proxy-still-sexism/596752/.

65. See Amanda Arnold, "All the Women Who Have Spoken Out Against Joe Biden," The Cut, April 5, 2019, https://www.thecut .com/2019/04/joe-biden-accuser-accusations-allegations.html; and Emma Tucker, "Sanders Backtracks on Promise to Release Medical Records: 'I'm in Good Health,'" The Daily Beast, February 9, 2020, https://www.thedailybeast.com/bernie -sanders-backtracks-promise-to-release-medical-records-says-im -in-good-health.

TEN Undespairing—On the Entitlement of Girls

1. See, for example, the research showing that, in the wake of the Me Too movement, attitudes about gender in the workplace have

shifted in a less than salutary direction for many people. In early 2019, researchers found that "19% of men said they were reluctant to hire attractive women, 21% said they were reluctant to hire women for jobs involving close interpersonal interactions with men (jobs involving travel, say), and 27% said they avoided one-on-one meetings with female colleagues." This was a bigger backlash than was anticipated by survey participants in 2017, in the immediate aftermath of the initial Me Too revelations—and these numbers have actually *increased* in that time frame, in all but one instance. Tim Bower, "The #MeToo Backlash," *Harvard Business Review,* September–October 2019, https://hbr.org/2019/09/the-metoo-backlash.

2.   One way of getting at the distinction here: beliefs aim to reflect the world accurately, whereas desires, commitments, and actions aim to actively *change* the world (or, again, prevent it from backsliding). I'm channeling a distinction first formulated by the famous twentieth-century English philosopher Elizabeth Anscombe in her classic book *Intention* (Oxford: Basil Blackwell, 1957). And for a compelling argument that the intelligibility of perpetual political struggle does not depend on hopefulness or optimism about the future, see Kathryn J. Norlock, "Perpetual Struggle," *Hypatia* 34, no. 1 (2019): 6–19.

3.   That is, we are alive to and actively embrace the possibility that our child may turn out to be a trans boy or non-binary.

4.   However, it may be worth recording that one common idea in liberal circles about raising boys—that they need much more help to become in touch with and expressive of their emotions, as compared with girls—appears to lack robust empirical foundations. In a large meta-analysis, researchers found that the differences between boys' versus girls' emotional expressions were generally small, subtle, and highly context-dependent. Tara M. Chaplin and Amelia Aldao, "Gender Differences in Emotion Expression in Children: A Meta-Analytic Review," *Psychological Bulletin* 139, no. 4 (2013): 735–65.

5.   Obviously we should celebrate these feminine-coded paths, when freely chosen by people of any gender; but the point here is just that it is a shame to have children's horizons winnowed early on, and that the father's choices appear to make an important difference for girls when it comes to this winnowing. It's also worth

noting that, sadly, *boys'* choices appear to be winnowed more consistently: identifying a gender-typical path was the norm for boys, regardless of parental division of labor. For an overview of this research, see Emily Chung, "Dads Who Do Housework Have More Ambitious Daughters," CBS News, May 28, 2014, https://www.cbc.ca/news/technology/dads-who-do-housework-have-more-ambitious-daughters-1.2655928.

6.   Of course, boys and men also face sexual abuse, assault, and harassment, though generally at lower rates than girls and women (and, I suspect, non-binary people, who are likely to be at least as vulnerable as their female counterparts). But whatever the gender of the victim, a large majority of those who *perpetrate* sexual violence are male. See, e.g., Liz Plank, "Most Perpetrators of Sexual Violence Are Men, So Why Do We Call It a Women's Issue?" *Divided States of Women,* November 2, 2017, https://www.dividedstatesofwomen.com/2017/11/2/16597768/sexual-assault-men-himthough, for relevant discussion.

7.   See David Sadker and Karen R. Zittleman, *Still Failing at Fairness: How Gender Bias Cheats Girls and Boys in School and What We Can Do About It* (New York: Scribner, 2009).

ableism, 11, 146, 248–49, 254
abortion rights and restrictions,
    97–112, 188. *See also* anti-
    abortion movement
abortion restrictions after
    twenty weeks, 100–102, 232
male partners and the abortion
    debate, 108–9
medical rationales for
    abortions, 100–102,
    103–4
restrictions as social control,
    99–100, 106–8, 109–11
Roe v. Wade, 97–98, 231,
    235–36
state restriction efforts, 97–99,
    109, 230, 231
Abramson, Kate, 149, 156, 249,
    250–51
Ackland, Richard, 219–20
Acosta, Alexander, 216
aggrievement. *See* himpathy;
    victimhood
Akin, Todd, 103
Alabama abortion restrictions,
    97–98, 109, 230, 231

Alana's Involuntary Celibacy
    Project, 17, 201
Allen, Sandra, 218
Alstead, Jim, 44–45
Andrews, Lori, 31
andronormativity, 91–95
anger, gender-biased perceptions
    of, 166–69, 174–75, 178,
    257–58
Anonymous: "We Need to Talk
    About Sexual Assault in
    Marriage," 67–68, 224
Ansari, Aziz, 57–58, 59–62,
    68–69, 221
Anscombe, Elizabeth, 267
anti-abortion movement, 97–110,
    199. *See also* abortion rights
    and restrictions
extreme views and rhetoric in,
    99–100, 232
hypocrisy in, 105–6, 109, 110,
    234, 236
and late-term abortions,
    100–102, 232
medical misinformation in,
    103–5, 232

anti-abortion movement (*cont.*)
  parallels with the anti-trans
    movement, 114–15, 239
  political and activist roots of,
    98, 106–9
  and religious culture, 106, 109,
    235–36
anti-trans movement, 114–19,
  239
Araujo, Gwen, 117–19
Ardern, Jacinda, 157–58, 253,
  254, 260
Arndt, Bettina, 41, 212–13
authority. *See* epistemic
  entitlement; female power
  and authority
autism, 94–95
Avdeef, Thomas, 251–52

Ball, W. David, 108–9
bathroom bills, 114–16
Baxter, Rowan, 40–41, 212
Beauchamp, Zack, 201, 202,
  203–4, 207
Beierle, Scott Paul, 16, 18,
  20–21, 23–24, 25–26, 203,
  205, 206
believing women. *See* testimonial
  injustice
Bettcher, Talia Mae, 11, 116–18
Biden, Joe, 167, 169, 183
  and the 2019–2020 primary,
    174–75, 177, 179–80, 181,
    262, 265
Black, Ashley Nicole, 175
Black Lives Matter, 106
Black women, 11, 144. *See also*
  specific authors and thinkers
  and health care inequities,
    75–78, 105, 234

and reproductive oppression,
  113–14, 238–39
blaming women, 9, 12, 36, 52–
  53, 229. *See also* punishing
  women
  self-blame, 67, 112
  victim blaming, 37, 60, 61–62,
    118
Blasey Ford, Christine, 3-7, 8,
  12-13, 195-96,198
Bloomberg, Michael, 177, 262
Bolt, Andrew, 254
Boorman, Georgi, 104, 112, 234
Bowles, Nellie, 202–3
Braincels, 202, 204
Broidy, Elliott, 236
Brooks, David, 144
Brown, Julie K., 216–17
Buckle, Dwayne, 54
Bullen, Paul, 138–39, 140,
  246–47
Burke, Tarana, 50
Bussone, Dave, 247
Buttigieg, Pete, 177, 262

Calef, Zach, 118
capital punishment, 105, 109, 112
cardiovascular disease, 93–94
caring/caregiving, 11, 89–91,
  108, 109–11, 127, 128–29,
  179. *See also* communality;
  domestic labor
"Cat Person" (Roupenian),
  56–57, 58, 60, 69
Cazares, Jason, 118, 241
celibacy, 24–25. *See also* incels
  and incel culture
Chambliss, Clyde, 109
Chemaly, Soraya, 174
Cherry, Myisha, 174

childbirth. *See* pregnancy and childbirth

child care, 120–21. *See also* caring/caregiving; domestic labor

Chumley, Cheryl K., 195–96

Clark, Brandon, 30–32

Clarke, Hannah, 41

climate change denialism, 157, 260

Clinton, Hillary, 160, 162, 172, 264

coercion. *See* consent and coercion

Coetzee, J. M., 70–72, 73

Collins, Susan, 196

Coltrane, Scott, 122–23

communality, gendered expectations of, 164–83
and female emotional expression, 174–75
and female politicians, 169–71, 172–73, 174, 175–78, 259, 260–61, 262–63
and political values, 173–74, 260–61
research on, 164–65, 169, 171–72, 256–57, 258–59

competence/incompetence. *See also* female power and authority; testimonial injustice
and gaslighting, 146, 154, 251, 252
gender-biased perceptions of, 161–62, 165, 260
and health care inequities, 86
and women as caregivers, 89, 229

consent and coercion, 56–74
female agency and social pressures, 58, 61, 62–65, 71–72, 223
and female fear, guilt, and shame, 67–69, 74
fictional explorations of, 56–57, 58, 60, 69–74
and men's feelings, 59–62, 69–70, 73
and power imbalances, 66, 72–73
real-life illustrations of, 57–62, 65–69, 224

Cooper, Brittney, 174

Crenshaw, Kimberlé W., 10, 177, 199

Criado Perez, Caroline, 91–92, 93, 96, 226

criminal justice and criminal justice inequities, 106, 108–9
and abortion, 108–9, 111–12
bathroom bills, 114–16
capital punishment, 105, 109, 112
parental rights of rapists, 240
reproductive oppression, 113–14, 237–39

Cruz, Nikolas, 201

dating violence/rape, 32. *See also* consent and coercion; intimate partner violence
the Florek-Vanett case, 33–36, 42–45, 55, 209

death penalty, 105, 109, 112

De Caunes, Emma, 66

DesJarlais, Scott, 236

Devins, Bianca, 30–32

Dirty John (podcast), 149–56

distrust of women. *See also*
testimonial injustice
in the anti-abortion
movement, 102
and health care inequities,
75–78, 80–81, 85–89,
228–29
Dodsworth, Laura, 138–39, 140
domestic abuse and violence, 32.
See also gaslighting; intimate
partner violence
domestic labor, division of,
120–37, 189
and the capacity for
multitasking, 245
and economic status, 127, 243
emotional labor as facet of,
123–27, 242–43
and female labor force
participation, 120, 121, 122,
133
gendered double standards,
132–33, 244–45
and hired help, 243, 246
and male leisure, 129–32
and "masculine" jobs, 128–29
research quantifying, 120–23
women's validation of their
partners' failures, 131,
133–37
Dotson, Kristie, 85, 141, 248
Douthat, Ross, 202
Down Girl (Manne), 7, 10, 184,
200
Dunham, Lena, 70
Girls, 69–70, 72–73, 74
Dunn, Jancee, 130–32, 133–37

economic status
and domestic labor, 127, 243

and reproductive oppression,
113–14, 238–39
Ehrlichman, John, 235
electability (of women), 159–62,
181–83, 255, 257. *See also*
female power and authority;
*specific candidates and office
holders*
Emily Doe rape case, 37–39,
210–11
emotional expression, 174–75,
190–91, 267
gender-biased perceptions of
anger, 166–69, 174–75, 178,
257–58
emotional labor, 123–27,
242–43
empathy, 31, 209–10. *See also*
communality; himpathy
entitlement, 4–5, 196–97. *See
also* epistemic entitlement;
male entitlement; sexual
entitlement
legitimate vs. illegitimate, 12,
186, 247–48
epistemic entitlement, 138–59,
247–48
attacks on female expression
of views, 156–59, 253,
254
gaslighting, 145–56, 190–91
mansplaining, 12, 138–44, 190,
246–47
self-silencing by women, 141,
248
vs. testimonial injustice,
140–41, 248, 249–50
epistemic injustice, 140. *See
also* epistemic entitlement;
testimonial injustice

Epstein, Jeffrey, 48, 216–17
Equal Rights Amendment
    (ERA), 108
exceptional clearances (rape
    cases), 45–47, 214–15
executions and the death penalty,
    105, 109

feelings. *See* emotional
    expression; himpathy
female power and authority,
    160–83. *See also*
    communality; electability;
    specific politicians
    double standards for female
        politicians, 161–63, 165–71,
        172, 175–83
    and female communality,
        163–66, 169–75, 256–57,
        259–60
fetal heartbeat bills, 98–99,
    231
Fisher, Shana, 40
Flanagan, Caitlin, 59–62,
    68–69
Flavin, Jeanne, 237–39
Florek, Rae, 33–36, 42–45, 55,
    209
Franken, Al, 169–71, 259
Fricker, Miranda, 86, 140

Gabbard, Tulsi, 262
Garbes, Angela, 90
gaslighting, 145–56, 157,
    190–91, 248–49
    in *Gas Light*, 145–48
    moral dimensions of, 146,
        148–49, 153–54, 249–50
    real-life examples of,
        149–56

Gay, Roxane, 49–50, 262
Gillard, Julia, 172, 253, 264
Gillibrand, Kirsten, 169–71, 178,
    258–59
Girls (TV show), 69–70,
    72–73, 74
Gladwell, Malcolm, 211
Goffard, Christopher, 151–52,
    155, 251–52, 252–53
Grace (Aziz Ansari's date), 57–58,
    59–62, 68–69
Graham, Lindsey, 5–7
Green, Anneke E., 195
Greenblatt, Mark, 42–44
Greenhouse, Linda, 106–8,
    235–36
Gunter, Jen, 104
Gutierrez, Ambra, 65–66

Hamilton, Patrick: *Gas Light*,
    145–48
Harper-Mercer, Chris, 16, 18,
    205
Harris, Kamala, 262–63
Hart, Arlane, 251
Hartley, Gemma, 125, 126–27,
    129–30
Hayek, Salma, 69
health care inequities, 75–96.
    See also reproductive
    justice
    distrust/dismissal of female
        experience and testimony,
        75–78, 80–81, 85–89,
        228–29
    gendered pain experiences
        and treatment, 78–85, 226,
        227
    health care usage differences,
        82–83

health care inequities (*cont.*)
  medical research disparities,
    91–96
  prenatal/maternal care, 77–78,
    90–91, 95–96, 225
  and race, 77–78, 86–89,
    228–29
  and women viewed as
    caregivers, 89–91
health care work, 128–29
heartbeat bills, 98–99, 231
heart disease, 93–94
Heilman, Madeline, 161–62,
    163–65, 171–72, 255,
    256–57, 259–60
Heintz, Paul, 168
herasure, 37, 38
Hill Collins, Patricia, 89
himpathy, 5–7, 11–12, 36–37,
    197, 209–10
  and the Araujo murder, 118
  and domestic labor inequities,
    125–26, 131, 133–34
  and the Grace/Ansari incident,
    60–62, 68–69
  for incels, 29–30, 202–3
  the pressure to protect men's
    feelings, 59–62, 73, 125–26,
    134
  for rapists, 36–39, 44–45, 211
  and the Vickers murder,
    251–52
Hochschild, Arlie Russell, 120,
    125, 242–43
Hoffmann, Diane E., 79, 80, 226
Holland, Cindy, 62
homicide. *See* murder
household labor. *See* domestic
    labor
Hunt, Kate, 82, 83

Ibrahim, Layla, 53, 218
incels and incel culture,
    14–30, 32
  dehumanizing rhetoric about
    women, 25–27, 205–6
  and the Devins murder,
    31–32
  empathetic views of, 29–30,
    202–3, 207
  incel demographics, 17, 202,
    204
  incel psychology and behavior
    patterns, 17–22, 27–29, 205,
    207
  the notion of involuntariness,
    24–25, 206
  racism and white supremacy,
    21–24
  threats and violent behavior,
    14–16, 18, 20, 203,
    206–7
incompetence. *See* competence/
    incompetence
information and knowledge. *See*
    epistemic entitlement
intersectionality, 10–11, 86–90,
    115, 197, 199, 209, 227–28.
    *See also specific marginalized
    groups*
intimate partner violence, 30–32,
    33, 44, 67–68, 209, 224.
    See also consent and
    coercion
Ivey, Kay, 97, 105, 112

Johnson, Charles, 112
Jones, Alan, 157–58, 159, 253,
    254
Joyner, Jazmine, 11, 87–89
Judge, Mark, 4

Kamp Dush, Claire, 121, 122, 123
Kavanaugh, Brett, 3–7, 8, 13, 48, 195–96, 197, 198, 231
Kimmel, Michael, 204
Kinnersly, Patty, 159
Klobuchar, Amy, 5, 166–68, 169, 178, 258, 262, 263
knowledge and information. *See* epistemic entitlement

labor force participation, by men: and domestic labor, 128–29, 244
labor force participation, by women, 133, 244, 245–46
    gendered career aspirations of children, 189, 267–68
    Me Too and perceptions about women in the workplace, 266–67
LeBrun, Aren R., 264
likability, 161–62, 165, 182, 259–60. *See also* communality; female power and authority
Lloyd, Scott, 236
Lockman, Darcy, 123–24, 129, 132, 135
Love Not Anger, 201

Magidson, Michael, 118, 241
male entitlement, 4–5, 11–12, 110, 196–97. *See also* epistemic entitlement; himpathy; sexual entitlement
male privilege
    entitlement as a facet of, 4–5, 196

and health care inequities, 85, 227–28
Manne: *Down Girl,* 7, 10, 184, 200
mansplaining, 12, 138–44, 190, 246–47
marital sex and rape. *See* consent and coercion; intimate partner violence
Master of None (TV show), 62, 221
maternal mortality rates, 77–78, 105
McDevitt, Tom, 45, 215
McGovern, George, 107
McKnight, Regina, 114, 238–39
McMillan Cottom, Tressie, 11, 75–77, 78, 87, 144
"Me and My Vulva: 100 Women Reveal All" (Dodsworth), 138–39, 140
medical care inequities. *See* health care inequities
medical research, 92–96, 234
Meehan, John, 150–56, 252–53
mental competence/illness
    and gaslighting, 146, 154, 248–49, 251, 252
    mothers of mentally ill children, 229
Merel, Jose, 118, 241
Me Too movement, 50–52, 266–67. *See also* sexual abuse/assault/harassment; *specific associated individuals*
Milgram (Stanley) experiments, 62–65, 222–23
Miller, Chanel, 37–39, 210–11
Minassian, Alek, 16, 18, 203, 205–6

miscegenation, 22–24, 229–30
misogynoir, 11, 86–90, 216,
    227–29. *See also* Black
    women; race
misogyny, 7–12, 36–37, 52–55
    as policing of patriarchal
        norms, 7–8, 36–37, 52–55
    resisting, 184–85, 191–92,
        267
Morrison, Scott, 158
motherhood. *See also* abortion
    rights and restrictions;
    caring/caregiving; domestic
    labor; parenthood;
    pregnancy and childbirth
    and perceptions of
        competence and likability,
        229, 259–60
    social policing of, 110–11
multitasking, 245
murder, 32
    abortion framed as, 111–12,
        115
    the Araujo murder, 117–19,
        241
    the Devins murder, 30–32
    exceptional clearances in
        homicide cases, 46, 215
    incels as murderers, 14–16, 18,
        203
    the McKnight case, 113–14,
        238–39
    reframed by himpathy, 39–41
    school shootings, 39–40, 201
    statistics, 32
    trans girls and women as
        victims of, 117–19, 240–41
    the Vickers case, 251–52
Murphy, Tim, 236

Nabors, Jaron, 118, 241
Nassar, Larry, 149
Newell, Debra, 149–56, 251–52
Newell, Terra, 156, 252–53
niceness. *See* likability
Nixon, Richard, 107, 235–36
non-binary people, 188, 236
nonconsensual pornography, 55,
    220
Norvill, Eryn Jean, 53–54,
    219–20
nurturing behaviors. *See* caring/
    caregiving; communality
Nyden, Tammy, 229

Oberman, Michelle, 108–9
objectification of women, 25–27,
    236
Ocasio-Cortez, Alexandria, 173,
    174
Ohio fetal heartbeat law, 99
Okimoto, Tyler, 163–65, 171–72,
    256–57, 259–60
O'Neil, Michael R., 155, 156
O'Rourke, Beto, 169

Pagourtzis, Dimitrios, 40
pain, gendered experience and
    treatment of, 78–85, 226,
    227–28
Palmieri, Jen, 170
Paltrow, Lynne M., 237–39
parenthood. *See also* abortion
    rights and restrictions;
    domestic labor;
    motherhood; pregnancy and
    childbirth
    raising boys, 186, 267
    raising girls, 185–92

Parkland shootings, 201
patriarchy. *See also* policing; social
    control; social pressures
    misogyny and sexism as facets
        of, 7–9
    misogyny as policing of
        patriarchal norms, 7–8,
        36–37, 52
Paul, David, 162, 255–56
Pence, Mike, 101
Penny, Laurie, 99, 236
Persky, Aaron, 38, 39
Peterson, Jordan, 202–3
Phillips, Kevin, 107
Pierson, Kate, 16
police violence, 106, 216
policing. *See also* abortion rights
    and restrictions; criminal
    justice
    misogyny as, 7–8, 36–37,
        52–55
    of pregnancy and motherhood,
        110–14, 236–37
    of trans people's bodies,
        114–19
political power. *See* electability;
    female power and authority
pornography, nonconsensual, 55,
    220
Porter, Janet, 98, 112
poverty
    and domestic labor inequities,
        127
    and reproductive oppression,
        113–14, 238–39
power, female. *See* female power
    and authority
power imbalances, 66, 72–73, 229
Powers, Kirsten, 247

pregnancy and childbirth. *See
    also* abortion rights and
    restrictions; motherhood;
    parenthood; reproductive
    justice/reproductive
    oppression
    health care and research
        inequities, 77–78, 90–91,
        95–96, 225
    maternal mortality rates,
        77–78, 105
    social policing of, 110,
        236–37
privilege. *See also* male privilege;
    white privilege
    entitlement as facet of, 4–5,
        196–97
    recognizing, 187–88, 196
    youth-based, 50–52
pro-life movement. *See* abortion
    rights and restrictions; anti-
    abortion movement
punishing women. *See also*
    blaming women; incels and
    incel culture; policing
    for speaking out/fighting back,
        12, 53–55, 218–20

queer women, as sexual assault
    victims, 54

race. *See also* Black women; white
    privilege
    and health/health care
        inequities, 77–78, 86–89,
        91, 105, 227–28, 228–29
    and the Miller-Turner rape
        case, 211
    miscegenation, 22–24, 229–30

race (*cont.*)
racial demographics of incel culture, 21, 204
racism and white supremacy, 10, 21–24, 91
and rape investigations, 47–48
RAINN (Rape, Abuse and Incest National Network), 49
Ramirez, Deborah, 195
Rape, Abuse and Incest National Network (RAINN), 49
rape and rape culture, 33–39, 42–55. *See also* consent and coercion; sexual abuse/assault/harassment
date rape/marital rape, 33, 44, 209
disbelief/silencing of victims, 53–54, 157, 218–20, 229
the Florek/Vanett case, 33–36, 42–45, 55, 209
himpathy for rapists, 36–39, 44–45, 211
incarceration rates, 49
the Miller/Turner case, 37–39, 210–11
offenders' ages, 49–50, 51
parental rights of rapists, 240
prosecutorial standards and practices, 42–49, 213, 214–15
rape and abortion, 99, 103
victim blaming and erasure, 37, 38
victim demographics, 198
Real, Terry, 131–32, 133
religious culture, and abortion, 106, 109, 235–36
reproductive justice/reproductive oppression, 113–14, 188, 237–39. *See also* abortion rights and restrictions
resistance, 184–85, 191–92, 267
revenge porn, 61–62, 68–69
Richardson, Nigel, 218
Rios, Tracy, 48–49
Rodger, Elliot, 14–15, 17–18, 20, 21–22, 200
as inspiration to others, 16, 201, 205–6
and Chanel Miller, 210
writings and videos by, 14–15, 20, 21–22, 25, 28, 200, 204–5, 206
Rodriguez, Sadie, 40
Roe v. Wade, 97–98, 231, 235–36
Rollins, Austin, 39
Roth, Philip, 74
Roupenian, Kristen: "Cat Person," 56–57, 58, 60, 69
Rubin, Jennifer, 178
Rudd, Kevin, 172
Rush, Geoffrey, 53–54, 219–20
Rutledge, Pamela, 31

Sabini, John, 223
Samulowitz, Anke, 80–81, 226
Sanders, Bernie, 168, 169, 177, 179, 183, 262, 265
and Warren, 176, 180–81, 265
Schlafly, Phyllis, 108, 112
school shootings, 39–40, 201
Schoppe-Sullivan, Sarah, 121
sexism
and the anti-trans movement, 114–17, 239
and gaslighting, 249
vs. misogyny, 8

sexual abuse/assault/harassment, 7, 12, 190, 198, 268. *See also* consent and coercion; Me Too movement; rape and rape culture
age of offenders, 49–52
disbelief/silencing of victims, 53–54, 157, 218–20, 229
the Epstein cases, 48, 216
by incels, 20–21, 203–4
Kavanaugh allegations and hearing, 3–7, 8, 13, 195–96, 197, 198
the Norvill/Rush case, 53–54, 219–20
and testimonial injustice, 229
the Weinstein cases, 51, 65–66, 69, 223–24
sexual entitlement. *See also* consent and coercion; incels; rape; sexual abuse/assault/harassment
male, 48, 58, 110
Sharone, Ofer, 128
Sherf, Dean, 35–37, 42–44
Siegel, Riva B., 106–8, 235–36
silencing women. *See* epistemic entitlement; testimonial injustice and testimonial quieting
Silverman, Sarah, 59
Silver, Maury, 223
Silver, Nate, 181–82
Smith, Jessi, 162, 255–56
social control. *See also* policing
abortion restrictions as, 99–100, 106–8, 109–11
social pressures. *See also* patriarchy
power of, 62–65

to protect men's feelings, 59–62, 73, 125–26
Solnit, Rebecca, 141–43, 157
Southworth, Cindy, 32
Spacey, Kevin, 51
Srinivasan, Amia, 174
Stephens, Kyle, 149
Swetnick, Julie, 195

The Talented Mr. Ripley (film), 86
Tarzian, Anita J., 79, 80, 226
testimonial injustice and testimonial quieting, 86, 88–89, 140–41, 190, 248, 249–50
disbelief/dismissal of sexual abuse/assault victims, 53–54, 157, 218–20, 229
and health care inequities, 75–78, 80–81, 85–89, 228–29
testimonial smothering (self-silencing), 141, 248
Thunberg, Greta, 173, 174, 254
Tolentino, Jia, 101
Traister, Rebecca, 174
transmisogyny and transphobia, 11, 114–17, 239
trans people, 188, 236, 237
as victims of violence, 117–19, 240–41
Trump, Donald, 13, 48, 100, 160, 197, 247, 257, 265
trusting women. *See* distrust of women; testimonial injustice
Turner, Brock, 37–39, 210–11
Tuteur, Amy, 237

2016 presidential campaign and election, 160, 172, 257

2019–2020 Democratic presidential primary campaign, 170–71, 258–59, 262, 265, 266. *See also specific candidates*

unemployment, among men, 128

Vanderbilt, Tom, 130–32, 133–37

Vanett, Randy, 33–36, 42–45, 55

Vickers, Billy, 251–52

Vickers, Cindi, 251–52

victim blaming, 37, 60, 61–62, 118

victim erasure, 37, 38

victimhood. *See also* himpathy and gaslighting, 151–53 in incel psychology, 27–29, 205

Villarosa, Linda, 78

Wallace, George, 107

Warren, Elizabeth, 174–83 and the electability narrative, 178, 180–82, 183, 254–55, 265 and expectations of communality, 175–76 and gendered double standards, 178–80 perceived failures of, 176–77, 178–79, 180–81, 264

primary polling and results, 176, 178, 181, 262, 263

Way, Katie: the Grace/Ansari story, 57–58, 59–62, 68–69

Webb, Todd, 44

Weinstein, Harvey, 51, 65–66, 69, 223–24

Weiss, Bari, 57, 58

Westwick, Ed, 51–52, 62

When She Was Good (Roth), 74

white privilege, 196–97. *See also* race

white women's privilege/entitlement, 11, 98, 112–13, 187–88, 197, 246

white supremacy, 10, 21–22, 91

Willey, Jaelynn, 39

Williamson, Kevin, 112

Williams, Serena, 78

women of color. *See also* Black women and health care inequities, 77–78, 90, 225 as sexual assault victims, 54 trans women as victims of violence, 117–19, 241 as victims of reproductive oppression, 113–14, 238–39

work. *See* domestic labor; female power and authority; labor force participation

Worthy, Kym, 47

Wray, Susan, 95–96

Yavorsky, Jill, 121

ABOUT THE AUTHOR

Kate Manne is an associate professor of philosophy at Cornell University, where she has taught since 2013. She did her graduate work at MIT and was a junior fellow in the Harvard Society of Fellows. The author of *Down Girl*, she has written for *The New York Times*, *Boston Review*, *HuffPost*, *The Times Literary Supplement*, and Politico, among other publications. She was recently named one of the "World's Top 10 Thinkers" by *Prospect Magazine* (U.K.).

ABOUT THE TYPE

This book was set in Bembo, a typeface based on an old-style Roman face that was used for Cardinal Pietro Bembo's tract *De Aetna* in 1495. Bembo was cut by Francesco Griffo (1450–1518) in the early sixteenth century for Italian Renaissance printer and publisher Aldus Manutius (1449–1515). The Lanston Monotype Company of Philadelphia brought the well-proportioned letterforms of Bembo to the United States in the 1930s.